- Go to **awmi.net/sg432** to download PDFs of the following resources for each lesson in this study guide:
  - o Outlines
  - o Discipleship Questions
  - o Scriptures

- Share as many copies as you'd like.

- These documents are not for resale.

FINANCIAL STEWARDSHIP

STUDY GUIDE

Andrew Wommack

Unless otherwise indicated, all Scripture quotations are taken from the *King James Version* of the Bible.

Some Scripture quotations are taken from the *Amplified® Bible*. Copyright © 1954, 1958, 1962, 1964, 1965, 1987 by The Lockman Foundation. Used by permission. (www.Lockman.org).

The author has emphasized some words in Scripture quotations with underline.

Financial Stewardship Study Guide
ISBN: 978-1-59548-327-0

Copyright © 2012 by Andrew Wommack Ministries Inc.
PO Box 3333
Colorado Springs CO 80934-3333

awmi.net

CONTENTS

PREFACE

I remember giving my tithes faithfully to the Lord as a young child. I don't think I have ever received a dollar that I didn't give a tithe of. I was blessed to a degree, but the traditions and doctrines of man made financial prosperity come hard for me (Mark 7:13).

I was married with two children and had been in ministry for over twenty-five years before I really began to get the revelation of the things I'm sharing with you in this study guide. And I'm telling you, it has made a huge difference. It has not only made a big difference in my life personally, but I could not be fulfilling God's instructions to me without the financial abundance these truths have produced in my ministry.

There was a time when I loved God with all my heart and was serving Him to the best of my ability and understanding, yet I was so strapped financially that I couldn't fulfill the instructions He was giving me. I've struggled more in this area than any other area of my Christian life.

And I'm not alone in this. I remember being a part of a group of ministers that went to Oral Roberts' home in 2009 to visit with him less than a year before he died. He ministered to all of us, and then he let each one of us ask him a question. One minister asked, "What is the hardest thing you have ever endured in your ministry?"

That question got my attention. Here was a man who had survived an assassination attempt, was persecuted for his beliefs as few ministers of our day have been, and dealt with scandals that eventually cost him the university he founded. I was eager to hear his response.

He didn't hesitate one moment. He said, "The hardest thing I have ever endured was financial problems." He spoke of many sleepless nights spent in agony over finances. He spoke of being pressed at every turn in his ministry by the restraints that lack of money had placed upon him. I could relate, as I'm sure many of you can.

There was a time in my life when it didn't matter how excited I was about the direction the Lord was giving me. Regardless of the enthusiasm or opportunity, my one dominant thought was, *How can I afford to do this?* Praise the Lord, that is no longer an issue.

I'm not saying I have an unlimited supply of money; I am saying I have come to a place in my faith where I know I can always get the finances needed to accomplish God's instructions. I am no longer limited by money. That is liberating.

I believe these truths the Lord has shown me will work for anyone. I believe they will work for you. I pray that as you read this study guide, the Holy Spirit will enlighten you in a way that only He can. I believe a spirit of poverty will be broken off of you, and you will come into a new place where the only factor that limits you is God's will, not whether or not you have the money to do it. Amen!

INTRODUCTION

The Sunday comics and money are both printed on paper, but one makes people laugh and the other makes them cry. The actual paper that money is printed on is pretty much worthless—not much different from the stuff used to manufacture Kleenex. In reality, money only has value because people agree to view it as valuable. The dollar, the euro, and the yen are nothing more than creations of man used to trade for services, but arguing about the real value of money isn't going to put food on the table. The world's system of trade is based on money, and everyone has to use it to survive.

The influence of money in people's lives is very real, so it isn't surprising that Jesus taught on the subject of finances more than on any other single topic. He taught more about managing resources than He did on prayer or even faith—which tells us that the topic of money, and how we handle it, is very important. I believe that one of the reasons the church hasn't made more of an impact on modern society is because it hasn't successfully applied the Gospel to everyday concerns. Most people are so occupied with trying to deal with earthly problems that they aren't thinking about the eternal. But the Gospel has a lot to say about everyday, earthly concerns—especially finances.

I know that money is a sore subject that a lot of us want to avoid, but learning how God views finances is basic Christianity. Jesus said that if we can't be faithful in our finances, then we can't be trusted with anything! Not surprisingly, what the Bible has to say about financial stewardship is different from most of what we will hear from business sources that teach on "asset management." God doesn't operate by this world's system, and it's more important for us to understand how God's financial system works than it is to understand Wall Street.

Some people have a tendency to get offended when ministers start talking about money—especially when that minister is on television. The truth is, everyone's been given plenty of reason to get offended. A lot of people have been taken advantage of in this area.

Recently I was appalled by what I saw going on during a fundraiser on a Christian television network. It was pure manipulation and hype. It was totally wrong. I'm not saying that to be critical of other ministers, but we have to acknowledge that dishonest practices are used sometimes. What really bothers me is that those carnal techniques work! The body of Christ is so uninformed in the area of finances that people fall for manipulation tactics all the time. Somebody says "Send me a thousand dollars and your prayers will be answered," and people send money by the truckload. But the kingdom of God doesn't operate that way. God's favor can't be bought.

So, yes, there are abuses in the body of Christ regarding money, but don't miss out on benefiting from the truths in God's Word about finances just because some people are abusing the topic. I encourage you to set aside any past upsets or offenses you might have suffered, and allow the Word of God to reveal finances to you from a godly perspective. I promise you'll be glad you did.

I won't be outlining the steps involved in forming a budget, or the nuts and bolts of managing your income. Other resources for that kind of practical wisdom are already available. I'm going to be teaching the scriptural principles that go to the heart of financial problems—and success. By fixing your heart, you deal with the root cause of financial situations, and then money will take care of itself. Once your heart is right, using wisdom in how you spend your money comes naturally.

We can't fall into the trap of compartmentalizing our lives into the spiritual realm (where we relate to God) and everyday life (where we deal with jobs, family, finances, and everything else). A house divided will not stand for long, and confining our interaction with God to a couple of hours on Sunday isn't going to produce the fruit we desire in life. Our relationship with God needs to permeate every area of our lives: marriages, businesses, relationships, recreation, and finances.

Finances are important and you'll be amazed at how letting God into your finances can bring peace and healing to other areas of your life—because how you view money affects a lot more than just your bank balance. My goal in this teaching is to help you discover how to turn your finances over to God and to help you step into true prosperity in every area of your life.

HOW TO USE YOUR STUDY GUIDE

Whether you are teaching a class, leading a small group, discipling an individual, or studying *Financial Stewardship* on your own, this study guide is designed for you! Here's how it works:

Each study consists of a **Lesson**, **Outline**, **Teacher's Guide**, **Discipleship Questions**, **Answer Key**, and **Scriptures**. Some studies also have additional information.

The teacher reads the **Lesson** or **Teacher's Guide** aloud. Each student follows along with their copy of the **Outline**.

Once the **Lesson** or **Teacher's Guide** is read, the teacher then facilitates discussion and study using the **Discipleship Questions** or **Teacher's Guide** questions (the questions are all the same). The teacher reads aloud one question at a time and has the group discuss and answer it. Then, repeat the process for the next numbered section. For the teacher's use and convenience, the **Answer Key** is provided, or the answers can be found underlined and boldface under each numbered section of the **Teacher's Guide**. The group should use their **Outlines** to assist them in answering the questions.

Whenever a question mentions a specific scripture, the teacher should be sure to have the group look it up in their Bibles and read it together before answering the question. Interaction with the group over the scriptures and points from the **Lesson** or **Teacher's Guide** is encouraged. One individual should not dominate the discussion, but the teacher should try to draw out the quieter ones for the group conversation. As much as possible, keep the discussion centered on the scriptures and the **Lesson** or **Teacher's Guide** points at hand. Remember, the goal is understanding (Matt. 13:19).

Then, the process is repeated until all of the questions are discussed/answered. As a brief review before launching into the next lesson, the teacher may wish to go over the answers from the previous **Lesson** or **Teacher's Guide** with the group.

The additional information in some studies is geared toward the teacher and contains resource recommendations for further study.

Scriptures from the *King James Version* of the Bible are included as another tool for reference and meditation.

For personal study, read the **Lesson** or **Teacher's Guide**. Then, answer the questions and check your work with the **Answer Key/Teacher's Guide** answers. For maximum impact, the teacher should utilize the additional information, if provided, and **Scriptures** section.

Outline for Group Study:
  I. Briefly review the previous study by going over the **Answer Key/Teacher's Guide** answers for the **Discipleship Questions/Teacher's Guide** questions.
  II. Read the current **Lesson** or **Teacher's Guide** aloud.
      A. Be sure that each student has a copy of the **Outline**.
      B. While the **Lesson** or **Teacher's Guide** is being read, students should use their **Outlines** to follow along.
  III. Once the **Lesson** or **Teacher's Guide** is read, facilitate discussion and study using the **Discipleship Questions/Teacher's Guide** questions.
      A. Read aloud one question at a time.
      B. The group should use their **Outlines** to assist them in answering the questions.
      C. Have them read aloud each specifically mentioned scripture before answering the question.
      D. Discuss the answer/point from the Lesson, as desired.
      E. Then repeat the process until all of the questions are discussed/answered.
  IV. Distribute copies of the **Discipleship Questions** to be worked on as homework.

Materials Needed:
  Study guide, Bible, and enough copies of the **Outline**, **Discipleship Questions**, and **Scriptures** for each student. (PDFs of the **Outlines**, **Discipleship Questions**, and **Scriptures** can be downloaded via the URL located on the first page of this study guide.)

Outline for Personal Study:
  I. Read **Lesson** or **Teacher's Guide**.
      A. Read additional information, if provided.
      B. Meditate on the given scriptures, as desired.
  II. Answer **Discipleship Questions/Teacher's Guide** questions.
  III. Check your work with the **Answer Key/Teacher's Guide** answers.

Materials Needed:
  Study guide, Bible, and a writing utensil.

BEING A STEWARD

I teach on financial stewardship on Thursday mornings at Charis Bible College in Colorado. Almost all of the students who have enrolled have moved in from out of state to attend the college. A lot of them have left behind careers and the security of good-paying jobs. They also have to pay the cost of tuition, and being in school for several hours a day means that most of them have to take part-time jobs or get shift work. So, the average student coming to school faces a decrease in salary, an increase in the cost of living, additional tuition costs, and part-time work to make ends meet. In the natural sense, it's a recipe for disaster.

Without God's intervention, those students would be in big trouble. But at the end of every year, I ask the students how many of them are better off financially than they were when they came, and 80 percent or more always say they are better off. The reason they are able to prosper in spite of natural obstacles is that through CBC, they have received a revelation on the scriptural truths related to finances.

This doesn't just work for Bible college students; any of you who apply the scriptural principles I'm going to talk about will see financial prosperity begin to work in your life—and I don't mean just an increase in wealth. You will have a totally different attitude toward money. Instead of being dominated and controlled by money, you will begin to see that money is your servant. Money will become a tool you use in life, instead of a master that rules over you. Too many Christians are slaves to money. They work at jobs they don't like and do things they don't want to do just to make ends meet. God has a better way for you to live.

> **MONEY IS MEANT TO BE YOUR SERVANT, NOT A MASTER THAT RULES OVER YOU.**

Not long ago, I was in Hong Kong teaching on grace. The people were really receiving what I was teaching, but I felt a nudging in my heart to teach on the subject of finances. I was a little hesitant to follow the leading, though, because of the reputation American ministers have when it comes to teaching about money. I knew there could be some prejudice against me, so even though I really felt a quickening in my heart to teach on finances, I didn't do it right away.

The conference went on for a few more days, and then the pastor of the church I was at took me out to lunch. Several of his leaders came with us, and while we were waiting for the food to arrive, they started asking me questions. Nearly every question they asked was about finances. They wanted to know how to reconcile teaching on prosperity with God's grace. Giving is often presented as something people have to do in order to make God bless them, and they wanted to know how finances fit into the true Gospel message: God blesses His people because Christ made them righteous, not because of their works.

After visiting with the pastor and his people, I knew for sure that God had been leading me to teach on finances. So, during the conference the next day, I decided to change the focus of my preaching. As I stood in front of the people, I asked, "What is the one thing you do not want to hear an American pastor preach about?"

People immediately began to shout "prosperity," "finances," "giving and receiving."

"Well, that is exactly what God has led me to teach on," I said.

The room went completely silent—you could've heard a pin drop. I pressed on anyway and taught prosperity from a grace perspective. In the end, they loved it. As a matter of fact, the pastor emailed me after the conference to say he was still getting responses. It helped people tremendously, which shows that sometimes, the things people least want to hear about will help them the most.

The very first thing we need to understand about finances is that we are stewards of what God has given us. Jesus taught on stewardship in His parable about the shrewd manager:

> *And he said also unto his disciples, There was a certain rich man, which had*
> *a steward; and the same was accused unto him that he had wasted his goods.*
>
> LUKE 16:1

This is an important parable that I will teach on in depth later, but for now, I just want to point out the function and attitude of being a steward. The *American Heritage Dictionary* defines a steward as a person "who manages another's property, finances, or other affairs." As Christians, we are stewards, and we need to recognize that the money we have is not really ours; it's a gift from God.

I know some of you are thinking, *I can guarantee you God didn't give me the money I have! I've worked hard for it. I've earned it.* Maybe you work two jobs, or you have scrimped for years to get a little savings, and so the money you have accumulated seems like the result of your own efforts. I understand that way of thinking, but in reality, it isn't true.

Every good and perfect gift comes from God (James 1:17). Ultimately, God is the source of all the good you have. First of all, God gave you life. You didn't cause yourself to exist—you were created. God made you and He is the source of every good thing in your life. The Apostle Paul said,

> *For in him we live, and move, and have our being.*
>
> ACTS 17:28

God not only gave you physical life, but He is also the source of your wisdom and abilities. He gave you the talents you use to earn a living. God is also the reason you were born at this time in history—the most prosperous period ever. So, even though you are working hard at your job, God is still the source of your financial success. Without the blessing of God upon your life, you wouldn't even have the ability to prosper.

I know you are out in the world actually doing the work you get paid for, but you need to develop the mindset that the money you receive doesn't belong to you; it belongs to God. Remember, God gave you your talents and abilities, and every good thing you have is a blessing from Him. God has entrusted you with all of your finances, and it is important to develop the mindset of being a steward—over God's money, not yours.

Most people see making a living as resulting from the sweat of their brow, and they don't see God as their source. They separate their lives into "spiritual" matters like heaven and hell, and private, personal matters like career and finances. When it comes to money, they think it's all up to them. As a result, many Christians are struggling financially. God wants to be the source of everything in their lives. The Lord never intended people to carry the burden of financial responsibility, and He wants to lift that burden from them.

A lot of Christians say they know God is the source of everything, but their lives don't reflect an understanding of that truth. I was in a meeting one time when the man receiving the offering told everyone to reach into the back pocket or the purse of the person in front of them and "give like you've always wanted to give." Of course, no one actually did it. The point he was making is that we are much more likely to be generous with someone else's money. We would probably take more money from our neighbors' wallets to put in the offering than we would from our own.

When you think that money comes by your own sweat and tears, then you keep a much tighter hold on it. You become attached to your money, and it actually becomes your master. But when you see yourself as a steward and recognize money as God's blessing—even though you work for your paychecks—it totally changes the role money plays in your life. It ceases to control you and simply becomes a tool. This simple change in mindset from owner to steward will make a tremendous difference for you.

Many Christians have made a firm commitment of their lives to the Lord concerning spiritual things, but when it comes to finances, they see money as a private possession. The pressures of life lead them to view money as something they must control, and that kind of ownership mentality leads to a lot of problems.

The first step toward becoming responsible with your finances is to get this mindset that money does not belong to you. Instead of clinging to your money, you need to think, *I am a steward of what God has entrusted to me. God has blessed me with these talents and abilities. God has blessed me with my job. God has put me in a prosperous nation at the most prosperous time in all of history. God is blessing me, and God has given me all of the resources I have. It is not up to me to run my finances the way I want to. I'm a steward.*

People with an ownership mentality end up trying to do everything themselves, but stewards freely receive God's blessing. Look at how blessed Abraham was:

> *Now the LORD had said unto Abram, Get thee out of thy country, and from thy kindred, and from thy father's house, unto a land that I will shew thee: And I will make of thee a great nation, and I will bless thee, and make thy name great; and thou shalt be a blessing: And I will bless them that bless thee, and curse him that curseth thee: and in thee shall all families of the earth be blessed.*
>
> GENESIS 12:1-3

God said here that He would bless Abraham and that He would make Abraham's name great. When you read the entire story of Abraham, you see that God wasn't talking about intangible spiritual benefits; He was talking about physical earthly blessings. Abraham didn't become rich through his own hard work; he became wealthy because the blessing of God was on his life. Abraham was blessed in everything he did. Even though he made mistakes, God blessed him.

During a famine in Canaan, Abraham traveled down into Egypt with his wife, Sarah. She was sixty-something at the time, but she was so beautiful that Abraham was afraid Pharaoh would kill him in order to take her from him. So, Abraham lied and told Pharaoh that Sarah was his sister, and not his wife! It was absolutely the wrong thing to do, and he put his wife in a terrible situation. Abraham was willing to sacrifice Sarah just to save his own neck. God had to intervene by sending plagues upon Pharaoh's house in order to get Sarah restored to Abraham.[1]

Not even thirty years later, Abraham did the exact same thing again! He told Abimelech, King of Gerar, that Sarah was his sister. This time, God came to Abimelech in a dream and told him to restore Sarah, or he would die. When Abimelech saw that God was with Abraham, he returned Sarah and gave him gold, silver, cattle, sheep, and servants. Then he told Abraham that he could live anywhere in the kingdom he desired. Abraham was in the wrong in both situations, but the blessing of God never stopped causing him to prosper.[2]

Abraham was not wealthy because of his shrewd business sense, or because God rewarded his great integrity; he was prosperous because God promised to bless him and make his name great. The blessing was independent of his performance, or what he deserved. It was purely the favor of God that made him rich. In the same way, your efforts are not the source of prosperity in your life.

THE BLESSING OF GOD IS NOT DEPENDENT ON YOUR PERFORMANCE, OR ACCORDING TO WHAT YOU DESERVE.

---

[1]See Genesis 12
[2]See Genesis 20

Even Abraham's nephew, Lot, benefited from the blessing of God on Abraham. In fact, both their flocks and herds grew to be so big that they couldn't occupy the same land. Their servants began fighting with one another over the grazing land, and they were forced to separate. Abraham's conversation with Lot is revealing:

> *And Abram said unto Lot, Let there be no strife, I pray thee, between me*
> *and thee, and between my herdmen and thy herdmen; for we be brethren.*
> *Is not the whole land before thee? separate thyself, I pray thee, from me:*
> *if thou wilt take the left hand, then I will go to the right; or if thou depart*
> *to the right hand, then I will go to the left. And Lot lifted up his eyes, and*
> *beheld all the plain of Jordan, that it was well watered every where.*
> GENESIS 13:8-10

Abraham took Lot up to a hilltop so they could look out over the whole land. One part of the land was a well-watered plain, lush with grass. The other part was dry. Keep in mind that the survival of their herds depended on there being plenty of natural grass to graze on. They couldn't go to a feed store and buy food for their flocks and cattle. Fields of grass were the only source of food they had. So, it isn't surprising that Lot chose the well-watered land for himself.

This story reveals how confident Abraham was in God as his source. No one who relies on natural circumstances and their own efforts for prosperity would ever give up a well-watered plain for their animals. Looking at the natural facts, the decision whether to choose a grassy plain or the desert was a no-brainer. But Abraham knew God was his source, no matter what things looked like to the naked eye. He was saying, "It doesn't matter where I go; the Lord is going to bless me." Right after Abraham allowed Lot to take the better land, God appeared to him and promised even more prosperity than Abraham had already experienced.

> *And the LORD said unto Abram, after that Lot was separated from him,*
> *Lift up now thine eyes, and look from the place where thou art northward,*
> *and southward, and eastward, and westward: For all the land which thou*
> *seest, to thee will I give it, and to thy seed for ever. And I will make thy seed*
> *as the dust of the earth: so that if a man can number the dust of the earth,*
> *then shall thy seed also be numbered. Arise, walk through the land in the*
> *length of it and in the breadth of it; for I will give it unto thee.*
> GENESIS 13:14-17

In the natural, it is impossible for a man who grazes his flocks and herds in the desert to prosper as much as a man whose cattle graze in lush pastures, but nothing is impossible for God. The blessing of God made Abraham rich, and he prospered much more than Lot did.

Not long after Lot and Abraham separated, foreign kings raided the city of Sodom, where Lot lived, and took everyone captive. When Abraham heard that his nephew had been seized, he armed his servants who were trained for war and pursued the foreign kings.

His party consisted of 318 men, which gives you an idea of how many servants he had.[3] Abraham's men defeated the foreign kings and brought back all of the spoil and the people who had been taken captive. The king of Sodom was grateful, so he offered to let Abraham keep the spoil.

> *And the king of Sodom said unto Abram, Give me the persons, and take the goods to thyself.*
>
> GENESIS 14:21

The king recognized that if it hadn't been for Abraham, his entire kingdom would have been lost. We don't know how much spoil the king was offering Abraham, but it isn't unreasonable to think it would have been the equivalent of millions of dollars today. Abraham had recovered all the goods, food, and valuables of five cities, so the spoil was certainly worth a lot of money. But Abraham didn't accept the king's offer.

> *And Abram said to the king of Sodom, I have lift up mine hand unto the Lord, the most high God, the possessor of heaven and earth, That I will not take from a thread even to a shoelatchet, and that I will not take any thing that is thine, lest thou shouldest say, I have made Abram rich: Save only that which the young men have eaten, and the portion of the men which went with me, Aner, Eshcol, and Mamre; let them take their portion.*
>
> GENESIS 14:22-24

Abraham refused to take any money from the king, because he didn't want anyone to have a reason to claim they had made him rich. He knew he was rich because of the blessing of God. His confidence in God as the source of his wealth was so strong that he gave away millions of dollars' worth of spoil, which he had rightfully earned by conquest. Abraham had a lot of possessions and many people working for him, but he saw himself as a recipient of God's blessing—not as a man who was earning wealth through his own efforts.

The foundation for Abraham's confidence goes back to when God appeared to him and said, "I will bless you, and I will make your name great." I'm sure Abraham put effort into maintaining his flocks and herds, and he had hundreds of servants helping him, but he still saw God as his source. He trusted in God, and because of that, God prospered him supernaturally. This same attitude is necessary for any Christian to really begin to walk in the financial prosperity God desires for them.

ONE OF THE REASONS WE DON'T SEE GREATER PROSPERITY IN OUR LIVES IS THAT WE HAVEN'T LEARNED THE LESSON OF BEING A STEWARD.

You need to see God as your source and develop the attitude that the resources you have are a gift from God. Yes,

---

[3]Genesis 14:14

you may have worked forty or sixty hours a week at your job, but God is the source! God gave you life, health, and abilities, and God is the one who opens doors of opportunity. God is your source, and just like Abraham, you need to recognize that the money you have belongs to God.

After Abraham boldly declared that God was his source, and had given away a fortune so the king had no basis for saying he made Abraham rich, the Lord appeared to Abraham in a vision and said, **"Fear not, Abram: I am thy shield, and thy exceeding great reward"** (Gen. 15:1). This statement had spiritual meaning, but it also had financial significance. Abraham gave away millions to preserve God as his sole source, but God gave back to Abraham even more financial increase. Abraham received from God an equivalent of all that bounty plus interest.

Until you recognize God as your source, nothing else the Bible says about finances is going to work. As long as you are hoarding possessions and holding on to your money with a clenched fist, God's method of prosperity won't work in your life. You have to change your mindset and recognize that God is the source of everything you own, seeing yourself as a steward managing the financial blessings He has given you.

God is the source of your resources just as surely as He was the source of Abraham's. The difference is that Abraham knew God was his source, and his trust in God caused him to prosper. One of the reasons you don't see greater prosperity in your life is that you haven't learned the lesson of being a steward. You see everything you own as being the result of your own sweat and tears, and because of that, you have a stingy, selfish attitude toward money. The first step toward walking in financial prosperity is to recognize that you are not the source of your financial blessing.

Seeing God as your source doesn't mean you sit at home and do nothing. You are supposed to work, but you need to recognize that even though you work, it is God who gives the increase. A farmer has to prepare the soil and plant seeds in order to get a crop, but God created the natural laws that govern sowing and reaping. God sends the rain and sun that make plants grow, He gave the land to farm on, and He is the source of the farmer's health. Likewise, it is the blessing of God that makes it possible for you to prosper, and the foundation of prosperity is seeing yourself as a steward.

— OUTLINE —

I.   I teach on financial stewardship on Thursday mornings at Charis Bible College in Colorado.

  A. The average student coming to school faces a decrease in salary, an increase in the cost of living, additional tuition costs, and part-time work to make ends meet.

  B. But at the end of every year, I ask the students how many of them are better off financially than they were when they came, and 80 percent or more always say they are better off.

  C. The reason they are able to prosper in spite of natural obstacles is that through CBC, they have received a revelation on the scriptural truths related to finances.

  D. Any of you who apply the scriptural principles I'm going to talk about will see financial prosperity begin to work in your life.

  E. Money will become a tool you use in life, instead of a master that rules over you.

  F. Too many Christians work at jobs they don't like and do things they don't want to do just to make ends meet.

  G. God has a better way for you to live.

II. The very first thing we need to understand about finances is that we are stewards of what God has given us.

  A. The *American Heritage Dictionary* defines a steward as a person "who manages another's property, finances, or other affairs."

  B. As Christians, we need to recognize that the money we have is not really ours; it's a gift from God.

  C. Without the blessing of God upon our lives, we wouldn't even have the ability to prosper.

  D. I know we are out in the world actually doing the work we get paid for, but we need to develop the mindset that the money we receive doesn't belong to us; it belongs to God.

  E. Remember, God gave us our talents and abilities, and every good thing we have is a blessing from Him.

  F. God has entrusted us with all of our finances, and it is important to develop the mindset of being a steward—over God's money, not ours.

III. Most separate their lives into "spiritual" matters like heaven and hell, and private, personal matters like career and finances.

A. When it comes to money, they think it's all up to them.

B. As a result, many Christians are struggling financially, but God wants to be the source of everything in their lives.

C. He never intended people to carry the burden of financial responsibility, and He wants to lift that burden from them.

D. This simple change in mindset from owner to steward will make a tremendous difference for you.

E. The first step toward becoming responsible with your finances is to get this mindset that money does not belong to you.

F. Instead of clinging to your money, you need to think,

    i. *I am a steward of what God has entrusted to me.*
    ii. *God has blessed me with these talents and abilities.*
    iii. *God has blessed me with my job.*
    iv. *God has put me into a prosperous nation at the most prosperous time in all of history.*
    v. *God is blessing me, and God has given me all of the resources I have.*
    vi. *It is not up to me to run my finances the way I want to.*
    vii. *I'm a steward.*

G. People with an ownership mentality end up trying to do everything themselves, but stewards freely receive God's blessing.

IV. Look at how blessed Abraham was:

> *Now the Lord had said unto Abram, Get thee out of thy country, and from thy kindred, and from thy father's house, unto a land that I will shew thee: And I will make of thee a great nation, and I will bless thee, and make thy name great; and thou shalt be a blessing: And I will bless them that bless thee, and curse him that curseth thee: and in thee shall all families of the earth be blessed.*
>
> GENESIS 12:1-3

A. When you read the entire story of Abraham, you see that God wasn't talking about intangible spiritual benefits; He was talking about physical earthly blessings.

B. Abraham was not wealthy because of his shrewd business sense, or because God rewarded his great integrity; he was prosperous because God promised to bless him and make his name great.

C. It was purely the favor of God that made him rich.

D. In the same way, your efforts are not the source of prosperity in your life.

V. Even Abraham's nephew, Lot, benefited from the blessing of God on Abraham.

A. Both their flocks and herds grew to be so big that they couldn't occupy the same land.

B. Abraham took Lot up to a hilltop so they could look out over the whole land: one part of the land was a well-watered plain, lush with grass; the other part was dry.

C. It isn't surprising that Lot chose the well-watered land for himself—no one who relies on natural circumstances and their own efforts for prosperity would ever give up a well-watered plain for their animals.

D. But Abraham knew God was his source, no matter what things looked like to the naked eye.

E. Right after Abraham allowed Lot to take the better land, God appeared to him and promised even more prosperity than Abraham had already experienced.

F. The blessing of God made Abraham rich, and he prospered much more than Lot did.

VI. Not long after Lot and Abraham separated, foreign kings raided the city of Sodom, where Lot lived, and took everyone captive.

A. When Abraham heard that his nephew had been seized, he armed his servants who were trained for war and pursued the foreign kings.

B. His party consisted of 318 men, which gives you an idea of how many servants he had (Gen. 14:14).

C. Abraham's men defeated the foreign kings and brought back all of the spoil and the people who had been taken captive.

D. The king of Sodom was grateful, so he offered to let Abraham keep the spoil.

E. But Abraham didn't accept the king's offer:

> *And Abram said to the king of Sodom, I have lift up mine hand unto the LORD, the most high God, the possessor of heaven and earth, That I will not take from a thread even to a shoelatchet, and that I will not take any thing that is thine, lest thou shouldest say, I have made Abram rich: Save only that which the young men have eaten, and the portion of the men which went with me, Aner, Eshcol, and Mamre; let them take their portion.*
>
> GENESIS 14:22-24

F. Abraham's confidence in God as the source of his wealth was so strong that he gave away millions of dollars' worth of spoil, which he had rightfully earned by conquest.

G. I'm sure Abraham put effort into maintaining his flocks and herds, and he had hundreds of servants helping him, but he still saw God as his source.

H. He trusted in God, and because of that, God prospered him supernaturally.

I. This same attitude is necessary for any Christian to really begin to walk in the financial prosperity God desires for them.

VII. After Abraham boldly declared that God was his source, and had given away a fortune so the king had no basis for saying he made Abraham rich, the Lord appeared to Abraham in a vision and said, **"Fear not, Abram: I am thy shield, and thy exceeding great reward"** (Gen. 15:1).

   A. This statement had spiritual meaning, but it also had financial significance.

   B. Abraham gave away millions to preserve God as his sole source, but God gave back to Abraham even more financial increase.

   C. Until you recognize God as your source, nothing else the Bible says about finances is going to work.

   D. As long as you are hoarding possessions and holding on to your money with a clenched fist, God's method of prosperity won't work in your life.

   E. You have to see yourself as a steward managing the financial blessings He has given you.

VIII. God is the source of your resources just as surely as He was the source of Abraham's.

   A. The difference is that Abraham knew God was his source, and his trust in God caused him to prosper.

   B. One of the reasons you don't see greater prosperity in your life is that you haven't learned the lesson of being a steward.

   C. You see everything you own as being the result of your own sweat and tears, and because of that, you have a stingy, selfish attitude toward money.

   D. The first step toward walking in financial prosperity is to recognize that you are not the source of your financial blessing.

IX. Seeing God as your source doesn't mean you sit at home and do nothing.

   A. You are supposed to work, but you need to recognize that even though you work, it is God who gives the increase.

   B. A farmer has to prepare the soil and plant seeds in order to get a crop, but God created the natural laws that govern sowing and reaping.

   C. God sends the rain and sun that make plants grow, He gave the land to farm on, and He is the source of the farmer's health.

   D. Likewise, it is the blessing of God that makes it possible for you to prosper, and the foundation of prosperity is seeing yourself as a steward.

TEACHER'S
—— GUIDE ——

1. I teach on financial stewardship on Thursday mornings at Charis Bible College in Colorado. The average student coming to school faces a decrease in salary, an increase in the cost of living, additional tuition costs, and part-time work to make ends meet. But at the end of every year, I ask the students how many of them are better off financially than they were when they came, and 80 percent or more always say they are better off. The reason they are able to prosper in spite of natural obstacles is that through CBC, they have received a revelation on the scriptural truths related to finances. Any of you who apply the scriptural principles I'm going to talk about will see financial prosperity begin to work in your life. Money will become a tool you use in life, instead of a master that rules over you. Too many Christians work at jobs they don't like and do things they don't want to do just to make ends meet. God has a better way for you to live.

    1a. Why are at least 80 percent of Charis Bible College students better off financially after a year of school?
        A. Because the other 20 percent didn't mail in the CBC cash-back rebate
        B. Because they pooled their money together
        C. Because 80 percent of the students worked harder than the others
        D. Because they have received a revelation on the scriptural truths related to finances
        E. Because God decided to prosper them over the others
    1b. What is the very first thing you need to understand about finances?
        That you are a steward of what God has given you

2. The very first thing we need to understand about finances is that we are stewards of what God has given us. The *American Heritage Dictionary* defines a steward as a person "who manages another's property, finances, or other affairs." As Christians, we need to recognize that the money we have is not really ours; it's a gift from God. Without the blessing of God upon our lives, we wouldn't even have the ability to prosper. I know we are out in the world actually doing the work we get paid for, but we need to develop the mindset that the money we receive doesn't belong to us; it belongs to God. Remember, God gave us our talents and abilities, and every good thing we have is a blessing from Him. God has entrusted us with all of our finances, and it is important to develop the mindset of being a steward—over God's money, not ours.

    2a. What wouldn't you have without the blessing of God on your life?
        Even the ability the prosper
    2b. How do you know you are a steward of every good thing in your life?
        Because every good thing in your life belongs to God

3. Most separate their lives into "spiritual" matters like heaven and hell, and private, personal matters like career and finances. When it comes to money, they think it's all up to them. As a result, many Christians are struggling financially, but God wants to be the source of everything in their lives. He never intended people to carry the burden of financial responsibility, and He wants to lift that burden from them. This simple change in mindset from owner to steward will make a tremendous difference for you. The first step toward becoming responsible with your finances is to get this mindset that money does not belong to you. Instead of clinging to your money, you need to think, *I am a steward of what God has entrusted to me. God has blessed me with these talents and abilities. God has blessed me with my job. God has put me into a prosperous nation at the most prosperous time in all of history. God is blessing me, and God has given me all of the resources I have. It is not up to me to run my finances the way I want to. I'm a steward.* People with an ownership mentality end up trying to do everything themselves, but stewards freely receive God's blessing.

    3a. Why doesn't God want you to carry the burden of financial responsibility?
        A. Because of your past experience with money
        B. Because He wants to be the source of everything in your life
        C. Because you're not mature enough
        D. All of the above
        E. None of the above
    3b. What should you think about your finances?
        A. *The money is mine, all mine!*
        B. *God has blessed me with my job*
        C. *I don't give, but God knows my heart*
        D. *It is not up to me to run my finances the way I want to*
        E. B. and D.

4. Look at how blessed Abraham was:

> *Now the LORD had said unto Abram, Get thee out of thy country, and from thy kindred, and from thy father's house, unto a land that I will shew thee: And I will make of thee a great nation, and I will bless thee, and make thy name great; and thou shalt be a blessing: And I will bless them that bless thee, and curse him that curseth thee: and in thee shall all families of the earth be blessed.*
>
> GENESIS 12:1-3

When you read the entire story of Abraham, you see that God wasn't talking about intangible spiritual benefits; He was talking about physical earthly blessings. Abraham was not wealthy because of his shrewd business sense, or because God rewarded his great integrity; he was prosperous because God promised to bless him and make his name great. It was purely the favor of God that made him rich. In the same way, your efforts are not the source of prosperity in your life.

    4a. Read Genesis 12:1-3. True or False: If Abraham stayed where he was, God would have blessed him anyway.
        False

    4b. According to the lesson, why did God bless Abraham and make his name great?
        Because He promised to

5. Even Abraham's nephew, Lot, benefited from the blessing of God on Abraham. Both their flocks and herds grew to be so big that they couldn't occupy the same land. Abraham took Lot up to a hilltop so they could look out over the whole land: one part of the land was a well-watered plain, lush with grass; the other part was dry. It isn't surprising that Lot chose the well-watered land for himself—no one who relies on natural circumstances and their own efforts for prosperity would ever give up a well-watered plain for their animals. But Abraham knew God was his source, no matter what things looked like to the naked eye. Right after Abraham allowed Lot to take the better land, God appeared to him and promised even more prosperity than Abraham had already experienced. The blessing of God made Abraham rich, and he prospered much more than Lot did.

    5a. Read Genesis 13:14-17. What did God do after Abraham allowed Lot to take the better land?
        He promised Abraham even more prosperity than he had already experienced

6. Not long after Lot and Abraham separated, foreign kings raided the city of Sodom, where Lot lived, and took everyone captive. When Abraham heard that his nephew had been seized, he armed his servants who were trained for war and pursued the foreign kings. His party consisted of 318 men, which gives you an idea of how many servants he had (Gen. 14:14). Abraham's men defeated the foreign kings and brought back all of the spoil and the people who had been taken captive. The king of Sodom was grateful, so he offered to let Abraham keep the spoil. But Abraham didn't accept the king's offer:

> *And Abram said to the king of Sodom, I have lift up mine hand unto the*
> *LORD, the most high God, the possessor of heaven and earth, That I will not*
> *take from a thread even to a shoelatchet, and that I will not take any thing*
> *that is thine, lest thou shouldest say, I have made Abram rich: Save only*
> *that which the young men have eaten, and the portion of the men which*
> *went with me, Aner, Eshcol, and Mamre; let them take their portion.*
> GENESIS 14:22-24

Abraham's confidence in God as the source of his wealth was so strong that he gave away millions of dollars' worth of spoil, which he had rightfully earned by conquest. I'm sure Abraham put effort into maintaining his flocks and herds, and he had hundreds of servants helping him, but he still saw God as his source. He trusted in God, and because of that, God prospered him supernaturally. This same attitude is necessary for any Christian to really begin to walk in the financial prosperity God desires for them.

    6a. Why didn't Abraham accept the spoil from the king of Sodom?
       Abraham didn't want to give the king any basis for saying he made Abraham rich

7. After Abraham boldly declared that God was his source, and had given away a fortune so the king had no basis for saying he made Abraham rich, the Lord appeared to Abraham in a vision and said, **"Fear not, Abram: I am thy shield, and thy exceeding great reward"** (Gen. 15:1). This statement had spiritual meaning, but it also had financial significance. Abraham gave away millions to preserve God as his sole source, but God gave back to Abraham even more financial increase. Until you recognize God as your source, nothing else the Bible says about finances is going to work. As long as you are hoarding possessions and holding on to your money with a clenched fist, God's method of prosperity won't work in your life. You have to see yourself as a steward managing the financial blessings He has given you.

    7a. After this, what did God say to Abraham, according to Genesis 15:1?
       "Fear not, Abram: I am thy shield, and thy exceeding great reward."
    7b. Until you recognize God as your source, what will work concerning your finances?
       Nothing

8. God is the source of your resources just as surely as He was the source of Abraham's. The difference is that Abraham knew God was his source, and his trust in God caused him to prosper. One of the reasons you don't see greater prosperity in your life is that you haven't learned the lesson of being a steward. You see everything you own as being the result of your own sweat and tears, and because of that, you have a stingy, selfish attitude toward money. The first step toward walking in financial prosperity is to recognize that you are not the source of your financial blessing.

    8a. Since Abraham knew God was his source, what did his trust in God cause him to do?
        A. Prosper
        B. Jump
        C. Fast
        D. Gloat
        E. Tithe
    8b. If you haven't seen greater prosperity in your life, what is one reason why?
        You don't see yourself as a steward

9. Seeing God as your source doesn't mean you sit at home and do nothing. You are supposed to work, but you need to recognize that even though you work, it is God who gives the increase. A farmer has to prepare the soil and plant seeds in order to get a crop, but God created the natural laws that govern sowing and reaping. God sends the rain and sun that make plants grow, He gave the land to farm on, and He is the source of the farmer's health. Likewise, it is the blessing of God that makes it possible for you to prosper, and the foundation of prosperity is seeing yourself as a steward.

    9a. Just seeing God as your source doesn't mean you can what?
        Sit at home and do nothing
    9b. What are you supposed to do, then?
        You are supposed to work and recognize that even though you work, it is God who gives the increase
    9c. What is a good example of this?
        A farmer who prepares the soil and plants seed but depends on God to send the rain, make the plants grow, provide the land, and keep him or her healthy

DISCIPLESHIP
——QUESTIONS——

1. Why are at least 80 percent of Charis Bible College students better off financially after a year of school?
    A. Because the other 20 percent didn't mail in the CBC cash-back rebate
    B. Because they pooled their money together
    C. Because 80 percent of the students worked harder than the others
    D. Because they have received a revelation on the scriptural truths related to finances
    E. Because God decided to prosper them over the others

2. What is the very first thing you need to understand about finances?
    _____
    _____
    _____

3. What wouldn't you have without the blessing of God on your life?
    _____
    _____
    _____

4. How do you know you are a steward of every good thing in your life?
    _____
    _____
    _____

5. Why doesn't God want you to carry the burden of financial responsibility?
    A. Because of your past experience with money
    B. Because He wants to be the source of everything in your life
    C. Because you're not mature enough
    D. All of the above
    E. None of the above

6. What should you think about your finances?
    A. *The money is mine, all mine!*
    B. *God has blessed me with my job*
    C. *I don't give, but God knows my heart*
    D. *It is not up to me to run my finances the way I want to*
    E. B. and D.

7. Read Genesis 12:1-3. True or False: If Abraham stayed where he was, God would have blessed him anyway.

8. According to the lesson, why did God bless Abraham and make his name great?

_____

_____

_____

9. Read Genesis 13:14-17. What did God do after Abraham allowed Lot to take the better land?

_____

_____

_____

10. Why didn't Abraham accept the spoil from the king of Sodom?

_____

_____

_____

11. After this, what did God say to Abraham, according to Genesis 15:1?

_____

_____

_____

12. Until you recognize God as your source, what will work concerning your finances?

_____

_____

_____

13. Since Abraham knew God was his source, what did his trust in God cause him to do?
    A. Prosper
    B. Jump
    C. Fast
    D. Gloat
    E. Tithe

14. If you haven't seen greater prosperity in your life, what is one reason why?

_____

_____

_____

15. Just seeing God as your source doesn't mean you can what?

_____

_____

_____

16. What are you supposed to do, then?

_____
_____
_____

17. What is a good example of this?

_____
_____
_____

ANSWER
—KEY—

1. D. Because they have received a revelation on the scriptural truths related to finances

2. That you are a steward of what God has given you

3. Even the ability the prosper

4. Because every good thing in your life belongs to God

5. B. Because He wants to be the source of everything in your life

6. E. B. and D.

7. False

8. Because He promised to

9. He promised Abraham even more prosperity than he had already experienced

10. Abraham didn't want to give the king any basis for saying he made Abraham rich

11. **"Fear not, Abram: I am thy shield, and thy exceeding great reward."**

12. Nothing

13. A. Prosper

14. You don't see yourself as a steward

15. Sit at home and do nothing

16. You are supposed to work and recognize that even though you work, it is God who gives the increase

17. A farmer who prepares the soil and plants seed but depends on God to send the rain, make the plants grow, provide the land, and keep him or her healthy

——SCRIPTURES——

LUKE 16:1

And he said also unto his disciples, There was a certain rich man, which had a steward; and the same was accused unto him that he had wasted his goods.

JAMES 1:17

Every good gift and every perfect gift is from above, and cometh down from the Father of lights, with whom is no variableness, neither shadow of turning.

ACTS 17:28

For in him we live, and move, and have our being; as certain also of your own poets have said, For we are also his offspring.

GENESIS 12:1-3

Now the LORD had said unto Abram, Get thee out of thy country, and from thy kindred, and from thy father's house, unto a land that I will shew thee: [2] And I will make of thee a great nation, and I will bless thee, and make thy name great; and thou shalt be a blessing: [3] And I will bless them that bless thee, and curse him that curseth thee: and in thee shall all families of the earth be blessed.

GENESIS 13:8-10

And Abram said unto Lot, Let there be no strife, I pray thee, between me and thee, and between my herdmen and thy herdmen; for we be brethren. [9] Is not the whole land before thee? separate thyself, I pray thee, from me: if thou wilt take the left hand, then I will go to the right; or if thou depart to the right hand, then I will go to the left. [10] And Lot lifted up his eyes, and beheld all the plain of Jordan, that it was well watered every where, before the LORD destroyed Sodom and Gomorrah, even as the garden of the LORD, like the land of Egypt, as thou comest unto Zoar.

GENESIS 13:14-17

And the LORD said unto Abram, after that Lot was separated from him, Lift up now thine eyes, and look from the place where thou art northward, and southward, and eastward, and westward: [15] For all the land which thou seest, to thee will I give it, and to thy seed for ever. [16] And I will make thy seed as the dust of the earth: so that if a man can number the dust of the earth, then shall thy seed also be numbered. [17] Arise, walk through the land in the length of it and in the breadth of it; for I will give it unto thee.

GENESIS 14:14

And when Abram heard that his brother was taken captive, he armed his trained servants, born in his own house, three hundred and eighteen, and pursued them unto Dan.

GENESIS 14:21-15:1

And the king of Sodom said unto Abram, Give me the persons, and take the goods to thyself. [22] And Abram said to the king of Sodom, I have lift up mine hand unto the LORD, the most high God, the possessor of heaven and earth, [23] That I will not take from a thread even to a shoelatchet, and that I will not take any thing that is thine, lest thou shouldest say, I have made Abram rich: [24] Save only that which the young men have eaten, and the portion of the men which went with me, Aner, Eshcol, and Mamre; let them take their portion. [1] After these things the word of the LORD came unto Abram in a vision, saying, Fear not, Abram: I am thy shield, and thy exceeding great reward.

GOD IS A GIVER

Many people are afraid to loosen the death grip they have on their money because they think God will take it all away. Actually, God will treat you better than you treat yourself. God is El Shaddai, not El Cheapo. He might make different choices than you would, but He will certainly treat you better.

The church has promoted so many wrong ideas over the years that people think the Lord wants Christians to live in little shacks with no money in their pockets. The Word of God says differently. God wants to bless His children. In fact, if you aren't embarrassed by your level of prosperity, then there is a good chance you aren't depending upon God as your source. I know that sounds a little shocking, but I believe it's true.

A man I used to know bought me cars for a number of years—and he didn't buy me cheap cars; he bought me top of the lines. He gave me a Chevy Suburban so nice that everywhere I went, people would ask me where I got it and what I did for a living. When they found out I was a preacher, the look on their faces said, "This car is way too nice for a preacher." It got to be embarrassing for me to take the vehicle out in public.

I went to the man who gave me the Suburban and said, "Look, I love this vehicle—and I'm not complaining—but it's embarrassing. People don't think a preacher should be driving something this nice." He looked at me for a moment and then said, "If you aren't embarrassed at your level of prosperity, then God isn't really your source." Those words went straight to my heart. It's true. If you can look at everything you have and say "I did this. This is all the result of my effort," then you haven't tapped into God's supernatural ability—you're just depending on yourself.

Of course, godly prosperity is different from coveting riches. Yes, God wants you to have nice things, but you shouldn't get them by hoarding your money and spending it all on yourself. When you give and handle your assets like a steward of God's money, then God will bless you—and the blessing of God adds no sorrow with it. You'll have nice things, but you won't be in hock up to your eyeballs or working yourself sick.

When you open up your hand and begin to trust God, you'll see that God is not a taker—He's a multiplier. He has not come into your life to take from you. The Bible is full of stories of men and women whom God blessed and prospered—and they all had the attitude of a steward. They all recognized God as their source.

David is a good example of a steward. He wanted to build the Lord a temple, but God told him he couldn't. God wanted David's son Solomon to build the temple. David obeyed God, but he started setting aside the money and materials Solomon would need one day in order to build the temple. It was his way of contributing. David set aside the equivalent of thirty-six billion dollars in gold and fourteen billion dollars in silver while Solomon was growing up. Then, right before he handed over the throne to Solomon, he made one last gift. He said,

Moreover, because I have set my affection to the house of my God, I have of mine own proper good, of gold and silver, which I have given to the house of my God, over and above all that I have prepared for the holy house, Even three thousand talents of gold, of the gold of Ophir, and seven thousand talents of refined silver, to overlay the walls of the houses withal: The gold for things of gold, and the silver for things of silver, and for all manner of work to be made by the hands of artificers. And who then is willing to consecrate his service this day unto the LORD?

1 CHRONICLES 29:3-5

For this one gift, David gave 110 tons of gold and 260 tons of silver. By today's prices, that is 6 billion dollars in gold and over 300 million dollars in silver.[1] After giving this huge gift, David encouraged other people to give. All the leaders of the tribes caught the spirit of giving and began to donate large sums of money. The leaders gave even more than David: 190 tons of gold and 375 tons of silver. All together, they gave 17 billion dollars in gold and silver in that one day.

Wherefore David blessed the LORD before all the congregation: and David said, Blessed be thou, LORD God of Israel our father, for ever and ever. Thine, O LORD, is the greatness, and the power, and the glory, and the victory, and the majesty: for all that is in the heaven and in the earth is thine; thine is the kingdom, O LORD, and thou art exalted as head above all. Both riches and honour come of thee, and thou reignest over all; and in thine hand is power and might; and in thine hand it is to make great, and to give strength unto all.

1 CHRONICLES 29:10-12

David saw himself as a steward. He knew that all of his assets had been given to him by God. David gave God the credit for being the source of all his riches. God had taken the people of Israel out of slavery and made them a rich and prosperous nation, able to donate more than sixteen billion dollars in one day. God had made them great. Then David said,

O LORD our God, all this store that we have prepared to build thee an house for thine holy name cometh of thine hand, and is all thine own. I know also, my God, that thou triest the heart, and hast pleasure in uprightness. As for me, in the uprightness of mine heart I have willingly offered all these things: and now have I seen with joy thy people, which are present here, to offer willingly unto thee.

1 CHRONICLES 29:16-17

Notice how David said they had only given what God first gave to them. All they had done was give back to God what was rightfully His anyway. This is the attitude I'm trying to

---

[1]Gold at $1,730 per ounce, and silver at $40 per ounce.

describe. In order to begin to prosper, you have to stop thinking of money as belonging to you. You need to quit seeing yourself as the source of your prosperity, and recognize that all blessings and riches come from God.

The reason people are so stressed out about money is that they think they are in control of their finances. They tend to think they are responsible for all of the factors that lead to prosperity and the money needed to survive. They are worried about losing their jobs or a downturn in the economy because they see themselves as the source of their provision.

Seeing yourself as the source of blessing in your life puts a lot of pressure on you to control circumstances that are really beyond your control. One of the benefits of seeing yourself as a steward is peace of mind and a sense of security. When you know that God is your source, you aren't worried about the natural circumstances. If God can prosper Abraham and feed his flocks and herds in a desert, then He can bless and prosper you in any economic situation. It doesn't matter what is going on around you. God is responsible for you, and even the hairs of your head are all numbered (Matt. 10:30). The Lord meets your needs according to His riches in glory, not this country's economy (Phil. 4:19).

If you are stressed out about finances—maybe you are single and trying to figure out how to make ends meet, or you're married and arguing with your spouse about money—then I encourage you to start looking to God as the source of your prosperity. God will take better care of your finances than you can.

Sometimes it's hard to look beyond the physical or natural challenges you face and see into the spiritual realm, but you can do it with a steward's mentality. Being a steward gives you a sense of confidence that you will never have as long as you see yourself as your source. I'm telling you, adopting the attitude of a steward will really help you.

In my own life, I recognize that I am not the one who has caused my success. It isn't my great wisdom or ability that has caused our ministry to succeed; it's the blessing of God. I haven't forgotten the poverty that God lifted my wife, Jamie, and me out of. I know God is my source. I have resources, but it's not really my money—it's God's money, and I'm a steward.

SEEING YOURSELF AS A STEWARD BRINGS PEACE OF MIND AND A SENSE OF SECURITY.

My mother was ninety-six at her death in 2009. Just one month before she died, she asked me to tell her again all the things the Lord was doing through my ministry. I shared with her about changed lives all over the world. As I was going on and on about all the Lord was doing, she interrupted with, "Andy, you know this is God." I replied, "Yes, Mother, I know this is God." Then she said, "You aren't smart enough to do this." Wow! There is nothing like a mother to put you in your place.

But I totally agree with her. As I look back on my life and ministry, I could not have planned what has happened. I had a vision and desire planted by the Lord, but I didn't have a clue about how to bring it to pass. All Jamie and I have done is hold on to Jesus for dear life, and the Lord has taken us on the most incredible journey. I truly see God as the source of all good things in our lives.

Every one of us needs to see our income as something God has entrusted us with. And then we need to ask ourselves what God wants us to do with it. Knowing that our incomes are really God's money makes us approach finances with a totally different attitude—and our attitudes toward money are actually more important than what we do with our money. Let's look at what is written in the book of Psalms:

> *Hear, O my people, and I will speak; O Israel, and I will testify against thee: I am God, even thy God. I will not reprove thee for thy sacrifices or thy burnt offerings, to have been continually before me. I will take no bullock out of thy house, nor he goats out of thy folds. For every beast of the forest is mine, and the cattle upon a thousand hills. I know all the fowls of the mountains: and the wild beasts of the field are mine. If I were hungry, I would not tell thee: for the world is mine, and the fulness thereof. Will I eat the flesh of bulls, or drink the blood of goats? Offer unto God thanksgiving; and pay thy vows unto the most High.*
>
> PSALM 50:7-14

God was saying that His disagreement with them wasn't about a lack of sacrifices on their part; they had been offering sacrifices continually. His complaint against them was the heart attitude they had in making the offerings. They were missing the point! God didn't need the sacrifices. He was trying to illustrate the need for blood to be spilled in order to be made righteous. They were a prophetic foreshadowing of how Christ would offer His blood in payment for man's sins. It was a type and shadow of a future New Testament reality. The Israelites were going through the motions of making the offerings, but they weren't giving their hearts to God.

They thought they were making sacrifices because God somehow needed their bulls and goats. In this passage, God was making it clear that He didn't need anything from them; everything already belonged to the Lord. God said, "If I were hungry, I wouldn't tell you! The world is mine, and everything in it." He doesn't need to ask anyone for food. The truth was that the *Israelites* needed those sacrifices. They needed to give back to God and show their trust and dependence upon Him. It wasn't for God—it was for them.

Do you know why God asked you to give 10 percent of your income to the church? It isn't because He needs your money! All of the gold, silver, and riches in the earth already belong to Him. He doesn't need your donations. God could have set up church finances differently. He could have made every minister of the Gospel independently wealthy like He made Abraham, Isaac, David, Solomon, and all the rest. The tithe exists for your benefit, not God's.

God doesn't need your money any more than He needed those Old Testament sacrifices. The point of the tithe is for you to learn to recognize God as the source of all of your money. It's one thing to say you believe God is your source, but it's another thing to prove it. The way you prove to yourself—not God—that you believe God is your source is to give a portion of what you make back to Him. If you don't really see God as your source, your are going to balk at giving away part of what you have. You are going to think, *I need that money!* But giving back some of what God has already given you is nothing when you see Him as your source.

Money is difficult to come by when you think of yourself as the provider. Money reminds you of how hard you have to work just to get by, and giving it away would only seem to put you further away from the goal of having all your needs met. All of that would be true if God wasn't your source. In God's economy, you move closer toward your goals by giving than you do by clinging to everything you have.

It all comes down to faith, and that's why God told you to give. He doesn't need your money. God could establish His kingdom using other principles. He could give every person in ministry creative ideas that would generate incredible wealth. He could have done all sorts of things, but God set up His kingdom around giving because He wants you to trust Him and recognize Him as your source. He wants you to remember that even though you have money, you didn't get it by your own power. Moses wrote,

> *But thou shalt remember the LORD thy God: for it is he that giveth thee power to get wealth, that he may establish his covenant which he sware unto thy fathers, as it is this day.*
>
> DEUTERONOMY 8:18

God gives us the power to get wealth, and it's important for us to recognize that He is our source—regardless of how much effort we put into earning a living. All prosperity comes from God. He blesses us so that **"he may establish his covenant"** and so we can be blessings to others. Yes, God gives us money to survive and pay our bills, but the primary reason He has blessed us is so that we can be blessings (Gen. 12:3, Eph. 4:28, and 2 Cor. 9:8).

Giving is a problem when you see yourself as the owner of your finances, because when God leads you to give or when you see instructions in the Word that tell you to give, you'll start thinking, *What right does God have to tell me what to do with my own money?* But the truth is that whatever wealth you have came from God. He is the one who gives you the power and ability to prosper.

The interesting thing about this scripture from Deuteronomy is that God was talking to the children of Israel who would eventually enter into the Promised Land. They were going to be living in homes built for giants. The fields already had the rocks cleared out of them, the furrows were dug, and the crops were planted. The Israelites were going to step in and benefit from the labor of others. God was telling them not to forget the source of their wealth when they went from living in the desert to living in mansions with abundant prosperity. In context, God was saying, "Don't think you got wealthy by your own might or power. I'm the one who made you rich, and I did it to establish My covenant upon the earth."

The same is true for us today. God is the one who makes us wealthy. I know that a lot of us don't feel wealthy, but that is partly because the standard for wealth is a little out of balance in the developed world. We are prosperous so far beyond our physical needs that we don't feel like we have enough unless we drive brand-new luxury cars and own five flat-screen televisions. Our level of poverty doesn't even compare to what most people on this earth have lived through. Most of us have no idea what it means to struggle to survive.

We live at a level of relative prosperity that most people throughout history couldn't have dreamed of, yet we didn't do anything to be born at this time. We didn't cause ourselves to be born into such opportunity and freedom. Even today, some people are born into social systems that don't permit them to seek prosperity, or into dictatorships that control their financial status. Others have suffered through war, persecution, and imprisonment. We are super blessed to be born into such a time of prosperity. It should help us see that even the ability to prosper is a gift from God, and we can't boast of the opportunities we have been given. The Apostle Paul said,

> *For who maketh thee to differ from another? and what hast thou that thou didst not receive? now if thou didst receive it, why dost thou glory, as if thou hadst not received it?*
>
> 1 CORINTHIANS 4:7

Everything we have has been given to us by God, and since we received it, there is no room for boasting that we earned it. The Corinthians worked just like we do, but Paul still said that everything they were, and all that they had, came from God. I have probably spent tens of thousands of hours studying the Word, but it would be wrong for me to adopt the attitude that I am a self-made man. I have worked to make sure our ministry does well, but I am not the reason it is successful. God called me into the ministry and blessed me with success by His grace, not because of anything I have done.

Many Christians recognize God as the cause of professional success, but far fewer people make the connection that God is also the source of financial success. A lot of people see the hand of God in granting them professional opportunities, but the truth is that they don't have a single thing that God didn't give them. What gets you into financial trouble is failing to recognize your roles as a steward of God's resources. A steward knows that their master wouldn't want them going into debt and paying two or three times the actual value of something in interest. A steward doesn't make impulse purchases, because they just can't wait to get a new toy, and they don't mortgage their future to buy things on credit.

The Word of God is full of instructions to help us make good financial decisions. For instance, the Word tells us to set money aside and be prepared. The reason a little dip in finances devastates a lot of us is that we don't have any savings, and often it's because we haven't made the best use of our money. Some of us have plenty of money coming in, but we are living so close to the limit that it only takes a slight economic downturn to send us into financial disaster. Following God's financial advice will save us from making those mistakes, but we have to adopt the mindset of a steward before we can understand what the Word says about managing money.

It's possible to prosper without God, but it comes with heartache. The Word says that the blessing of the Lord makes you rich, and He adds no sorrow with it (Prov. 10:22). When you're doing it all yourself, you carry the load of responsibility also. That's why people are so stressed out about what's going to happen in the stock market or how they're going to pay their bills. When God is your source, there is no sorrow added to your prosperity. Scripture says,

> *But they that will be rich fall into temptation and a snare, and into many*
> *foolish and hurtful lusts, which drown men in destruction and perdition. For*
> *the love of money is the root of all evil: which while some coveted after, they*
> *have erred from the faith, and pierced themselves through with many sorrows.*
> 1 TIMOTHY 6:9-10

The way the world goes about trying to prosper is ungodly, and those who gain prosperity in an ungodly way bring grief upon themselves. The world's attitude toward finances is causing people to be totally stressed out. They need a pill to get through the day and another pill to get to sleep at night. We need to quit following the example of the world. The godly way to seek prosperity is to remember that God has given us the power to get wealth, and our role is to be stewards of what God has blessed us with. We seek first of all God's kingdom, and He adds to us all the physical things we need (Matt. 6:33).

The two most important steps toward prosperity are to realize that God is your source and to develop the mindset of a steward. Once you do those two things, the Word of God will cause you to prosper. It also takes away the stress and worry associated with finances because it's not your money! You don't have to fear that God is going to take from you if you loosen your grip on money. God is a multiplier, not a subtracter. I promise you, being a steward puts everything into perspective and enables you to receive greater blessings from God. You'll be blessed and you'll be a greater blessing to other people.

— OUTLINE —

I.   Many people are afraid to loosen the death grip they have on their money because they think God will take it all away.

    A. Actually, God will treat you better than you treat yourself—He wants to bless His children.

    B. In fact, this will sound a little shocking, but if you aren't embarrassed by your level of prosperity, then there is a good chance you aren't depending upon God as your source.

    C. Godly prosperity is different from coveting riches.

    D. Yes, God wants you to have nice things, but you shouldn't get them by hoarding your money and spending it all on yourself.

    E. When you give and handle your assets like a steward of God's money, then God will bless you—and the blessing of God adds no sorrow with it.

    F. You'll have nice things, but you won't be in hock up to your eyeballs or working yourself sick.

    G. When you open up your hand and begin to trust God, you'll see that God is not a taker—He's a multiplier.

    H. He has not come into your life to take from you.

II.   The Bible is full of stories of men and women whom God blessed and prospered, and they all had the attitude of a steward—they all recognized God as their source.

    A. David is a good example of a steward.

    B. He started setting aside the money and materials Solomon would need one day in order to build the temple.

    C. Then, right before he handed over the throne to Solomon, he made one last gift: 110 tons of gold and 260 tons of silver (by today's prices, that is 6 billion dollars in gold and over 300 billion dollars in silver).

    D. After giving this huge gift, David encouraged other people to give.

    E. All the leaders of the tribes caught the spirit of giving and began to donate large sums of money.

    F. The leaders gave even more than David.

    G. God had taken the people of Israel out of slavery and made them a rich and prosperous nation.

O Lord our God, all this store that we have prepared to build thee an house for thine holy name cometh of thine hand, and is all thine own. I know also, my God, that thou triest the heart, and hast pleasure in uprightness. As for me, in the uprightness of mine heart I have willingly offered all these things: and now have I seen with joy thy people, which are present here, to offer willingly unto thee.

1 CHRONICLES 29:16-17

H. Notice how David said they had only given what God first gave to them.

I. All they had done was give back to God what was rightfully His anyway.

J. In order to begin to prosper, you have to stop thinking of money as belonging to you.

K. You need to quit seeing yourself as the source of your prosperity, and recognize that all blessings and riches come from God.

III. The reason people are so stressed out about money is that they think they are in control of their finances.

A. People tend to think they are responsible for all of the factors that lead to prosperity and the money needed to survive.

B. They are worried about losing their jobs or a downturn in the economy because they see themselves as the source of their provision.

C. Seeing yourself as the source of blessing in your life puts a lot of pressure on you to control circumstances that are really beyond your control.

D. One of the benefits of seeing yourself as a steward is peace of mind and a sense of security.

E. When you know that God is your source, you aren't worried about the natural circumstances.

F. The Lord meets your needs according to His riches in glory, not this country's economy (Phil. 4:19).

G. If you are stressed out about finances—maybe you are single and trying to figure out how to make ends meet, or you're married and arguing with your spouse about money—then I encourage you to start looking to God as the source of your prosperity.

H. God will take better care of your finances than you can.

I. Sometimes it's hard to look beyond the physical or natural challenges you face and see into the spiritual realm, but you can do it with a steward's mentality.

J. Being a steward gives you a sense of confidence that you will never have as long as you see yourself as your source.

K. I'm telling you, adopting the attitude of a steward will really help you.

IV. In my own life, I recognize that I am not the one who has caused my success—it's the blessing of God.

    A. I haven't forgotten the poverty that God lifted my wife and me out of.

    B. Just one month before my mother died, she asked me to tell her again all the things the Lord was doing through my ministry.

    C. I shared with her about changed lives all over the world.

    D. As I was going on and on about all the Lord was doing, she interrupted with, "Andy, you know this is God." I replied, "Yes, Mother, I know this is God." Then she said, "You aren't smart enough to do this."

    E. There is nothing like a mother to put you in your place, but I totally agree with her.

    F. As I look back on my life and ministry, I could not have planned what has happened.

    G. I had a vision and desire planted by the Lord, but I didn't have a clue about how to bring it to pass.

    H. All Jamie and I have done is hold on to Jesus for dear life, and the Lord has taken us on the most incredible journey.

    I. I truly see God as the source of all good things in our lives.

    J. Every one of us needs to see our income as something God has entrusted us with.

    K. And then we need to ask ourselves what God wants us to do with it.

V. Knowing that our incomes are really God's money makes us approach finances with a totally different attitude—and our attitudes toward money are actually more important than what we do with our money.

    A. Let's look at what is written in the book of Psalms:

Hear, O my people, and I will speak; O Israel, and I will testify against thee: I am God, even thy God. I will not reprove thee for thy sacrifices or thy burnt offerings, to have been continually before me. I will take no bullock out of thy house, nor he goats out of thy folds. For every beast of the forest is mine, and the cattle upon a thousand hills. I know all the fowls of the mountains: and the wild beasts of the field are mine. If I were hungry, I would not tell thee: for the world is mine, and the fulness thereof. Will I eat the flesh of bulls, or drink the blood of goats? Offer unto God thanksgiving; and pay thy vows unto the most High.

PSALM 50:7-14

B. God's complaint against them was the heart attitude they had in making the offerings.

C. God didn't need the sacrifices.

D. They were a prophetic foreshadowing of how Christ would offer His blood in payment for our sins.

E. The Israelites were going through the motions of making the offerings, but they weren't giving their hearts to God.

F. They thought they were making sacrifices because God somehow needed their bulls and goats.

G. In this passage, God was making it clear that He didn't need anything from them; everything already belonged to the Lord.

H. The truth was that the *Israelites* needed those sacrifices.

I. They needed to give back to God and show their trust and dependence upon Him.

J. It wasn't for God—it was for them.

VI. God could have set up church finances differently.

A. He could have made every minister of the Gospel independently wealthy like He made Abraham, Isaac, David, Solomon, and all the rest.

B. God doesn't need your money any more than He needed those Old Testament sacrifices.

C. The reason God asked you to give a tithe of your finances is for you to learn to recognize God as the source of all of your money.

D. It's one thing to say you believe God is your source, but it's another thing to prove it.

E. The way you prove to yourself—not God—that you believe God is your source is to give a portion of what you make back to Him.

F. If you don't really see God as your source, you are going to balk at giving away part of what you have.

G. But giving back some of what God has already given you is nothing when you see Him as your source.

H. Money is difficult to come by when you think of yourself as the provider.

I And giving it away would only seem to put you further away from the goal of having all your needs met—which would be true if God wasn't your source.

J. In God's economy, you move closer toward your goals by giving than you do by clinging to everything you have.

K. It all comes down to faith, and that's why God told you to give.

L. God set up His kingdom around giving because He wants you to trust Him and recognize Him as your source.

VII. He wants us to remember that even though we have money, we didn't get it by our own power.

A. Moses wrote,

But thou shalt remember the LORD thy God: for it is he that giveth thee power to get wealth, that he may establish his covenant which he sware unto thy fathers, as it is this day.

DEUTERONOMY 8:18

B. God gives us the power to get wealth, and it's important for us to recognize that He is our source—regardless of how much effort we put into earning a living.

C. Yes, God gives us money to survive and pay our bills, but the primary reason He has blessed us is so that we can be blessings (Gen. 12:3, Eph. 4:28, and 2 Cor. 9:8).

D. God was saying, "Don't think you got wealthy by your own might or power. I'm the one who made you rich, and I did it to establish My covenant upon the earth."

E. I know that a lot of people don't feel wealthy, but that is partly because the standard for wealth is a little out of balance in the developed world.

F. We live at a level of relative prosperity that most people throughout history couldn't have dreamed of, yet we didn't do anything to be born at this time.

G. The Apostle Paul said,

For who maketh thee to differ from another? and what hast thou that thou didst not receive? now if thou didst receive it, why dost thou glory, as if thou hadst not received it?

1 CORINTHIANS 4:7

H. Everything we have has been given to us by God, and since we received it, there is no room for boasting that we earned it.

I. The Corinthians worked just like we do, but Paul still said that everything they were, and all that they had, came from God.

J. Many Christians recognize God as the cause of professional success, but far fewer people make the connection that God is also the source of financial success.

K. A lot of people see the hand of God in granting them professional opportunities, but the truth is that they don't have a single thing that God didn't give them.

VIII. What gets you into financial trouble is failing to recognize your role as a steward of God's resources.

A. A steward knows that his master wouldn't want him to go into debt and pay two or three times the actual value of something in interest.

B. A steward doesn't make impulse purchases, because they just can't wait to get a new toy, and they don't mortgage their future to buy things on credit.

C. The Word of God is full of instructions to help you make good financial decisions.

D. For instance, the Word tells you to set money aside and be prepared.

E. The reason a little dip in finances devastates a lot of people is that they don't have any savings, and often it's because they haven't made the best use of their money.

F. Some people have plenty of money coming in, but they are living so close to the limit that it only takes a slight economic downturn to send them into financial disaster.

G. Following God's financial advice will save you from making those mistakes, but you have to adopt the mindset of a steward before you can understand what the Word says about managing money.

IX. It's possible to prosper without God, but it comes with heartache.

A. The Word says that the blessing of the Lord makes us rich, and He adds no sorrow with it (Prov. 10:22).

B. When we're doing it all ourselves, we carry the load of responsibility also.

C. That's why people are so stressed out about what's going to happen in the stock market or how they're going to pay their bills.

D. Scripture says,

But they that will be rich fall into temptation and a snare, and into many foolish and hurtful lusts, which drown men in destruction and perdition. For the love of money is the root of all evil: which while some coveted after, they have erred from the faith, and pierced themselves through with many sorrows.
1 TIMOTHY 6:9-10

E. The way the world goes about trying to prosper is ungodly, and those who gain prosperity in an ungodly way bring grief upon themselves.

F. We need to quit following the example of the world.

G. The godly way to seek prosperity is to remember that God has given us the power to get wealth, and our role is to be stewards of what God has blessed us with.

H. We seek first of all God's kingdom, and He adds to us all the physical things we need (Matt. 6:33).

X. The two most important steps toward prosperity are to realize that God is your source and to develop the mindset of a steward.

    A. I promise you, being a steward puts everything into perspective and enables you to receive greater blessings from God.

    B. You'll be blessed and you'll be a greater blessing to other people.

TEACHER'S
——— GUIDE ———

1. Many people are afraid to loosen the death grip they have on their money because they think God will take it all away. Actually, God will treat you better than you treat yourself—He wants to bless His children. In fact, this will sound a little shocking, but if you aren't embarrassed by your level of prosperity, then there is a good chance you aren't depending upon God as your source. Godly prosperity is different from coveting riches. Yes, God wants you to have nice things, but you shouldn't get them by hoarding your money and spending it all on yourself. When you give and handle your assets like a steward of God's money, then God will bless you—and the blessing of God adds no sorrow with it. You'll have nice things, but you won't be in hock up to your eyeballs or working yourself sick. When you open up your hand and begin to trust God, you'll see that God is not a taker—He's a multiplier. He has not come into your life to take from you.

    1a. There is a good chance you aren't depending on God as your source if you aren't what?
        Embarrassed by your level of prosperity
    1b. What do you have to do to see that God is not a taker but a multiplier?
        A. Do the math again
        B. You have to give to get, so get with it!
        C. Follow the money
        D. Get all you can, can all you get, and sit on the can
        E. Open your hands and begin to trust God

2. The Bible is full of stories of men and women whom God blessed and prospered, and they all had the attitude of a steward—they all recognized God as their source. David is a good example of a steward. He started setting aside the money and materials Solomon would need one day in order to build the temple. Then, right before he handed over the throne to Solomon, he made one last gift: 110 tons of gold and 260 tons of silver (by today's prices, that is 6 billion dollars in gold and over 300 billion dollars in silver). After giving this huge gift, David encouraged other people to give. All the leaders of the tribes caught the spirit of giving and began to donate large sums of money. The leaders gave even more than David. God had taken the people of Israel out of slavery and made them a rich and prosperous nation.

> *O Lord our God, all this store that we have prepared to build thee an house for thine holy name cometh of thine hand, and is all thine own. I know also, my God, that thou triest the heart, and hast pleasure in uprightness. As for me, in the uprightness of mine heart I have willingly offered all these things: and now have I seen with joy thy people, which are present here, to offer willingly unto thee.*
> 1 CHRONICLES 29:16-17

Notice how David said they had only given what God first gave to them. All they had done was give back to God what was rightfully His anyway. In order to begin to prosper, you have to stop thinking of money as belonging to you. You need to quit seeing yourself as the source of your prosperity, and recognize that all blessings and riches come from God.

    2a. After David and the leaders had given gold and silver for the building of the temple, what did he say?
        That they had only given what God first gave to them

3. The reason people are so stressed out about money is that they think they are in control of their finances. People tend to think they are responsible for all of the factors that lead to prosperity and the money needed to survive. They are worried about losing their jobs or a downturn in the economy because they see themselves as the source of their provision. Seeing yourself as the source of blessing in your life puts a lot of pressure on you to control circumstances that are really beyond your control. One of the benefits of seeing yourself as a steward is peace of mind and a sense of security. When you know that God is your source, you aren't worried about the natural circumstances. The Lord meets your needs according to His riches in glory, not this country's economy (Phil. 4:19). If you are stressed out about finances—maybe you are single and trying to figure out how to make ends meet, or you're married and arguing with your spouse about money—then I encourage you to start looking to God as the source of your prosperity. God will take better care of your finances than you can. Sometimes it's hard to look beyond the physical or natural challenges you face and see into the spiritual realm, but you can do it with a steward's mentality. Being a steward gives you a sense of confidence that you will never have as long as you see yourself as your source. I'm telling you, adopting the attitude of a steward will really help you.

    3a. What is the reason people are stressed out about money?
        A. They are in control of their finances
        B. They want to be in control of their finances
        C. They think they are in control of their finances
        D. All of the above
        E. None of the above
    3b. What is one benefit of seeing yourself as a steward?
        Peace of mind and a sense of security
    3c. Read Philippians 4:19. How does God meet your needs?
        A. According to your job and promotion
        B. According to others sowing into your life
        C. According to your efforts and ideas
        D. According to His riches in glory by Christ Jesus
        E. According to how good you've been lately
    3d. What can you do with a steward's mentality?
        Look beyond the physical or natural challenges you face and see into the spiritual realm

4. In my own life, I recognize that I am not the one who has caused my success—it's the blessing of God. I haven't forgotten the poverty that God lifted my wife and me out of. Just one month before my mother died, she asked me to tell her again all the things the Lord was doing through my ministry. I shared with her about changed lives all over the world. As I was going on and on about all the Lord was doing, she interrupted with, "Andy, you know this is God." I replied, "Yes, Mother, I know this is God." Then she said, "You aren't smart enough to do this." There is nothing like a mother to put you in your place, but I totally agree with her. As I look back on my life and ministry, I could not have planned what has happened. I had a vision and desire planted by the Lord, but I didn't have a clue about how to bring it to pass. All Jamie and I have done is hold on to Jesus for dear life, and the Lord has taken us on the most incredible journey. I truly see God as the source of all good things in our lives. Every one of us needs to see our income as something God has entrusted us with. And then we need to ask ourselves what God wants us to do with it.

5. Knowing that our incomes are really God's money makes us approach finances with a totally different attitude—and our attitudes toward money are actually more important than what we do with our money. Let's look at what is written in the book of Psalms:

> *Hear, O my people, and I will speak; O Israel, and I will testify against thee:*
> *I am God, even thy God. I will not reprove thee for thy sacrifices or thy*
> *burnt offerings, to have been continually before me. I will take no bullock*
> *out of thy house, nor he goats out of thy folds. For every beast of the forest*
> *is mine, and the cattle upon a thousand hills. I know all the fowls of the*
> *mountains: and the wild beasts of the field are mine. If I were hungry, I*
> *would not tell thee: for the world is mine, and the fulness thereof. Will I eat*
> *the flesh of bulls, or drink the blood of goats? Offer unto God thanksgiving;*
> *and pay thy vows unto the most High.*
>
> PSALM 50:7-14

God's complaint against them was the heart attitude they had in making the offerings. God didn't need the sacrifices. They were a prophetic foreshadowing of how Christ would offer His blood in payment for our sins. The Israelites were going through the motions of making the offerings, but they weren't giving their hearts to God. They thought they were making sacrifices because God somehow needed their bulls and goats. In this passage, God was making it clear that He didn't need anything from them; everything already belonged to the Lord. The truth was that the *Israelites* needed those sacrifices. They needed to give back to God and show their trust and dependence upon Him. It wasn't for God—it was for them.

5a. What's more important than what you do with your money?
    Your attitude toward money
5b. Read Psalm 50:7-14. True or False: God wanted the Israelites' sacrifices because He needed them.
    False
5c. What were the sacrifices for?
    A.   They were to foreshadow how Christ would offer His blood in payment for sins
    B.   They were to take away the Israelites' sins
    C.   They were to clear the Israelites' consciences for one whole year
    D.   All of the above
    E.   None of the above

6. God could have set up church finances differently. He could have made every minister of the Gospel independently wealthy like He made Abraham, Isaac, David, Solomon, and all the rest. God doesn't need your money any more than He needed those Old Testament sacrifices. The reason God asked you to give a tithe of your finances is for you to learn to recognize God as the source of all of your money. It's one thing to say you believe God is your source, but it's another thing to prove it. The way you prove to yourself—not God—that you believe God is your source is to give a portion of what you make back to Him. If you don't really see God as your source, you are going to balk at giving away part of what you have. But giving back some of what God has already given you is nothing when you see Him as your source. Money is difficult to come by when you think of yourself as the provider. And giving it away would only seem to put you further away from the goal of having all your needs met—which would be true if God wasn't your source. In God's economy, you move closer toward your goals by giving than you do by clinging to everything you have. It all comes down to faith, and that's why God told you to give. God set up His kingdom around giving because He wants you to trust Him and recognize Him as your source.

    6a. True or False: God doesn't need your money.
       True
    6b. It's one thing to say you believe God is your source, but it's another thing to _____ it.
       Prove
    6c. How do you prove to yourself that you believe God is your source?
       By giving a portion of what you make back to Him
    6d. What is nothing when you see God as your source?
       Giving back some of what God has already given you
    6e. You move closer toward your goals by doing what?
       A. Depositing your money in the bank
       B. Clinging to everything you have
       C. Receiving
       D. Giving
       E. Budgeting
    6f. Why did God set up His kingdom around giving?
       Because He wants you to trust Him and recognize Him as your source

7. He wants us to remember that even though we have money, we didn't get it by our own power. Moses wrote,

> *But thou shalt remember the LORD thy God: for it is he that giveth thee power to get wealth, that he may establish his covenant which he sware unto thy fathers, as it is this day.*
>
> DEUTERONOMY 8:18

God gives us the power to get wealth, and it's important for us to recognize that He is our source—regardless of how much effort we put into earning a living. Yes, God gives us money to survive and pay our bills, but the primary reason He has blessed us is so that we can be blessings (Gen. 12:3, Eph. 4:28, and 2 Cor. 9:8). God was saying, "Don't think you got wealthy by your own might or power. I'm the one who made you rich, and I did it to establish My covenant upon the earth." I know that a lot of people don't feel wealthy, but that is partly because the standard for wealth is a little out of balance in the developed world. We live at a level of relative prosperity that most people throughout history couldn't have dreamed of, yet we didn't do anything to be born at this time. The Apostle Paul said,

> *For who maketh thee to differ from another? and what hast thou that thou didst not receive? now if thou didst receive it, why dost thou glory, as if thou hadst not received it?*
>
> 1 CORINTHIANS 4:7

Everything we have has been given to us by God, and since we received it, there is no room for boasting that we earned it. The Corinthians worked just like we do, but Paul still said that everything they were, and all that they had, came from God. Many Christians recognize God as the cause of professional success, but far fewer people make the connection that God is also the source of financial success. A lot of people see the hand of God in granting them professional opportunities, but the truth is that they don't have a single thing that God didn't give them.

7a. Read Deuteronomy 8:18. Regardless of how much effort you put into earning a living, what do you need to recognize?
   That it is God who gives you the power to get wealth

7b. According to 1 Corinthians 4:7, since everything you have you received, what can you boast about?
   Nothing

8. What gets you into financial trouble is failing to recognize your role as a steward of God's resources. A steward knows that his master wouldn't want him to go into debt and pay two or three times the actual value of something in interest. A steward doesn't make impulse purchases, because they just can't wait to get a new toy, and they don't mortgage their future to buy things on credit. The Word of God is full of instructions to help you make good financial decisions. For instance, the Word tells you to set money aside and be prepared. The reason a little dip in finances devastates a lot of people is that they don't have any savings, and often it's because they haven't made the best use of their money. Some people have plenty of money coming in, but they are living so close to the limit that it only takes a slight economic downturn to send them into financial disaster. Following God's financial advice will save you from making those mistakes, but you have to adopt the mindset of a steward before you can understand what the Word says about managing money.

    8a. What gets you into financial trouble?
        A. Taking out a loan
        B. Buying stuff you cannot afford
        C. Failing to recognize your role as a steward of God's resources
        D. B. and C.
        E. None of the above

9. It's possible to prosper without God, but it comes with heartache. The Word says that the blessing of the Lord makes us rich, and He adds no sorrow with it (Prov. 10:22). When we're doing it all ourselves, we carry the load of responsibility also. That's why people are so stressed out about what's going to happen in the stock market or how they're going to pay their bills. Scripture says,

> *But they that will be rich fall into temptation and a snare, and into many*
> *foolish and hurtful lusts, which drown men in destruction and perdition. For*
> *the love of money is the root of all evil: which while some coveted after, they*
> *have erred from the faith, and pierced themselves through with many sorrows.*
> 1 TIMOTHY 6:9-10

The way the world goes about trying to prosper is ungodly, and those who gain prosperity in an ungodly way bring grief upon themselves. We need to quit following the example of the world. The godly way to seek prosperity is to remember that God has given us the power to get wealth, and our role is to be stewards of what God has blessed us with. We seek first of all God's kingdom, and He adds to us all the physical things we need (Matt. 6:33).

    9a. Is it possible to prosper without God?
        Yes
    9b. What does it come with?
        Heartache
    9c. Read Proverbs 10:22. What is not added to the blessing of the Lord?
        Sorrow
    9d. What do you need to quit following?
        The example of the world
    9e. According to Matthew 6:33, when you seek first God's kingdom, what will He add to you?
        All the physical things you need

10. The two most important steps toward prosperity are to realize that God is your source and to develop the mindset of a steward. I promise you, being a steward puts everything into perspective and enables you to receive greater blessings from God. You'll be blessed and you'll be a greater blessing to other people.

    10a. What are the two most important steps toward prosperity?
         <u>Realizing that God is your source and developing the mindset of a steward</u>

DISCIPLESHIP
——— QUESTIONS ———

1. There is a good chance you aren't depending on God as your source if you aren't what?

   _____
   _____
   _____

2. What do you have to do to see that God is not a taker but a multiplier?
   A. Do the math again
   B. You have to give to get, so get with it!
   C. Follow the money
   D. Get all you can, can all you get, and sit on the can
   E. Open your hands and begin to trust God

3. After David and the leaders had given gold and silver for the building of the temple, what did he say?

   _____
   _____
   _____

4. What is the reason people are stressed out about money?
   A. They are in control of their finances
   B. They want to be in control of their finances
   C. They think they are in control of their finances
   D. All of the above
   E. None of the above

5. What is one benefit of seeing yourself as a steward?

   _____
   _____
   _____

6. Read Philippians 4:19. How does God meet your needs?
   A. According to your job and promotion
   B. According to others sowing into your life
   C. According to your efforts and ideas
   D. According to His riches in glory by Christ Jesus
   E. According to how good you've been lately

7. What can you do with a steward's mentality?

    _____
    _____
    _____

8. What's more important than what you do with your money?

    _____
    _____
    _____

9. Read Psalm 50:7-14. True or False: God wanted the Israelites' sacrifices because He needed them.

10. What were the sacrifices for?
    A. They were to foreshadow how Christ would offer His blood in payment for sins
    B. They were to take away the Israelites' sins
    C. They were to clear the Israelites' consciences for one whole year
    D. All of the above
    E. None of the above

11. True or False: God doesn't need your money.

12. It's one thing to say you believe God is your source, but it's another thing to
    _____ it.

13. How do you prove to yourself that you believe God is your source?

    _____
    _____
    _____

14. What is nothing when you see God as your source?

    _____
    _____
    _____

15. You move closer toward your goals by doing what?
    A. Depositing your money in the bank
    B. Clinging to everything you have
    C. Receiving
    D. Giving
    E. Budgeting

16. Why did God set up His kingdom around giving?

_____

_____

_____

17. Read Deuteronomy 8:18. Regardless of how much effort you put into earning a living, what do you need to recognize?

_____

_____

_____

18. According to 1 Corinthians 4:7, since everything you have you received, what can you boast about?

_____

_____

_____

19. What gets you into financial trouble?
    A. Taking out a loan
    B. Buying stuff you cannot afford
    C. Failing to recognize your role as a steward of God's resources
    D. B. and C.
    E. None of the above

20. Is it possible to prosper without God?

_____

_____

_____

21. What does it come with?

_____

_____

_____

22. Read Proverbs 10:22. What is not added to the blessing of the Lord?

_____

_____

_____

23. What do you need to quit following?

_____

_____

_____

24. According to Matthew 6:33, when you seek first God's kingdom, what will He add to you?

_____
_____
_____

25. What are the two most important steps toward prosperity?

_____
_____
_____

ANSWER
—KEY—

1. Embarrassed by your level of prosperity

2. E. Open your hands and begin to trust God

3. That they had only given what God first gave to them

4. C. They think they are in control of their finances

5. Peace of mind and a sense of security

6. D. According to His riches in glory by Christ Jesus

7. Look beyond the physical or natural challenges you face and see into the spiritual realm

8. Your attitude toward money

9. False

10. A. They were to foreshadow how Christ would offer His blood in payment for sins

11. True

12. Prove

13. By giving a portion of what you make back to Him

14. Giving back some of what God has already given you

15. D. Giving

16. Because He wants you to trust Him and recognize Him as your source

17. That it is God who gives you the power to get wealth

18. Nothing

19. C. Failing to recognize your role as a steward of God's resources

20. Yes

21. Heartache

22. Sorrow

23. The example of the world

24. All the physical things you need

25. Realizing that God is your source and developing the mindset of a steward

──SCRIPTURES──

1 CHRONICLES 29:3-5

Moreover, because I have set my affection to the house of my God, I have of mine own proper good, of gold and silver, which I have given to the house of my God, over and above all that I have prepared for the holy house, [4] Even three thousand talents of gold, of the gold of Ophir, and seven thousand talents of refined silver, to overlay the walls of the houses withal: [5] The gold for things of gold, and the silver for things of silver, and for all manner of work to be made by the hands of artificers. And who then is willing to consecrate his service this day unto the LORD?

1 CHRONICLES 29:10-12

Wherefore David blessed the LORD before all the congregation: and David said, Blessed be thou, LORD God of Israel our father, for ever and ever. [11] Thine, O LORD, is the greatness, and the power, and the glory, and the victory, and the majesty: for all that is in the heaven and in the earth is thine; thine is the kingdom, O LORD, and thou art exalted as head above all. [12] Both riches and honour come of thee, and thou reignest over all; and in thine hand is power and might; and in thine hand it is to make great, and to give strength unto all.

1 CHRONICLES 29:16-17

O LORD our God, all this store that we have prepared to build thee an house for thine holy name cometh of thine hand, and is all thine own. [17] I know also, my God, that thou triest the heart, and hast pleasure in uprightness. As for me, in the uprightness of mine heart I have willingly offered all these things: and now have I seen with joy thy people, which are present here, to offer willingly unto thee.

MATTHEW 10:30

But the very hairs of your head are all numbered.

PHILIPPIANS 4:19

But my God shall supply all your need according to his riches in glory by Christ Jesus.

PSALM 50:7-14

Hear, O my people, and I will speak; O Israel, and I will testify against thee: I am God, even thy God. [8] I will not reprove thee for thy sacrifices or thy burnt offerings, to have been continually before me. [9] I will take no bullock out of thy house, nor he goats out of thy folds. [10] For every beast of the forest is mine, and the cattle upon a thousand hills. [11] I know all the fowls of the mountains: and the wild beasts of the field are mine. [12] If I were hungry, I would not tell thee: for the world is mine, and the fulness thereof. [13] Will I eat the flesh of bulls, or drink the blood of goats? [14] Offer unto God thanksgiving; and pay thy vows unto the most High.

DEUTERONOMY 8:18

But thou shalt remember the LORD thy God: for it is he that giveth thee power to get wealth, that he may establish his covenant which he sware unto thy fathers, as it is this day.

GENESIS 12:3

And I will bless them that bless thee, and curse him that curseth thee: and in thee shall all families of the earth be blessed.

——SCRIPTURES——

EPHESIANS 4:28

Let him that stole steal no more: but rather let him labour, working with his hands the thing which is good, that he may have to give to him that needeth.

2 CORINTHIANS 9:8

And God is able to make all grace abound toward you; that ye, always having all sufficiency in all things, may abound to every good work.

1 CORINTHIANS 4:7

For who maketh thee to differ from another? and what hast thou that thou didst not receive? now if thou didst receive it, why dost thou glory, as if thou hadst not received it?

PROVERBS 10:22

The blessing of the LORD, it maketh rich, and he addeth no sorrow with it.

1 TIMOTHY 6:9-10

But they that will be rich fall into temptation and a snare, and into many foolish and hurtful lusts, which drown men in destruction and perdition. [10] For the love of money is the root of all evil: which while some coveted after, they have erred from the faith, and pierced themselves through with many sorrows.

MATTHEW 6:33

But seek ye first the kingdom of God, and his righteousness; and all these things shall be added unto you.

GREATER THINGS

He that is faithful in that which is least is faithful also in much: and he that is unjust in the least is unjust also in much.

LUKE 16:10

People use this scripture to say that those who want to be entrusted with a lot of authority, they have to start small and work their way up. I even tell the students at Charis Bible College that they aren't going to leave school and jump right into pastoring a church of a thousand members, that they have to be faithful in the small things first—serving at their churches, teaching Bible studies, and other ministry work. As they become faithful through doing small things, God will increase their leadership responsibilities. Those are true statements, and it isn't wrong to use this scripture to demonstrate that truth, but it isn't really what Jesus was talking about here.

The context of a scripture determines its main application, and the context of this scripture is the steward who had wasted his master's money. In context, Jesus is saying that the least area of trusting God is money. What an incredible statement! It is also completely contrary to the way most believers think.

JESUS SAID THAT MONEY IS THE LEAST AREA OF TRUSTING GOD.

Many think that money is something for mature Christians to deal with and that salvation and living a holy life are the simple things. As a matter of fact, somebody always gets upset with me when I teach about finances on television or on radio. I actually received a letter one time from a listener who threatened to sue me for wasting airtime talking about money. He was absolutely livid that I would take time to talk about finances when I should—he thought—be talking about more important issues. But finances are the least area of trusting God! It's a starting place. In this parable, Jesus went on to say,

If therefore ye have not been faithful in the unrighteous mammon, who will commit to your trust the true riches? And if ye have not been faithful in that which is another man's, who shall give you that which is your own? No servant can serve two masters: for either he will hate the one, and love the other; or else he will hold to the one, and despise the other. Ye cannot serve God and mammon.

LUKE 16:11-13

Mammon means money! You need to talk about money because Jesus said that trusting God in the area of finances is the least area of trust, and you can't do greater things without doing the lesser things first. If you can't lift five pounds, then you certainly shouldn't go out and try to lift a hundred pounds. You have to start with what is least and work your way up. If you can't walk ten paces, then you can't climb a mountain. If you can't run a mile, then you can't run a marathon. When you start an exercise program, you don't start with the greatest; you start with that which is least and work your way up.

Remember, Jesus is saying that trusting God with your finances is the least area of trusting God. It's the least use of your faith. When Jesus said **"He that is faithful in that which is least,"** He was calling money **"that which is least."** Think about it: *If you aren't trusting God in your finances, then you are deceiving yourself to think you are trusting Him with your eternal salvation—or anything else.* Boy, that is profound!

The reason you aren't seeing greater things come to pass in your life may very well be that you aren't trusting God with **"that which is least."** Believing for your family to be restored, for healing to manifest in your body, or for mental and emotional healing are all infinitely greater than believing for finances. If you haven't started trusting God with your finances yet, how can you go beyond that and trust God to heal your body? How will you trust God to get over depression if you can't do that which is least and trust Him with your money? How can you trust God to give you eternal life, but not trust Him to provide for your physical needs?

Clinging to money out of fear that God won't provide for you but then trying to say you are believing God for healing or restoration is like saying, "I can't jump three feet, but I'm going to jump clear across the Grand Canyon." It just doesn't work that way. It isn't because God wants you to jump through a bunch of hoops before He will heal you—no, everything has already been provided. It's because you probably won't be able to trust God for big things until you can trust Him for little things first.

Trusting God with your finances is much more important than it has been given credit for. Many people are trying to bypass this issue and move on to bigger things, but it won't work. Just like other areas of life, you have to start at the beginning and work your way up. You can't jump from the ground to the top of a ladder. You have to start at the bottom rung and work your way up. Trusting God with your finances is the bottom rung. It's the starting place.

I taught this same message at a church in California one time, and God used it to really touch people's hearts. After I taught, I received an offering to give them an opportunity to act on what they had learned. I didn't want them to think I was doing it for selfish reasons, so I gave the entire offering to the pastor of the church. As they were passing the buckets, the Lord spoke to me and said, "Watch what happens now that these people have started trusting me with their finances." When the offering was finished, I stood up to pray and miracles started happening! People started receiving the healing power of God. It was such a dramatic demonstration of God's power that people were running to the front asking what they needed to do to be saved.

I saw with my own eyes that the reason some of those people hadn't been healed was because they had never fully trusted God in the area of finances. I know that a lot of ministers don't see things this way. They want to just preach about salvation and leave Christians to try to figure out finances on their own, but that isn't what Scripture teaches. Jesus said that trusting God with finances is foundational.

Please don't misunderstand what I'm saying. I'm not saying that if you just give money, then you will receive a miracle. You can't buy healing or any other blessing of God. You can only receive from God by faith. Faith is the only thing that makes anything God has done for you manifest in your life. What I *am* saying is that using your faith for finances is the least use of faith, and if you haven't done that which is least, then you won't be able to do greater things.

I meet people all the time who are seeking physical and emotional healing, but they haven't started trusting God with their money yet. Honestly, I'm probably not as bold in telling people about this as I should be. I should probably be stronger about this because I know in my heart that people have come to me wanting to receive healing from God for cancer when they have never started believing His simple promises concerning giving and receiving. They don't give or tithe, because they don't really believe that God's promises about financial provision are true. They don't really trust God. So, how are they going to trust Him to heal them of cancer? They won't believe God for the greater thing if they won't believe Him for money, which is the least use of faith.

On a few occasions, I have questioned people about their giving. I remember a friend of mine who came to one of my meetings in Atlanta asking me for prayer. As we were talking, the Lord quickened to me that she hadn't been giving. This was a Christian who knew better, so I asked her,

"Have you been faithful in your giving?"

She looked at me and then said, "No, I fell behind, and I haven't been doing it."

She was trying to believe God for healing, yet she wasn't doing that which is least. So, I told her, "Until you start acting on what you already know and using your faith for those smaller things, there is no point in me praying for you to receive bigger things."

> **USING YOUR FAITH FOR FINANCES IS THE LEAST USE OF FAITH, AND IF YOU HAVEN'T DONE THAT WHICH IS THE LEAST, THEN YOU WON'T BE ABLE TO DO GREATER THINGS.**

Some people might be shocked that I would tie being faithful in finances to receiving healing from God, but those things can be connected. It's not a matter of people pleasing God with giving before He will heal them; it's all about being able to trust Him for small things before trying to trust Him for big things. Jesus said the exact same thing when the rich young ruler came to Him and said, "What must I do to be saved?" Jesus recognized that the young man's heart wasn't right, so He told him to sell everything he had, give the proceeds to the poor, and then come follow Him. He was telling the young man, "If you can't trust Me in that which is least, then you won't trust Me for that which is greater."

In the parable of the unjust steward, Jesus said, **"If therefore ye have not been faithful in the unrighteous mammon, who will commit to your trust the true riches?"** (Luke 16:11).

People talk about money being true riches, but money is nothing compared to health. People pay millions of dollars trying to get well. Anyone who has ever been really sick can tell you that good health is priceless.

Some of you might think that once you get healed or after your marriage is restored or after you are delivered from depression, *then* you will start being a faithful steward of your finances. You want to receive a greater blessing before you start trusting God for the lesser blessings. You can't do that. You have to start with that which is least and work your way up.

It would be foolish to try to believe God for the healing of cancer but not trust Him with your finances. At the very least, you are going to be frustrated and disappointed if you don't see your physical body healed. Or worse, you might become bitter and think faith doesn't work or that God's Word isn't true. No, faith works and God wants you well, but faith is trust in God. If you don't trust God with your finances, then you probably won't be able to trust that Jesus has already paid the price for your healing. The Word says you can't serve two masters. You can't trust yourself when it comes to money and then try to trust God with everything else.

I'm not saying these things to hurt you—I'm saying them to enlighten you. If you have been standing in faith for healing but you haven't seen any physical manifestation, this could be the reason. Think about how you handle your finances: Are you trusting God with your finances? If not, then you don't need to look any further for why you haven't received healing. It isn't effective to compartmentalize your faith so that you are trying to trust God in one area but not in others. If you are going to trust God, then trust Him all the way. The same God who promised eternal life when you confess Jesus as your Lord and believe in your heart that God raised Him from the dead (Rom. 10:9), also said, "Give and it shall be given unto you."

Imagine if I had the resources to guarantee that I could give a thousand dollars back to every one of you who sent me ten dollars. If you really believed that I was telling the truth, then you would be dumb not to send me ten dollars. It wouldn't matter what kind of financial straits you were in, you could find ten dollars. If you really and truly believed that I was a man of my word, then it would be dumb not to invest ten dollars in order to receive a thousand dollars back. Even if you were living on the street, you would find a way to get me ten dollars. I think everyone can understand that. Well, Scripture says the same thing:

> *Give, and it shall be given unto you; good measure, pressed down, and shaken together, and running over, shall men give into your bosom.*
> LUKE 6:38

Jesus also said that anyone who sacrifices home or family will be rewarded with one hundred times what they sacrificed *in this life*, as well as the gift of eternal life (Mark 10:30). If you really believe God's promises, then why wouldn't you give of your finances and trust that

He will give back much more than you gave? One of God's promises is that He will give back to you abundantly, so if you aren't giving, you don't really believe the promises of God.

I could name a lot of verses that talk about God blessing you and prospering you when you give. It's an established principle in the Word of God. You are deceiving yourself if you say that you are trusting and believing in God but aren't giving financially. If you aren't giving to God, then you either don't know His promises to give back to you, or you don't really believe those promises are true.

Lack of trust in the area of finances will hinder your entire walk with the Lord. Let me put it this way: I don't know a single mature Christian who doesn't tithe and give. Everyone I know who has made a total commitment to the Lord trusts God with their finances. On the other hand, I could give you many examples of people who don't trust God with their finances, and their relationship with God is up and down like a yo-yo. They haven't learned to trust God in their finances, and they have no stability in their lives. The conclusion I draw is that people who don't trust God with their finances are not mature, stable Christians—and you won't become stable until you start trusting God in this area. Just keep in mind that sowing and reaping takes time. Likewise, learning to trust God with finances and moving into maturity and stability in this area is a process.

This isn't just for the people who want to be fanatics. This is for baby Christians. You cannot truly mature and fully walk in the blessings of God until you start trusting Him with your finances. As we just saw, the same God who promised that He would save you and give you eternal life also promised to prosper you financially. It's double minded (James 1:7-8) to say that you will trust God with your eternal salvation but not trust Him enough to give and see yourself as a steward of His resources.

Prosperity is a part of our salvation. The Word says that Jesus became poor so that we, through His poverty, might be made rich (2 Cor. 8:9). Some people try to spiritualize that verse and say it is talking about being rich emotionally, but the context of the verse is finances. Yes, Jesus came to make us rich emotionally and spiritually, but He also came to provide for our physical needs. Jesus became poor so that we could be made rich.

ONE REASON SO MANY CHRISTIANS ARE STUCK IN THEIR WALK WITH THE LORD IS THAT THEY HAVEN'T STARTED TRUSTING GOD IN THE AREA OF FINANCES.

We can't just pick and choose which portions of the Word we are going to believe. We shouldn't listen to those who try to spiritualize every scripture about finances and pretend like money doesn't matter   it does matter. In fact, Jesus told the rich young ruler that if he couldn't trust God for his financial needs, then he wouldn't trust God for his salvation. We touched on this story earlier, but the point is that Jesus used finances to demonstrate to the young ruler the true condition of his heart. He said that if we aren't faithful in that which is least, then we won't be faithful in something greater. Trusting God with our finances is where we start. Let's read about the rich young ruler:

> *And when he was gone forth into the way, there came one running, and kneeled to him, and asked him, Good Master, what shall I do that I may inherit eternal life? And Jesus said unto him, Why callest thou me good? there is none good but one, that is, God.*
>
> MARK 10:17-18

Sometimes we read through Scripture without thinking about it enough to let it have its full impact on us. Let's try to picture the situation here. Jesus was a radical and controversial figure in His day. The scribes and Pharisees had established that anyone who acknowledged Jesus as the Messiah was going to be kicked out of the synagogue, so there was persecution for those who associated with Jesus. Yet this rich young man ran and fell at the feet of Jesus, saying, **"Good Master, what shall I do that I may inherit eternal life?"**

This young man had some degree of commitment to fall down at Jesus' feet like that. He could have been kicked out of the synagogue. He certainly would have been ridiculed. It was a big deal for him to publicly acknowledge Jesus the way he did. Imagine yourself sitting in one of my meetings when all of a sudden somebody runs up and throws himself down at my feet and says, "How do I get saved?" Most people would think, *Wow, this guy is really sincere.* But Jesus recognized that the young man wasn't all that he appeared to be. He wasn't really willing to commit himself to the Lord, even though he made such a public demonstration.

Man looks on the outward appearance, but the Lord looks on the heart (1 Sam. 16:7). Jesus was God in the flesh, and He wasn't moved by outward appearances. The young man's actions looked good, but his heart was wrong. Jesus knew it, so He said, "Why are you calling Me good?" In those days "master" was just a term of respect, similar to the way we use Mr. or Mrs. It didn't mean the young man was submitting to Him. Jesus essentially said, "Look, you're calling Me a good master, but you have to go beyond that. You have to receive Me as Lord and accept Me as God. So, either call Me God, or quit calling Me good!" Then Jesus told the young man to keep the commandments.

What I'm trying to point out is that Jesus had to be God in order for His sacrifice to be able to atone for the young man's sin. One man's sacrifice isn't worth any more than one man's life. For Jesus to be the Savior of the entire world, He had to be more than a mere man; He had to be God manifest in the flesh (1 Tim. 3:16). Jesus had been saying that He was God. He called Himself God and referred to Himself as the Son of God. He also said that we have to honor Him exactly the way we honor the Father (John 5:23).

Some people today are saying Jesus was a great prophet, but they don't acknowledge Him as the Son of God. Others want to promote Jesus as a great example of love, but not as God. Contrary to those views, Jesus said, **"I am the way, the truth, and the life: no man cometh**

unto the Father, but by me" (John 14:6). Jesus was either the Son of God, or He was a liar—there are no other options. Our options today are the same ones the young ruler had: either make Jesus God, or quit calling Him good! Here's what the young ruler decided to do:

> *And he answered and said unto him, Master, all these have I observed from*
> *my youth.*
>
> MARK 10:20

He dropped the *good*! See, he never believed that Jesus was God manifest in the flesh. He believed that Jesus could offer something he wanted, but he wasn't willing to humble himself and acknowledge Jesus as his Lord. Instead, the young man had the audacity to say that he had kept all of the commandments from his youth. Nobody has ever observed all of the commandments (Rom. 3:23).

The New Testament reveals that it's not only your actions that count but what is in your heart. If you've been angry with a person without cause, you're guilty of murder (Matt. 5:21-22). If you have lusted after a person or coveted what someone owns, then you're guilty of lust, adultery, and covetousness (Matt. 5:27-28). So, it's not just whether you physically go out and disobey the commandments. If you've even lusted for these things in your heart, then you're guilty.

This man was deceiving himself to think he had kept all of the commandments. I believe that one of the main reasons the Lord told him to go sell everything he had and give it to the poor was because the first commandment is **"Thou shalt have no other gods before me"** (Ex. 20:3). This man's wealth was his god. He would have rather had his money and what his money could have bought than have God. He wanted all of his money because he coveted the things money could get him, which violates the last commandment: **"Thou shalt not covet"** (Ex. 20:17). I believe that Jesus was showing the man that he had broken the first and the last commandments, and probably everything in between. Look at how Jesus responded after the man claimed to have kept all of the commandments:

> *Then Jesus beholding him loved him, and said unto him, One thing thou*
> *lackest: go thy way, sell whatsoever thou hast, and give to the poor, and thou*
> *shalt have treasure in heaven: and come, take up the cross, and follow me.*
>
> MARK 10:21

Jesus loved the young man. He didn't say these things because He was mad. He wasn't trying to hurt him or drive him away by giving him an impossible task. No, Jesus loved this man and wanted to help him. In his heart, the man was trusting in money, and Jesus was trying to help him shift his trust to God.

You might think I've been insensitive because of some of the things I've said about trusting God with your finances. Maybe it seems like I don't understand how hard your situation is, or that I don't care. But I do care—that's the reason I wrote this study guide! I'm trying to help raise you up out of poverty and financial crisis. I'm trying to help you shift your trust to the Lord so that you can start receiving prosperity by faith instead of depending on yourself and stressing yourself out. It's the exact same motivation Jesus had with the rich man.

When the young man heard Jesus tell him to sell everything he had and give the proceeds to the poor, he hung his head and walked away (Mark 10:22). The man knew in his heart that he couldn't do it. After he left, the disciples began asking Jesus questions about what He had just taught on money. Finally, Jesus said to them,

> *Verily I say unto you, There is no man that hath left house, or brethren, or sisters, or father, or mother, or wife, or children, or lands, for my sake, and the gospel's, But he shall receive an hundredfold now in this time, houses, and brethren, and sisters, and mothers, and children, and lands, with persecutions; and in the world to come eternal life.*
>
> MARK 10:29-30

Jesus said this right after they saw the rich man walk away. In other words, if the man had sold everything he had and given it to the poor, he would have received a hundredfold return in this life. Jesus wasn't trying to take from him. He would have blessed the man back a hundred times over. You are a steward, and the money you have isn't really yours anyway, but God is never going to let you outgive Him. When you do give, the Lord will always bless you back—not just in heaven, but here on earth too.

The rich man's refusal to sell his possessions revealed the true condition of his heart. His trust in money was a hindrance to his relationship with God—money was his god. Likewise, if some of the things I am saying rub you the wrong way, it's probably because your heart isn't right in this matter. Just as Jesus used money to reveal the rich man's attitude, you can see what is in a person's heart by looking at how they operate financially.

GOD DOESN'T ASK FOR TITHES AND OFFERINGS BECAUSE HE NEEDS YOUR MONEY. HE ASKS BECAUSE HE WANTS YOU TO LEARN TO TRUST HIM WITH ALL OF YOUR HEART, AND FINANCES ARE THE FIRST STEP IN THAT DIRECTION.

Jesus didn't ask every rich person He met to sell everything they owned. He went to the house of a very wealthy tax collector named Zacchaeus and never mentioned money—and tax collectors earned a lot of money by stealing from people. Zacchaeus decided to give half of his goods to the poor and to restore four times any money he had stolen, but Jesus didn't ask him to do those things; Zacchaeus did them voluntarily. The reason Jesus didn't ask everyone to sell all they had was because the issue wasn't money—it's whether or not they were *trusting* money instead of God.

God gives us money because we need it to function in this world. We use it to buy the goods that meet our needs, but money is not what provides for us. The question is whether we are trusting in God as the source of our provision or whether we are operating out of fear and trusting in money itself. Money is just a delivery system—God is our source.

A lot of Christians say "My trust is in the Lord," but we can tell where their hearts really are by looking at how they give. Are they faithful givers, or are they hoarding everything they get? Jesus told the rich man to sell everything he had in an effort to reveal the condition of his heart. If Jesus was still on earth in His physical body today, He would be asking whether our trust is in God or in stocks, bonds, and pension funds. He would be urging us to administer our finances as stewards and to put our trust in God.

The desire of God's heart is to be involved in every area of your life. He doesn't just want to be part of one hour a week at church. He doesn't want just a scrap of time every once in a while. He wants all of you, and the most dominant area of your life is the forty, fifty, or sixty hours a week you spend earning a living. The way God gets you to trust Him in that area of your life is by asking you to give a portion of what you earn back to Him, and He promises to bless you back in return. It helps you remember that the power to get wealth comes from God, and it teaches you to trust God as your true source of prosperity.

You might not want to follow the leading of God, because you are afraid—especially when it comes to earning income—but you have to believe God. You have to trust that God has your best interests at heart and that He will prosper and take care of you. Finances are the least use of your faith. This isn't just for the "super saints." Baby Christians should start with trusting God in their finances. One reason is that they won't have the confidence to step out and do the things that God has called them to do until they can trust Him to be their source.

Sometimes you might be afraid to step out and do what God is leading you to do, but the blessing on your life is in doing what He has called you to do. When my wife, Jamie, and I really started to step out and trust God with our finances, we saw the Lord come through for us time and time again. I could easily spend hours telling stories of God's miraculous financial provision in my life. I'm telling you, it did something for me that I can't verbalize when I began to see God supernaturally prosper us and lift us out of poverty. My faith in God went through the roof. I believe that an important part of seeing my own son raised from the dead, and the countless other miracles I've seen, was learning to trust God in the area of finances. If I hadn't done that which is least, I couldn't have seen those greater things come to pass. That can be true for you too.

— OUTLINE —

I.   People use this scripture to say that those who want to be entrusted with a lot of authority, they have to start small and work their way up, but that isn't really what Jesus was talking about here.

   A.   The context of a scripture determines its main application, and the context of this scripture is the steward who had wasted his master's money.

   B.   In context, Jesus is saying that the least area of trusting God is money.

   C.   What an incredible statement that is completely contrary to the way most believers think.

   D.   I actually received a letter one time from a listener who threatened to sue me for wasting airtime talking about money.

   E.   He was absolutely livid that I would take time to talk about finances when I should—he thought—be talking about more important issues.

   F.   But finances are the least area of trusting God!

II. In this parable, Jesus went on to say,

   If therefore ye have not been faithful in the unrighteous mammon, who will commit to your trust the true riches? And if ye have not been faithful in that which is another man's, who shall give you that which is your own? No servant can serve two masters: for either he will hate the one, and love the other; or else he will hold to the one, and despise the other. Ye cannot serve God and mammon.
   LUKE 16:11-13

   A.   Mammon means money!

   B.   When Jesus said **"He that is faithful in that which is least,"** He was calling money **"that which is least."**

   C.   Think about it: *If you aren't trusting God in your finances, then you are deceiving yourself to think you are trusting Him with your eternal salvation—or anything else.*

   D.   The reason you aren't seeing greater things come to pass in your life may very well be that you aren't trusting God with **"that which is least."**

   E.   Believing for your family to be restored, for healing to manifest in your body, or for mental and emotional healing are all infinitely greater than believing for finances.

   F.   Clinging to money out of fear that God won't provide for you but then trying to say you are believing God for healing or restoration is like saying, "I can't jump three feet, but I'm going to jump clear across the Grand Canyon."

   G.   It just doesn't work that way.

III.   I taught this same message at a church.

    A.   After I taught, I received an offering to give them an opportunity to act on what they had learned.

    B.   I didn't want them to think I was doing it for selfish reasons, so I gave the entire offering to the pastor of the church.

    C.   As they were passing the buckets, the Lord spoke to me and said, "Watch what happens now that these people have started trusting me with their finances."

    D.   When the offering was finished, I stood up to pray and miracles started happening!

    E.   It was such a dramatic demonstration of God's power that people were running to the front asking what they needed to do to be saved.

IV.   I know that a lot of ministers don't see things this way.

    A.   They want to just preach about salvation and leave Christians to try to figure out finances on their own, but that isn't what Scripture teaches.

    B.   Jesus said that trusting God with finances is foundational.

    C.   I'm not saying that if you just give money, then you will receive a miracle.

    D.   You can't buy healing or any other blessing of God—you can only receive from God by faith.

    E.   What I *am* saying is that using your faith for finances is the least use of faith, and if you haven't done that which is least, then you won't be able to do greater things.

V.   I remember a friend of mine who came to one of my meetings in Atlanta asking me for prayer.

    A.   As we were talking, the Lord quickened to me that she hadn't been giving.

    B.   So, I told her, "Until you start acting on what you already know and using your faith for those smaller things, there is no point in me praying for you to receive bigger things."

    C.   Some people might be shocked that I would tie being faithful in finances to receiving healing from God, but those things can be connected.

    D.   It's not a matter of people pleasing God with giving before He will heal them; it's all about being able to trust Him for small things before they try trusting Him for big things.

VI.   People talk about money being true riches, but money is nothing compared to health.

    A.   People pay millions of dollars trying to get well.

    B.   Anyone who has ever been really sick can tell you that good health is priceless.

C. Some of you might think that once you get healed or after your marriage is restored or after you are delivered from depression, *then* you will start being a faithful steward of your finances—you want to receive a greater blessing before you start trusting God for the lesser blessings.

D. At the very least, you are going to be frustrated and disappointed.

E. Or worse, you might become bitter and think faith doesn't work or that God's Word isn't true.

F. No, faith works, but faith is trust in God.

G. You can't trust yourself when it comes to money and then try to trust God with everything else.

VII. If you have been standing in faith for healing but you haven't seen any physical manifestation, this could be the reason.

A. Think about how you handle your finances: Are you trusting God with your finances?

B. If not, then you don't need to look any further for why you haven't received healing.

C. It isn't effective to compartmentalize your faith so that you are trying to trust God in one area but not in others.

D. If you are going to trust God, then trust Him all the way.

VIII. The same God who promised eternal life when you confess Jesus as your Lord and believe in your heart that God raised Him from the dead (Rom. 10:9), also said, "Give and it shall be given unto you."

A. Imagine if I had the resources to guarantee that I could give a thousand dollars back to everyone who sent me ten dollars.

B. It wouldn't matter what kind of financial straits you were in, you could find ten dollars.

C. If you really and truly believed that I was a man of my word, then it would be dumb not to invest ten dollars in order to receive a thousand dollars back.

D. I think everyone can understand that.

E. Well, Scripture says the same thing:

Give, and it shall be given unto you; good measure, pressed down, and shaken together, and running over, shall men give into your bosom.
LUKE 6:38

F. Jesus also said that anyone who sacrifices home or family will be rewarded with one hundred times what they sacrificed *in this life*, as well as the gift of eternal life (Mark 10:30).

G. If you really believe God's promises, then why wouldn't you give of your finances and trust that He will give back much more than you gave?

H. If you aren't giving to God, then you either don't know His promises to give back to you, or you don't really believe those promises are true.

IX. Lack of trust in the area of finances will hinder your entire walk with the Lord.

A. Let me put it this way: I don't know a single mature Christian who doesn't tithe and give.

B. Everyone I know who has made a total commitment to the Lord trusts God with their finances.

C. On the other hand, I could give you many examples of people who don't trust God with their finances, and their relationship with God is up and down like a yo-yo.

D. The conclusion I draw is that people who don't trust God with their finances are not mature, stable Christians—and you won't become stable until you start trusting God in this area.

E. Learning to trust God with finances and moving into maturity and stability in this area is a process.

F. But you cannot truly mature and fully walk in the blessings of God until you start trusting Him with your finances.

X. The Word says that Jesus became poor so that we, through His poverty, might be made rich (2 Cor. 8:9).

A. Some people try to spiritualize that verse and say it is talking about being rich emotionally, but the context of the verse is finances.

B. Yes, Jesus came to make us rich emotionally and spiritually, but He also came to provide for our physical needs.

C. We shouldn't listen to those who try to spiritualize every scripture about finances and pretend like money doesn't matter—it does matter.

XI. Jesus told the rich young ruler that if he couldn't trust God for his financial needs, then he wouldn't trust God for his salvation.

> *And when he was gone forth into the way, there came one running, and kneeled to him, and asked him, Good Master, what shall I do that I may inherit eternal life? And Jesus said unto him, Why callest thou me good? there is none good but one, that is, God.*
>
> MARK 10:17-18

A. Sometimes we read through Scripture without thinking about it enough to let it have its full impact on us.

B. Let's try to picture the situation here: There was persecution for those who associated with Jesus.

C. This young man could have been ridiculed for publicly acknowledging Jesus the way he did.

D. Most people would think, *Wow, this guy is really sincere.*

E. But Jesus recognized that the young man wasn't really willing to commit himself to the Lord, even though he made such a public demonstration.

F. Man looks on the outward appearance, but the Lord looks on the heart(1 Sam. 16:7).

G. The young man's actions looked good, but his heart was wrong. Jesus knew it, so He said, "Look, you're calling Me a good master, but you have to go beyond that. You have to receive Me as Lord and accept Me as God. So, either call Me God, or quit calling Me good!"

H. Then Jesus told the young man to keep the commandments.

I. Here's what the young ruler decided to do:

And he answered and said unto him, Master, all these have I observed from my youth.

MARK 10:20

J. He dropped the *good*!

K. See, he never believed that Jesus was God manifest in the flesh.

L. He believed that Jesus could offer something he wanted, but he wasn't willing to humble himself and acknowledge Jesus as his Lord.

M. Instead, the young man had the audacity to say that he had kept all of the commandments from his youth.

N. This man was deceiving himself to think he had kept all of the commandments.

O. I believe that one of the main reasons the Lord told him to go sell everything he had and give it to the poor was because the first commandment is **"Thou shalt have no other gods before me"** (Ex. 20:3).

P. This man's wealth was his god.

Q. He would have rather had his money and what his money could have bought than have God.

R. He wanted all of his money because he coveted the things money could get him, which violates the last commandment: **"Thou shalt not covet"** (Ex. 20:17).

S. I believe that Jesus was showing the man that he had broken the first and the last commandments, and probably everything in between.

T. This is how Jesus responded after the man claimed to have kept all of the commandments:

Then Jesus beholding him loved him, and said unto him, One thing thou lackest: go thy way, sell whatsoever thou hast, and give to the poor, and thou shalt have treasure in heaven: and come, take up the cross, and follow me.
MARK 10:21

U. Jesus wasn't trying to hurt him or drive him away by giving him an impossible task.

V. No, Jesus loved this man and wanted to help him.

W. In his heart, the man was trusting in money, and Jesus was trying to help him shift his trust to God.

XII. You might think I've been insensitive because of some of the things I've said about trusting God with your finances.

A. Maybe it seems like I don't understand how hard your situation is, or that I don't care.

B. But I do care—that's the reason I wrote this study guide!

C. I'm trying to help raise you up out of poverty and financial crisis.

D. I'm trying to help you shift your trust to the Lord so that you can start receiving prosperity by faith instead of depending on yourself and stressing yourself out.

E. It's the exact same motivation Jesus had with the rich man.

XIII. When the young man heard Jesus tell him to sell everything he had and give the proceeds to the poor, he hung his head and walked away (Mark 10:22).

A. The man knew in his heart that he couldn't do it.

B. After he left, Jesus said to His disciples,

Verily I say unto you, There is no man that hath left house, or brethren, or sisters, or father, or mother, or wife, or children, or lands, for my sake, and the gospel's, But he shall receive an hundredfold now in this time, houses, and brethren, and sisters, and mothers, and children, and lands, with persecutions; and in the world to come eternal life.
MARK 10:29-30

C. In other words, if the man had sold everything he had and given it to the poor, he would have received a hundredfold return in this life.

D. Jesus wasn't trying to take from him—He would have blessed the man back a hundred times over.

E. You are a steward, and the money you have isn't really yours anyway, but God is never going to let you outgive Him.

F. The Lord will always bless you back—not just in heaven, but here on earth too.

G. The rich man's refusal to sell his possessions revealed the true condition of his heart.

H. His trust in money was a hindrance to his relationship with God—money was his god.

I. Likewise, if some of the things I am saying rub you the wrong way, it's probably because your heart isn't right in this matter.

J. Just as Jesus used money to reveal the rich man's attitude, you can see what is in a person's heart by looking at how they operate financially.

K. Jesus didn't ask every rich person He met to sell everything they owned.

L. He went to the house of a very wealthy tax collector named Zacchaeus and never mentioned money.

M. Zacchaeus decided to give half of his goods to the poor and to restore four times any money he had stolen, but Jesus didn't ask him to do those things.

N. The reason Jesus didn't ask everyone to sell all they had was because the issue wasn't money—it's whether or not they were *trusting* money instead of God.

XIV. We use money to buy the goods that meet our needs, but it is not what provides for us.

A. The question is whether we are trusting in God as the source of our provision or whether we are operating out of fear and trusting in money itself.

B. A lot of Christians say "My trust is in the Lord," but we can tell where their hearts really are by looking at how they give.

C. Are they faithful givers, or are they hoarding everything they get?

D. Jesus told the rich man to sell everything he had in an effort to reveal the condition of his heart.

E. If Jesus was still on earth in His physical body today, He would be asking whether our trust is in God or in stocks, bonds, and pension funds.

F. He would be urging us to administer our finances as stewards and to put our trust in God.

XV. The desire of God's heart is to be involved in every area of your life.

A. He doesn't just want to be part of one hour a week at church.

B. He wants all of you, and the most dominant area of your life is the forty, fifty, or sixty hours a week you spend earning a living.

C. The way God gets you to trust Him in that area of your life is by asking you to give a portion of what you earn back to Him, and He promises to bless you back in return.

D. It helps you remember that the power to get wealth comes from God, and it teaches you to trust God as your true source of prosperity.

E. You might not want to follow the leading of God, because you are afraid—especially when it comes to earning income—but you have to believe God.

F. You have to trust that God has your best interests at heart and that He will prosper and take care of you.

G. Finances are the least use of your faith.

H. This isn't just for the "super saints"; baby Christians should start with trusting God in their finances.

I. One reason is that they won't have the confidence to step out and do the things that God has called them to do until they can trust Him to be their source.

J. Sometimes you might be afraid to step out and do what He is leading you to do, but the blessing on your life is in doing what He has called you to do.

XVI. When my wife, Jamie, and I really started to step out and trust God with our finances, we saw the Lord come through for us time and time again.

A. I'm telling you, it did something for me that I can't verbalize when I began to see God supernaturally prosper us and lift us out of poverty.

B. My faith in God went through the roof.

C. I believe that an important part of seeing my own son raised from the dead, and the countless other miracles I've seen, was learning to trust God in the area of finances.

D. If I hadn't done that which is least, I couldn't have seen those greater things come to pass.

E. That can be true for you too.

TEACHER'S GUIDE

1. People use this scripture to say that those who want to be entrusted with a lot of authority, they have to start small and work their way up, but that isn't really what Jesus was talking about here. The context of a scripture determines its main application, and the context of this scripture is the steward who had wasted his master's money. In context, Jesus is saying that the least area of trusting God is money. What an incredible statement that is completely contrary to the way most believers think. I actually received a letter one time from a listener who threatened to sue me for wasting airtime talking about money. He was absolutely livid that I would take time to talk about finances when I should—he thought—be talking about more important issues. But finances are the least area of trusting God!

    1a. Read Luke 16:10. What was Jesus saying here?
        A. A person who is faithful with much is faithful with that which is least
        B. A person who is faithful with that which is least is faithful also with much
        C. A person who is faithful with their own is faithful with that which is another's
        D. All of the above
        E. None of the above
    1b. True or false: The least area of trusting God is money.
        True

2. In this parable, Jesus went on to say,

> *If therefore ye have not been faithful in the unrighteous mammon, who will commit to your trust the true riches? And if ye have not been faithful in that which is another man's, who shall give you that which is your own? No servant can serve two masters: for either he will hate the one, and love the other; or else he will hold to the one, and despise the other. Ye cannot serve God and mammon.*
>
> LUKE 16:11-13

Mammon means money! When Jesus said **"He that is faithful in that which is least,"** He was calling money **"that which is least."** Think about it: *If you aren't trusting God in your finances, then you are deceiving yourself to think you are trusting Him with your eternal salvation—or anything else.* The reason you aren't seeing greater things come to pass in your life may very well be that you aren't trusting God with **"that which is least."** Believing for your family to be restored, for healing to manifest in your body, or for mental and emotional healing are all infinitely greater than believing for finances. Clinging to money out of fear that God won't provide for you but then trying to say you are believing God for healing or restoration is like saying, "I can't jump three feet, but I'm going to jump clear across the Grand Canyon." It just doesn't work that way.

2a. What did Jesus call mammon?
   A. Bread
   B. Money
   C. Dough
   D. That which is most
   E. That which is least
2b. If you aren't trusting God in your finances, then you are deceiving yourself to think you are trusting Him with what?
   Your eternal salvation—or anything else
2c. Is it harder to trust God for healing or for finances?
   For healing

3. I taught this same message at a church. After I taught, I received an offering to give them an opportunity to act on what they had learned. I didn't want them to think I was doing it for selfish reasons, so I gave the entire offering to the pastor of the church. As they were passing the buckets, the Lord spoke to me and said, "Watch what happens now that these people have started trusting me with their finances." When the offering was finished, I stood up to pray and miracles started happening! It was such a dramatic demonstration of God's power that people were running to the front asking what they needed to do to be saved.

4. I know that a lot of ministers don't see things this way. They want to just preach about salvation and leave Christians to try to figure out finances on their own, but that isn't what Scripture teaches. Jesus said that trusting God with finances is foundational. I'm not saying that if you just give money, then you will receive a miracle. You can't buy healing or any other blessing of God—you can only receive from God by faith. What I *am* saying is that using your faith for finances is the least use of faith, and if you haven't done that which is least, then you won't be able to do greater things.

   4a. True or false: If you give money, you will receive a miracle.
   False

5. I remember a friend of mine who came to one of my meetings in Atlanta asking me for prayer. As we were talking, the Lord quickened to me that she hadn't been giving. So, I told her, "Until you start acting on what you already know and using your faith for those smaller things, there is no point in me praying for you to receive bigger things." Some people might be shocked that I would tie being faithful in finances to receiving healing from God, but those things can be connected. It's not a matter of people pleasing God with giving before He will heal them; it's all about being able to trust Him for small things before they try trusting Him for big things.

   5a. What did Andrew tell his friend in Atlanta who came to him for prayer?
   "Until you start acting on what you already know and using your faith for those smaller things, there is no point in me praying for you to receive bigger things"
   5b. Was Andrew trying to get her to please God through her giving?
   No
   5c. Giving is a matter of what?
   It's all about being able to trust God for small things before you try trusting Him for big things

6. People talk about money being true riches, but money is nothing compared to health. People pay millions of dollars trying to get well. Anyone who has ever been really sick can tell you that good health is priceless. Some of you might think that once you get healed or after your marriage is restored or after you are delivered from depression, *then* you will start being a faithful steward of your finances—you want to receive a greater blessing before you start trusting God for the lesser blessings. At the very least, you are going to be frustrated and disappointed. Or worse, you might become bitter and think faith doesn't work or that God's Word isn't true. No, faith works, but faith is trust in God. You can't trust yourself when it comes to money and then try to trust God with everything else.

   6a. What is more valuable: money or health?
   Health
   6b. What happens if you decide to start giving when your circumstances change?
   At the very least, you are going to be frustrated and disappointed. Or worse, you might become bitter and think faith doesn't work or that God's Word isn't true
   6c. If you trust yourself when it comes to money, what can't you do?
   Try to trust God with everything else

7. If you have been standing in faith for healing but you haven't seen any physical manifestation, this could be the reason. Think about how you handle your finances: Are you trusting God with your finances? If not, then you don't need to look any further for why you haven't received healing. It isn't effective to compartmentalize your faith so that you are trying to trust God in one area but not in others. If you are going to trust God, then trust Him all the way.

8. The same God who promised eternal life when you confess Jesus as your Lord and believe in your heart that God raised Him from the dead (Rom. 10:9), also said, "Give and it shall be given unto you." Imagine if I had the resources to guarantee that I could give a thousand dollars back to everyone who sent me ten dollars. It wouldn't matter what kind of financial straits you were in, you could find ten dollars. If you really and truly believed that I was a man of my word, then it would be dumb not to invest ten dollars in order to receive a thousand dollars back. I think everyone can understand that. Well, Scripture says the same thing:

> *Give, and it shall be given unto you; good measure, pressed down, and*
> *shaken together, and running over, shall men give into your bosom.*
> LUKE 6:38

Jesus also said that anyone who sacrifices home or family will be rewarded with one hundred times what they sacrificed *in this life*, as well as the gift of eternal life (Mark 10:30). If you really believe God's promises, then why wouldn't you give of your finances and trust that He will give back much more than you gave? If you aren't giving to God, then you either don't know His promises to give back to you, or you don't really believe those promises are true.

   8a. Read Luke 6:38. If you really believed God's promises concerning finances, what would you do?
   Give of your finances and trust that He will give back much more than you gave

9. Lack of trust in the area of finances will hinder your entire walk with the Lord. Let me put it this way: I don't know a single mature Christian who doesn't tithe and give. Everyone I know who has made a total commitment to the Lord trusts God with their finances. On the other hand, I could give you many examples of people who don't trust God with their finances, and their relationship with God is up and down like a yo-yo. The conclusion I draw is that people who don't trust God with their finances are not mature, stable Christians—and you won't become stable until you start trusting God in this area. Learning to trust God with finances and moving into maturity and stability in this area is a process. But you cannot truly mature and fully walk in the blessings of God until you start trusting Him with your finances.

   9a. Giving is a sign of what?
      A. Wealth
      B. Self-gratification
      C. Maturity
      D. All of the above
      E. None of the above
   9b. Until you start to trust God with your finances, what can't you do?
      Truly mature and fully walk in the blessings of God

10. The Word says that Jesus became poor so that we, through His poverty, might be made rich (2 Cor. 8:9). Some people try to spiritualize that verse and say it is talking about being rich emotionally, but the context of the verse is finances. Yes, Jesus came to make us rich emotionally and spiritually, but He also came to provide for our physical needs. We shouldn't listen to those who try to spiritualize every scripture about finances and pretend like money doesn't matter—it does matter.

   10a. Read 2 Corinthians 8:9. What is the context is this verse?
   Finances

11. Jesus told the rich young ruler that if he couldn't trust God for his financial needs, then he wouldn't trust God for his salvation.

> *And when he was gone forth into the way, there came one running, and kneeled to him, and asked him, Good Master, what shall I do that I may inherit eternal life? And Jesus said unto him, Why callest thou me good? there is none good but one, that is, God.*
>
> MARK 10:17-18

Sometimes we read through Scripture without thinking about it enough to let it have its full impact on us. Let's try to picture the situation here: There was persecution for those who associated with Jesus. This young man could have been ridiculed for publicly acknowledging Jesus the way he did. Most people would think, *Wow, this guy is really sincere.* But Jesus recognized that the young man wasn't really willing to commit himself to the Lord, even though he made such a public demonstration. Man looks on the outward appearance, but the Lord looks on the heart (1 Sam. 16:7). The young man's actions looked good, but his heart was wrong. Jesus knew it, so He said, "Look, you're calling Me a good master, but you have to go beyond that. You have to receive Me as Lord and accept Me as God. So, either call Me God, or quit calling Me good!" Then Jesus told the young man to keep the commandments. Here's what the young ruler decided to do:

> *And he answered and said unto him, Master, all these have I observed from my youth.*
>
> MARK 10:20

He dropped the *good*! See, he never believed that Jesus was God manifest in the flesh. He believed that Jesus could offer something he wanted, but he wasn't willing to humble himself and acknowledge Jesus as his Lord. Instead, the young man had the audacity to say that he had kept all of the commandments from his youth. This man was deceiving himself to think he had kept all of the commandments. I believe that one of the main reasons the Lord told him to go sell everything he had and give it to the poor was because the first commandment is **"Thou shalt have no other gods before me"** (Ex. 20:3). This man's wealth was his god. He would have rather had his money and what his money could have bought than have God. He wanted all of his money because he coveted the things money could get him, which violates the last commandment: **"Thou shalt not covet"** (Ex. 20:17). I believe that Jesus was showing the man that he had broken the first and the last commandments, and probably everything in between. This is how Jesus responded after the man claimed to have kept all of the commandments:

*Then Jesus beholding him loved him, and said unto him, One thing thou
lackest: go thy way, sell whatsoever thou hast, and give to the poor, and thou
shalt have treasure in heaven: and come, take up the cross, and follow me.*

MARK 10:21

Jesus wasn't trying to hurt him or drive him away by giving him an impossible task. No, Jesus loved this man and wanted to help him. In his heart, the man was trusting in money, and Jesus was trying to help him shift his trust to God.

11a. Read Mark 10:17-18. How did Jesus reply to the rich young ruler who knelt before Him and called Him good?
"You're calling Me a good master, but you have to go beyond that. You have to receive Me as Lord and accept Me as God. So, either call Me God, or quit calling Me good!"

11b. According to Mark 10:20, when Jesus told the young man to keep the commandments, what did he say?
He addressed Jesus simply as teacher and said that he'd kept the commandments from his youth

11c. Read Exodus 20:3 and 17. Had the rich young man broken both of these commandments?
Yes

11d. Read Mark 10:21. How did Jesus feel about this man?
Jesus loved him

11e. What did Jesus do to reveal that the man hadn't kept all the commandments?
A. He didn't thank him for it
B. He used the Scripture to embarrass him
C. He broke out in laughter
D. He told him to sell all he had
E. He walked away sorrowful

11f. What was Jesus trying to do for him?
Help him shift his trust to God instead of his money

12. You might think I've been insensitive because of some of the things I've said about trusting God with your finances. Maybe it seems like I don't understand how hard your situation is, or that I don't care. But I do care—that's the reason I wrote this study guide! I'm trying to help raise you up out of poverty and financial crisis. I'm trying to help you shift your trust to the Lord so that you can start receiving prosperity by faith instead of depending on yourself and stressing yourself out. It's the exact same motivation Jesus had with the rich man.

12a. How do you know that Andrew is trying to do the same thing?
He wrote this study guide!

13. When the young man heard Jesus tell him to sell everything he had and give the proceeds to the poor, he hung his head and walked away (Mark 10:22). The man knew in his heart that he couldn't do it. After he left, Jesus said to His disciples,

> *Verily I say unto you, There is no man that hath left house, or brethren, or sisters, or father, or mother, or wife, or children, or lands, for my sake, and the gospel's, But he shall receive an hundredfold now in this time, houses, and brethren, and sisters, and mothers, and children, and lands, with persecutions; and in the world to come eternal life.*
>
> MARK 10:29-30

In other words, if the man had sold everything he had and given it to the poor, he would have received a hundredfold return in this life. Jesus wasn't trying to take from him—He would have blessed the man back a hundred times over. You are a steward, and the money you have isn't really yours anyway, but God is never going to let you outgive Him. The Lord will always bless you back—not just in heaven, but here on earth too. The rich man's refusal to sell his possessions revealed the true condition of his heart. His trust in money was a hindrance to his relationship with God—money was his god. Likewise, if some of the things I am saying rub you the wrong way, it's probably because your heart isn't right in this matter. Just as Jesus used money to reveal the rich man's attitude, you can see what is in a person's heart by looking at how they operate financially. Jesus didn't ask every rich person He met to sell everything they owned. He went to the house of a very wealthy tax collector named Zacchaeus and never mentioned money. Zacchaeus decided to give half of his goods to the poor and to restore four times any money he had stolen, but Jesus didn't ask him to do those things. The reason Jesus didn't ask everyone to sell all they had was because the issue wasn't money—it's whether or not they were *trusting* money instead of God.

13a.   Read Mark 10:22. Why do you think the rich young man was sad at what Jesus said?
       Because, though he wanted eternal life, he knew he couldn't do what Jesus told him
13b.   According to Mark 10:29, if you give for Jesus' sake and the Gospel's, what will you receive?
       A hundredfold in this life and eternal life in the world to come
13c.   What was revealed when the rich man refused to sell his possessions?
       The true condition of his heart
13d.   Zacchaeus was wealthy too. Why didn't Jesus tell him to sell everything he owned?
       Because the issue isn't money—it's whether or not you are trusting money instead of God

14. We use money to buy the goods that meet our needs, but it is not what provides for us. The question is whether we are trusting in God as the source of our provision or whether we are operating out of fear and trusting in money itself. A lot of Christians say "My trust is in the Lord," but we can tell where their hearts really are by looking at how they give. Are they faithful givers, or are they hoarding everything they get? Jesus told the rich man to sell everything he had in an effort to reveal the condition of his heart. If Jesus was still on earth in His physical body today, He would be asking whether our trust is in God or in stocks, bonds, and pension funds. He would be urging us to administer our finances as stewards and to put our trust in God.

14a. Why is it wrong to think that money provides for you?
   A. Because that would be an indication of greed
   B. Because it is God who provides for you
   C. It's not a misconception
   D. All of the above
   E. None of the above
14b. If Jesus was still on earth in His physical body today, what is one thing He would be doing?
   He would be asking whether your trust is in God or in stocks, bonds, and pension funds

15. The desire of God's heart is to be involved in every area of your life. He doesn't just want to be part of one hour a week at church. He wants all of you, and the most dominant area of your life is the forty, fifty, or sixty hours a week you spend earning a living. The way God gets you to trust Him in that area of your life is by asking you to give a portion of what you earn back to Him, and He promises to bless you back in return. It helps you remember that the power to get wealth comes from God, and it teaches you to trust God as your true source of prosperity. You might not want to follow the leading of God, because you are afraid—especially when it comes to earning income—but you have to believe God. You have to trust that God has your best interests at heart and that He will prosper and take care of you. Finances are the least use of your faith. This isn't just for the "super saints"; baby Christians should start with trusting God in their finances. One reason is that they won't have the confidence to step out and do the things that God has called them to do until they can trust Him to be their source. Sometimes you might be afraid to step out and do what He is leading you to do, but the blessing on your life is in doing what He has called you to do.

15a. What does giving help you remember?
   That the power to get wealth comes from God
15b. When you give, what do you have to trust?
   That God has your best interests at heart and that He will prosper and take care of you
15c. What's one reason that even baby Christians should start trusting God in their finances?
   Because you won't have the confidence to step out and do the things that God has called you to do until you can trust Him to be your source

16. When my wife, Jamie, and I really started to step out and trust God with our finances, we saw the Lord come through for us time and time again. I'm telling you, it did something for me that I can't verbalize when I began to see God supernaturally prosper us and lift us out of poverty. My faith in God went through the roof. I believe that an important part of seeing my own son raised from the dead, and the countless other miracles I've seen, was learning to trust God in the area of finances. If I hadn't done that which is least, I couldn't have seen those greater things come to pass. That can be true for you too.

16a. What happened when Andrew and Jamie started to step out and trust God with their finances?
They saw the Lord come through for them time and time again

16b. What happened to Andrew's faith?
It went through the roof

16c. Andrew believes that learning to trust God in the area of finances was what?
An important part of seeing his own son raised from the dead and the countless other miracles he's seen

16d. If you do that which is least, what will you be able to see?
Greater things come to pass

DISCIPLESHIP
── QUESTIONS ──

1. Read Luke 16:10. What was Jesus saying here?
    A. A person who is faithful with much is faithful with that which is least
    B. A person who is faithful with that which is least is faithful also with much
    C. A person who is faithful with their own is faithful with that which is another's
    D. All of the above
    E. None of the above

2. True or false: The least area of trusting God is money.

3. What did Jesus call mammon?
    A. Bread
    B. Money
    C. Dough
    D. That which is most
    E. That which is least

4. If you aren't trusting God in your finances, then you are deceiving yourself to think you are trusting Him with what?

    _____
    _____
    _____

5. Is it harder to trust God for healing or for finances?

    _____
    _____
    _____

6. True or false: If you give money, you will receive a miracle.

7. What did Andrew tell his friend in Atlanta who came to him for prayer?

    _____
    _____
    _____

8. Was Andrew trying to get her to please God through her giving?

    _____
    _____
    _____

9. Giving is a matter of what?

_____
_____
_____

10. What is more valuable: money or health?

_____
_____
_____

11. What happens if you decide to start giving when your circumstances change?

_____
_____
_____

12. If you trust yourself when it comes to money, what can't you do?

_____
_____
_____

13. Read Luke 6:38. If you really believed God's promises concerning finances, what would you do?

_____
_____
_____

14. Giving is a sign of what?
    A. Wealth
    B. Self-gratification
    C. Maturity
    D. All of the above
    E. None of the above

15. Until you start to trust God with your finances, what can't you do?

_____
_____
_____

16. Read 2 Corinthians 8:9. What is the context is this verse?

_____
_____
_____

17. Read Mark 10:17-18. How did Jesus reply to the rich young ruler who knelt before Him and called Him good?

_____
_____
_____

18. According to Mark 10:20, when Jesus told the young man to keep the commandments, what did he say?

_____
_____
_____

19. Read Exodus 20:3 and 17. Had the rich young man broken both of these commandments?

_____
_____
_____

20. Read Mark 10:21. How did Jesus feel about this man?

_____
_____
_____

21. What did Jesus do to reveal that the man hadn't kept all the commandments?
      A. He didn't thank him for it
      B. He used the Scripture to embarrass him
      C. He broke out in laughter
      D. He told him to sell all he had
      E. He walked away sorrowful

22. What was Jesus trying to do for him?

_____
_____
_____

23. How do you know that Andrew is trying to do the same thing?

_____
_____
_____

24. Read Mark 10:22. Why do you think the rich young man was sad at what Jesus said?

_____
_____
_____

25. According to Mark 10:29, if you give for Jesus' sake and the Gospel's, what will you receive?

_____

_____

_____

26. What was revealed when the rich man refused to sell his possessions?

_____

_____

_____

27. Zacchaeus was wealthy too. Why didn't Jesus tell him to sell everything he owned?

_____

_____

_____

28. Why is it wrong to think that money provides for you?
    A. Because that would be an indication of greed
    B. Because it is God who provides for you
    C. It's not a misconception
    D. All of the above
    E. None of the above

29. If Jesus was still on earth in His physical body today, what is one thing He would be doing?

_____

_____

_____

30. What does giving help you remember?

_____

_____

_____

31. When you give, what do you have to trust?

_____

_____

_____

32. What's one reason that even baby Christians should start trusting God in their finances?

_____

_____

_____

33. What happened when Andrew and Jamie started to step out and trust God with their finances?

_____

_____

_____

34. What happened to Andrew's faith?

_____

_____

_____

35. Andrew believes that learning to trust God in the area of finances was what?

_____

_____

_____

36. If you do that which is least, what will you be able to see?

_____

_____

_____

ANSWER
—KEY—

1. B. A person who is faithful with that which is least is faithful also with much

2. True

3. E. That which is least

4. Your eternal salvation—or anything else

5. For healing

6. False

7. "Until you start acting on what you already know and using your faith for those smaller things, there is no point in me praying for you to receive bigger things"

8. No

9. It's all about being able to trust God for small things before you try trusting Him for big things

10. Health

11. At the very least, you are going to be frustrated and disappointed. Or worse, you might become bitter and think faith doesn't work or that God's Word isn't true

12. Try to trust God with everything else

13. Give of your finances and trust that He will give back much more than you gave

14. C. Maturity

15. Truly mature and fully walk in the blessings of God

16. Finances

17. "You're calling Me a good master, but you have to go beyond that. You have to receive Me as Lord and accept Me as God. So, either call Me God, or quit calling Me good!"

18. He addressed Jesus simply as teacher and said that he'd kept the commandments from his youth

19. Yes

20. Jesus loved him

21. D. He told him to sell all he had

22. Help him shift his trust to God instead of his money

23. He wrote this study guide!

24. Because, though he wanted eternal life, he knew he couldn't do what Jesus told him

25. A hundredfold in this life and eternal life in the world to come

26. The true condition of his heart

27. Because the issue isn't money—it's whether or not you are *trusting* money instead of God

28. B. Because it is God who provides for you

29. He would be asking whether your trust is in God or in stocks, bonds, and pension funds

30. That the power to get wealth comes from God

31. That God has your best interests at heart and that He will prosper and take care of you

32. Because you won't have the confidence to step out and do the things that God has called you to do until you can trust Him to be your source

33. They saw the Lord come through for them time and time again

34. It went through the roof

35. An important part of seeing his own son raised from the dead and the countless other miracles he's seen

36. Greater things come to pass

——SCRIPTURES——

LUKE 16:10-13

He that is faithful in that which is least is faithful also in much: and he that is unjust in the least is unjust also in much. [11] If therefore ye have not been faithful in the unrighteous mammon, who will commit to your trust the true riches? [12] And if ye have not been faithful in that which is another man's, who shall give you that which is your own? [13] No servant can serve two masters: for either he will hate the one, and love the other; or else he will hold to the one, and despise the other. Ye cannot serve God and mammon.

ROMANS 10:9

That if thou shalt confess with thy mouth the Lord Jesus, and shalt believe in thine heart that God hath raised him from the dead, thou shalt be saved.

LUKE 6:38

Give, and it shall be given unto you; good measure, pressed down, and shaken together, and running over, shall men give into your bosom. For with the same measure that ye mete withal it shall be measured to you again.

MARK 10:29-30

And Jesus answered and said, Verily I say unto you, There is no man that hath left house, or brethren, or sisters, or father, or mother, or wife, or children, or lands, for my sake, and the gospel's, [30] But he shall receive an hundredfold now in this time, houses, and brethren, and sisters, and mothers, and children, and lands, with persecutions; and in the world to come eternal life.

JAMES 1:7-8

For let not that man think that he shall receive any thing of the Lord. [8] A double minded man is unstable in all his ways.

2 CORINTHIANS 8:9

For ye know the grace of our Lord Jesus Christ, that, though he was rich, yet for your sakes he became poor, that ye through his poverty might be rich.

MARK 10:17-18

And when he was gone forth into the way, there came one running, and kneeled to him, and asked him, Good Master, what shall I do that I may inherit eternal life? [18] And Jesus said unto him, Why callest thou me good? there is none good but one, that is, God.

1 SAMUEL 16:7

But the LORD said unto Samuel, Look not on his countenance, or on the height of his stature; because I have refused him: for the LORD seeth not as man seeth; for man looketh on the outward appearance, but the LORD looketh on the heart.

1 TIMOTHY 3:16

And without controversy great is the mystery of godliness: God was manifest in the flesh, justified in the Spirit, seen of angels, preached unto the Gentiles, believed on in the world, received up into glory.

——SCRIPTURES——

JOHN 5:23

That all men should honour the Son, even as they honour the Father. He that honoureth not the Son honoureth not the Father which hath sent him.

JOHN 14:6

Jesus saith unto him, I am the way, the truth, and the life: no man cometh unto the Father, but by me.

MARK 10:20-22

And he answered and said unto him, Master, all these have I observed from my youth. [21] Then Jesus beholding him loved him, and said unto him, One thing thou lackest: go thy way, sell whatsoever thou hast, and give to the poor, and thou shalt have treasure in heaven: and come, take up the cross, and follow me. [22] And he was sad at that saying, and went away grieved: for he had great possessions.

ROMANS 3:23

For all have sinned, and come short of the glory of God.

MATTHEW 5:21-22

Ye have heard that it was said by them of old time, Thou shalt not kill; and whosoever shall kill shall be in danger of the judgment: [22] But I say unto you, That whosoever is angry with his brother without a cause shall be in danger of the judgment: and whosoever shall say to his brother, Raca, shall be in danger of the council: but whosoever shall say, Thou fool, shall be in danger of hell fire.

MATTHEW 5:27-28

Ye have heard that it was said by them of old time, Thou shalt not commit adultery: [28] But I say unto you, That whosoever looketh on a woman to lust after her hath committed adultery with her already in his heart.

EXODUS 20:3

Thou shalt have no other gods before me.

EXODUS 20:17

Thou shalt not covet thy neighbour's house, thou shalt not covet thy neighbour's wife, nor his manservant, nor his maidservant, nor his ox, nor his ass, nor any thing that is thy neighbour's.

HIDDEN
TREASURE

Looking at the world around you, you can see that money has power. It obviously enables you to do things you otherwise can't do, and it gives you a certain level of respect. For instance, when a rich man walks into a room, his financial status gives him authority that a poor person in the same room doesn't have. The danger is that unless you are careful, you will begin to trust more in the power of money than you do in the power of God. The Lord is aware of this temptation, and that is why He said so many things about finances. In one of His teachings, Jesus said,

> *Lay not up for yourselves treasures upon earth, where moth and rust*
> *doth corrupt, and where thieves break through and steal: But lay up for*
> *yourselves treasures in heaven, where neither moth nor rust doth corrupt,*
> *and where thieves do not break through nor steal: For where your treasure*
> *is, there will your heart be also.*
>
> MATTHEW 6:19-21

This is interesting: It says that your heart is where your treasure is—which means you can tell where a person's heart is by where their money goes! This scripture illustrates the point Jesus was making with the rich man when He told the man to sell all of his goods. Jesus was saying, "If you really love and trust Me more than your money, then put your treasure in heaven." The man wouldn't do it because his treasure—and his heart—were in earthly riches. Of course, the Lord would have blessed the man back with even more riches than he gave away, so God wasn't trying to take from him. Jesus was just trying to get the man to put his total trust and dependence on God.

The church doesn't preach on finances today the way Jesus did. You hear very little being taught about money, and usually the motivation is to get you to give and fund ministries or projects. The primary motivation behind teaching on finances should be that if you aren't faithful in that which is least, you won't be faithful in that which is greater. After the rich man walked away unwilling to part with his money, the Lord said,

> *How hardly shall they that have riches enter into the kingdom of God! And*
> *the disciples were astonished at his words. But Jesus answereth again, and*
> *saith unto them, Children, how hard is it for them that trust in riches to*
> *enter into the kingdom of God!*
>
> MARK 10:23-24

You could say it this way: "How hard it is for rich people to be born again." That's quite a statement, which is why the disciples were astonished. But Jesus clarified His meaning by saying "how hard it is for them that *trust* in riches." He wasn't saying that money itself makes it difficult to be saved; He was saying that having lots of money can trick people into putting faith in their money instead of in God. Money isn't the problem—it's where you put your trust.

Are you putting your trust in money or in the Lord? It's a question everyone should ask themselves. You can say "Oh, yeah, I'm trusting in the Lord," but you have to do more than just say it. As it says in the epistle of James, **"faith without works is dead"** (James 2:26). You can see where a person's heart is by where their money goes. Someone who is really trusting in the Lord will prove it by tithing and giving out of their resources. Again, the issue isn't money—it's where you put your trust. Whatever you serve becomes your master (Rom. 6:16), and putting your trust in finances places you in bondage to money.

While serving money enslaves you, the Bible is full of evidence that God freely blesses His servants. Isaac was so prosperous that a king asked him to leave the land because it couldn't sustain his wealth (Gen. 26:16). Jacob was even more prosperous than Isaac or his father, Abraham. David started life as the runt of his family with the responsibility of tending his father's sheep, but God made him king of Israel. David became so wealthy that he gave a six billion-dollar offering in one day toward the building of the temple. His son Solomon was even more prosperous.

The Lord knows how dependent we are upon money. He knows how fearful we can be about finances. People recognize that money gives them power. It enables them to put food on the table and pay their bills, so they see giving money away as losing power. They think they are losing leverage in life by giving. But God knows our frame (Ps. 103:14). He knows we are prone to fear in the area of finances, and that's the reason He made so many promises to prosper us when we trust in Him.

Once you step out and begin trusting God, realizing that finances are the least use of your faith, you will start to see God's supernatural provision. It will increase your faith, and you will begin believing God for bigger and better things. On the other hand, if you never learn to trust God with your finances, you are always going to have a lack of confidence in Him. At some point, when you find yourself in a tough situation, you'll try to stand on God's promises for a miracle, and it won't come to pass because you have lingering doubts. Your own heart will condemn you and say, "You never believed God's promises that say 'give and it will be given unto you.' How can you trust the words on this page about healing? What really makes you think that by Jesus' stripes, you are healed?"

Notice I didn't say God will condemn you—condemnation doesn't come from God. God doesn't withhold His miracle-working power from you based on your works or history of giving. But if you are condemning yourself and your heart is divided about whether or not God really desires good for you, then you are going to have a hard time believing in Him—and faith is how you receive from God. See, the danger with money is that you can get to where you trust in what money can do for you more than you trust in God. Then, when you come upon a problem that money can't solve, it will feel like the earth is crumbling beneath you. God will still be there to help you, but you won't have learned to trust in His ability to deliver you. This is a major reason giving is important: Learning to trust God starts with your finances.

Another word for trust is *reliance*. To rely on something is to depend on it. The dictionary defines reliance as "confident rest for support," as in, "We may have perfect *reliance* on the promises of God."[1] That's what the word "trust" means. What are you relying on? Are you relying on your money, or are you relying on God? Thinking *I want to give, but I can't—I need this money* means your confidence is in riches. After Jesus told His disciples that it is hard to enter the kingdom of God when your trust is in riches, He said,

> *It is easier for a camel to go through the eye of a needle, than for a rich man to enter into the kingdom of God. And they were astonished out of measure, saying among themselves, Who then can be saved?*
>
> MARK 10:25-26

The disciples were shocked before, but this statement put them over the top. This left them thinking no one could be saved! Jesus said it is easier for a camel to go through the eye of a needle than it is for one who trusts in riches to be saved. He was stressing the importance of turning your finances over to God and trusting Him as your source, yet many people today are not acknowledging the emphasis that He put on trusting God with finances.

A popular story has circulated that tries to reinterpret what Jesus meant in this teaching. You may have heard the story yourself. Supposedly, "the eye of the needle" was a special gate in the city of Jerusalem. During the day, the story goes, big gates in the walls of the city were open, but at night, the big gates were closed. The only way into the city was through a small opening in the gate. Supposedly, the smaller door was called the "eye of the needle," and in order to get a camel through, they had to unburden the camel and make it crawl through on its knees. In other words, getting a camel through "the eye of the needle" was hard work, but it wasn't impossible. It's a neat story, but no such gate existed.

Actually, I have a funny story about that. When I was in Israel, I asked our tour guide to show us "the eye-of-the-needle gate." At first, the guide told me that it was out of the way, and we didn't have time to go see it. I kept asking him about it, and he continued brushing me off. Finally, I asked him, "Is there really a gate called the eye of the needle?" "No," he said, "there isn't." I asked him why he didn't just tell me that in the first place, and he explained how the tour guides in Israel are trained to make sure tourists have a wonderful experience—not necessarily to tell them the truth.

The guide told me how one time he had a tour group that kept asking him to see the burning bush from the story of Moses. He remembered a bush catching fire the week before behind a gas station, so he had the bus driver stop at the station. They all got off the bus, and he told the tourists that the charred plant behind the gas station was Moses' burning bush! He said the tourists were lining up to take pictures next to it. They actually believed it was the same bush that burned in front of Moses thousands of years before—never mind that the whole reason Moses turned aside to inspect the bush was that it wasn't being consumed by the flames.

---

[1]*Century Dictionary Online.* "reliance"

The eye of the needle wasn't a gate any more than some burned plant behind a gas station was Moses' burning bush. Jesus was literally talking about the eye of a needle. He wasn't saying it is hard for those who trust in riches to enter the kingdom of God—He was saying it is *impossible*. That's why the disciples were shocked and wondered if anyone could be saved. In fact, Jesus specifically said it was impossible:

> *And Jesus looking upon them saith, With men it is impossible, but not with*
> *God: for with God all things are possible.*
>
> MARK 10:27

The point is that you can't sidestep the issue of trusting God with your finances. This is square one. Trusting God with your finances is the least use of your faith, and if you aren't faithful in that which is least, then you won't be faithful in greater things. In my own life, I couldn't be doing the things I am doing now if I hadn't started with trusting God in my finances.

I believe that God has a plan for every one of you, and I believe His plans are bigger than your dreams. I don't think anyone has maxed out God's plans for them. God will do great things, but you have to rely on Him. One of the first steps in that direction is becoming a faithful steward of His resources. Once you begin trusting God for that which is seen—money—then you will be able to trust Him for that which is unseen: health, peace, joy, prosperity, and God's favor in your life.

I've mentioned the parable of the unjust steward a few times, but now I want to take a closer look at what Jesus was teaching. This parable is one of Jesus' hardest teachings to understand. You have to have a pretty good revelation on prosperity before you can decipher what the Lord is talking about here. I think understanding this parable will make a big difference in the way you view and use money. The parable starts like this:

ONCE YOU BEGIN TRUSTING GOD FOR THAT WHICH IS SEEN—MONEY—THEN YOU WILL BE ABLE TO TRUST HIM FOR THAT WHICH IS UNSEEN: HEALTH, PEACE, JOY, PROSPERITY, AND GOD'S FAVOR IN YOUR LIFE.

> *And he said also unto his disciples, There was a*
> *certain rich man, which had a steward; and the same*
> *was accused unto him that he had wasted his goods. And he called him,*
> *and said unto him, How is it that I hear this of thee? give an account of thy*
> *stewardship; for thou mayest be no longer steward.*
>
> LUKE 16:1-2

So, a wealthy man had someone managing his money. The wealthy man thought that the steward was stealing from him, or somehow mismanaging his funds, so he told the steward to get his books in order.

Then the steward said within himself, What shall I do? for my lord taketh
away from me the stewardship: I cannot dig; to beg I am ashamed.

LUKE 16:3

You can tell from the steward's reaction that he was guilty. He didn't try to prove his innocence or defend himself in any way. He knew that when his master took a look at the books, he was going to get fired. It was basically an admission of guilt. So, the steward said, "What am I going to do? I can't dig." It's probably not true that he couldn't dig. It is probably more accurate to say he *wouldn't* dig.

This raises a good point: Not everyone who has financial problems is lazy, but lazy people usually have financial problems. They're looking for a quick fix. They're looking to win the lottery or something. That's not how God's system works. If you are looking to prosper through winning the lottery, then you have the wrong attitude toward finances. The lottery isn't sinful necessarily, but it is a compromise. Expecting to get rich quick is never God's system of prosperity. Even if you were to defy the odds and strike it rich, Scripture says that wealth obtained through vanity doesn't last (Prov. 13:11). Prosperity isn't about getting money any way you can—there is a right and a wrong way to do it.

I'm sure the steward could have found a job if he wanted to, but that isn't the way he thought. He didn't want to work to get his money. He wanted to steal it, inherit it, or come by it effortlessly somehow. He was always looking for some scheme instead of simply believing that God would bless his work. After concluding that he didn't want to look for work, he said, "I am ashamed to beg." It's too bad he wasn't ashamed to *steal*—he might have still had a job! Having ruled out working and begging, the steward struck upon a scheme he liked:

I am resolved what to do, that, when I am put out of the stewardship, they
may receive me into their houses. So he called every one of his lord's debtors
unto him, and said unto the first, How much owest thou unto my lord? And
he said, An hundred measures of oil. And he said unto him, Take thy bill,
and sit down quickly, and write fifty. Then said he to another, And how
much owest thou? And he said, An hundred measures of wheat. And he
said unto him, Take thy bill, and write fourscore.

LUKE 16:4-7

The parable only lists two debtors, but I believe those were simply given as examples of what the steward did. The wealthy man wouldn't have needed a steward to run his finances if only two people owed him money, so I'm sure many people were indebted to him. These examples show that the steward called in all of his master's debtors and cut their debts by huge margins. He gave them all discounts. He was too lazy to work and too proud to beg, so he kept on stealing money—but instead of putting the money into his own pocket, he put the money in the pockets of people who owed his master money.

I don't know how much a hundred measures of oil was worth, but I'm sure it was a lot of money. The steward probably cut this man's debt by the equivalent of tens of thousands of dollars today, and he did that for all of his master's debtors, which means there could have been dozens or even hundreds of people who saved thousands of dollars because of the steward's discounts. The logic behind this was that when the steward got fired, he could go back to all of those debtors and say, "Hey, remember how I saved you thousands of dollars? Well, I'm out of work now. Can you give me a hand?" All of those people would feel indebted to him, or responsible for his unemployment, and he could mooch off them instead of getting a job.

Up until this point, the parable isn't difficult to understand. It's about a man who didn't use his master's money properly and was going to be fired for it. We don't know if he was actually stealing or if he was just a bad steward, but either way, he was going to get fired. So, he essentially used his master's money to bribe other people. He used his master's money to influence people and win favors. People steal money from their employers all of the time, so nothing we've read so far is all that strange. What is unusual about this story is the master's response:

And the lord commended the unjust steward, because he had done wisely.
LUKE 16:8A

The simple fact that the master found something to commend the steward on says a lot about the master's attitude toward money. Think about it: Would you pay compliments to someone you caught stealing from you? If you came home one night and discovered a thief standing in your living room with a pillowcase stuffed full of your valuables, would you say, "Wow, you're doing a great job!" Would you compliment the thief for bypassing your security system and nabbing your most valuable goods?

The master's reaction to catching a thief is not what you'd expect. He didn't get angry or demand justice. He actually complimented the steward. It's possible that the master was so filthy rich that he didn't care if people stole from him, but I doubt it. If he didn't care about his money, he wouldn't have called the steward to account in the first place. I think this master understood that money is just a tool. It's not what is meant to be valued. The blessing and favor of God are what make you rich—not money.

The master knew that money isn't the important part of prosperity. Most people judge their worth by their savings and retirement fund, but those things are just physical manifestations of the real asset—which is God's favor. Wealth is just a byproduct of God's favor. The Lord told Abraham, **"I will bless thee, and make thy name great; and thou shalt be a blessing"** (Gen. 12:2). It was the spoken favor of God on Abraham's life that caused him to prosper. It was God's favor that allowed him to grow rich from grazing his cattle and sheep in a desert. The master had a revelation that his true wealth was the favor of God, not the money the steward was stealing.

THE BLESSING AND FAVOR OF GOD ARE WHAT MAKE YOU RICH—NOT MONEY.

This goes back to the first point I made about being a steward and recognizing that everything you have comes from God. God gives you resources, but the resources aren't your real asset. It's like the old children's fable about the goose that lays golden eggs. The golden eggs are not as valuable as the goose that produces them! The goose lays a golden egg every day, and when you have the goose, you get all of the golden eggs that come with it. In the same way, money isn't your true asset; the true treasure is the blessing and favor of God that *produces* riches.

A lot of people today are focused on gathering golden eggs, and they are completely overlooking the parent force that creates them. The person who owns the goose is going to end up with a lot more gold than someone who is running around looking for eggs. Likewise, once you realize that God is the source of prosperity, you understand how pointless it is to chase after riches. This is one reason Scripture reminds you that the power to get wealth comes from God:

> *But thou shalt remember the* LORD *thy God: for it is he that giveth thee power to get wealth, that he may establish his covenant which he sware unto thy fathers, as it is this day.*
>   DEUTERONOMY 8:18

God is the source of your prosperity, but notice the scripture doesn't say God *gives* you wealth. God doesn't send you checks in the mail; He gives you the power to *get* wealth. He releases an anointing on whatever you do and causes it to prosper—and the blessing of God is so powerful that it cannot be reversed. Balaam is the infamous prophet who was hired by a foreign king to curse the children of Israel, but he said,

> *Behold, I have received commandment to bless: and* [God] *hath blessed; and I cannot reverse it.*
>   NUMBERS 23:20, BRACKETS MINE

Once the favor of God is on your life, it cannot be stopped! The only thing that can derail the blessing of God is your own unbelief and negativity. As long as you keep believing, the blessings of God will keep coming. Understanding the true value of God's favor on your life will cause you to have the same attitude that the rich master had toward his steward. You can look at all of the things you possess and say, "It's just stuff." You'll know that money is merely a tool that helps you accomplish what God has called you to do—it isn't true prosperity.

Riches can be stolen and property can be taken away, but no one can rob you of God's favor. The rich master knew where his real treasure was, and that is why he didn't get angry with the steward. He wasn't counting his paper money or coins as his true net worth. Once you get that same mindset, you could catch a thief robbing you blind and not feel fear or panic. You can get to where your life isn't bound up in things. You can become so secure in your relationship with God and so certain of His favor in your life that you could actually find something to compliment a thief about.

The wealth you amass in life isn't important. The focus of your life should be your relationship with God, which is what causes wealth to accumulate. Money isn't that significant. On the other hand, God's favor in your life is priceless.

A good friend of mine, Pastor Bob Nichols, pastors Calvary Cathedral in Fort Worth, Texas. In April 2000, a tornado hit the area and destroyed his church. It was an eighteen million-dollar facility, not including the building's contents, and in less than sixty seconds, it was completely obliterated. Within one hour of the storm, CNN was standing in front of the wreckage interviewing Pastor Bob. He had his hard hat on, and he was saying, "God didn't do this. This is nothing but an attack of the devil." He said God was going to work it together for good, and they were going to end up with a facility twice as nice as the one that was destroyed.

Pastor Bob was expressing the same attitude that the rich master had. He could see all of his physical assets were destroyed, but it didn't shake his faith, because his faith wasn't in physical assets. He knew that the blessing of God was what produced all of those things, and he still had God's favor. The storm had taken his property, but God's blessing was still on his life. In the end, Pastor Bob did end up with a facility twice as nice as the one destroyed by the tornado. His confidence was in the Lord, and the Lord restored everything that was taken from him—and then some.

This is exactly the way the rich master was thinking. He found an employee stealing what could have been millions of dollars from him, and it didn't faze him one bit. People on Wall Street start jumping out of windows when they lose millions, because all of their trust and confidence is in money. Financial crisis pushes a lot of people over the edge, but—like the rich master—you won't be shaken if your trust is in the Lord.

You can only have that kind of confidence when you quit basing your life on physical things and rely on God. When your trust is in what money can do for you, then your security is in your bank account—and when your bank account gets low, you are going to feel frightened and insecure. But when you know God is your source, you won't cling to assets. This mindset will help you sleep at night! It will completely transform your life to learn to rely on God instead of trusting in assets or other people. You can actually live your life without being tied to, or a servant of, your money. Money is nothing! It's the blessing and the favor of God on you that is the real asset.

The other important point to understand from this parable is why the steward was commended. You wouldn't think there is anything commendable about stealing money and giving it to other people, yet Jesus tells us that the master praised the steward for stealing. Here's the reason the rich master was commending the steward: The steward had finally realized that the true power of money is in using it to affect the future. Instead of pocketing the stolen money, the steward was using it to bribe people and prepare for his future.

It's easy to see that prior to this, the steward had just been blowing the money on "things." He was buying fancy cars, caviar, flat-screen televisions, nice clothes, jewelry, and things like that, because he didn't have any money saved. He was going to have to dig ditches or beg (Luke 16:3).

> **THE TRUE POWER OF MONEY IS IN USING IT TO CHANGE YOUR FUTURE.**

The master wasn't commending the steward for the act of stealing—he was complimenting the steward for finally figuring out that money is a tool. It doesn't matter what country it is, or how much money is in the bank; most people make the critical mistake of using money only for temporary, short-term things. They spend their money on things that give a little bit of momentary reward, and they ignore the power money has to shape their future.

To a degree, lost people are better stewards of their assets than Christians are. That's not always the case, but often it is. I believe this is what Jesus was getting at when He said, **"The children of this world are in their generation wiser than the children of light"** (Luke 16:8b). Part of the reason is that Christians know this life isn't all there is. Lost people are planning for retirement and thinking death is the end, whereas Christians aren't as short-term in their thinking.

Christians don't have the same fear of death that unbelievers have, and they look beyond this life, into eternity. As a result, Christians often don't prepare for their later years in life or gather an inheritance to leave for their children. But money doesn't just give you power to shape your future on earth—it also influences eternity. When Jesus was done teaching about the rich master who commended the unjust steward, He said:

> *And I say unto you, Make to yourselves friends of the mammon of unrighteousness; that, when ye fail, they may receive you into everlasting habitations.*
>
> LUKE 16:9

The Greek word translated as "fail" here also means death. This scripture is telling you to use money to make friends who will receive you into everlasting habitations when you die. In other words, you can touch people's lives through giving, and when you die, those people will be lined up in heaven to thank you for the way you used your resources to help them. You can do it by giving to people directly or by giving to support the preaching of the Gospel, which saves, heals, and delivers.

Money is only temporary. It doesn't exist in heaven, and you can't take it with you when you die—that's why you'll never see a hearse pulling a trailer. Paper money, gold, coins, diamonds, and silver are all temporary. One day they will all be burned up. But by investing money in the lives of others, you can take something that is destined for destruction and turn it into something eternal. You can transform money into something that will never pass away by investing it in the Gospel and by using it to touch other people's lives.

The purpose of this parable is to show you that the best use of money isn't on temporary things that are going to pass away. Prosperity isn't about your house or car. It's not about having the latest gadgets and the fanciest clothes. The number one use of your money is to touch people's lives.

Every natural thing that you have used your money to purchase is going to be destroyed one day. It doesn't matter how much you have in this life. Some of the people who are greatly admired now because of all of their wealth aren't going to have a single person waiting in heaven to thank them for using their money to change lives. A lot of people who have put their trust in money won't even make it to heaven, but I also believe that there are Christians who won't have much treasure waiting in heaven. They'll still be blessed and overwhelmed by the love of God, because they weren't saved according to their works, but there won't be anybody waiting to welcome them into heaven, because they never used their money to spread the Gospel and change lives.

Other people who were not highly esteemed in this life will have people lined up by the thousands waiting to welcome them. They might not have lived in the nicest house on the block, but they will have given from their resources to bless others. Their giving will have transformed into eternal treasure. You won't know how many lives you have touched by giving to support the preaching of the Gospel until you get to heaven and see everyone lined up to greet you.

Yes, God wants you to take care of your needs. You aren't a good steward if your family is sleeping under a tree because you keep giving all of your money away. God wants you to live in comfort, dress well, and own nice things. He doesn't want you to be poor. God is not against you taking care of yourself. What I'm saying is that your attitude about money will change when you really get a revelation on prosperity. You'll be thinking, *How little money do I need to take care of my family, and how much can I invest in eternity?* A million years from now, people will still be stopping by your mansion in glory to thank you for the investment you made in the Gospel and for the way it touched their lives. No saint will be saying, "Oh, I sure wish I'd spent my money on a nicer car, or a third flat-screen television." No way.

God is in the people business! All material things are going to fade away, and the only thing that will matter is how much you invested in people. One day you will thank me for getting money out of your pocket and putting it into the Gospel. Everything you hold on to, you end up losing. It's only what you give away that you get to keep, and you are not a fool to give away something you can't keep in order to get something you can never lose.

When the master told the steward he was going to be fired, the steward finally got the message that he had better start planning for the future. He realized that he needed to take the money he had access to and use the influence and power it gave him to prepare his future. Jesus used that parable to teach us that the best use of money is not to buy things, but to touch lives and change people.

Unfortunately, I don't think many people have understood or embraced the mindset Jesus was teaching through this parable. Most people take care of themselves first and tip God from the remains. After every lust and desire of their hearts has been satisfied, they give God the leftovers. God isn't mad at them, but they are missing the benefits of good financial stewardship. It is far better to learn to live on less money and to use a portion of one's resources to affect the future.

I'm not saying you are supposed to keep your nose to the grindstone and not enjoy the journey of life. You need to keep a balance between planning for the future and living in the moment, but—at least in the United States—a lot of people have swung clear over to gratifying every whim and thinking only about the moment. People are mortgaging their futures so they can enjoy everything right now. They are indulging themselves by grabbing everything they can, and they aren't planning for the future at all. Like the unjust steward, they would do well to recognize that money is best spent on the future.

A MAN IS NOT A FOOL TO GIVE AWAY SOMETHING HE CAN'T KEEP IN ORDER TO GET SOMETHING HE CAN NEVER LOSE.

The two main points we learn from the parable of the dishonest steward are that money is not our greatest asset, and wise people invest their money in the future. The blessing of God is what makes us rich, not money. As long as we have God's blessing, wealth will find us. The key is learning not to blow all of our money on short-lived pleasures but to use some of it to help shape our futures. Money is not for treasures on earth but for the lives of multitudes of people, who will be waiting to welcome us into heaven.

— OUTLINE —

I.   Looking at the world around you, you can see that money has power.

    A. It obviously enables you to do things you otherwise can't do, and it gives you a certain level of respect.

    B. For instance, when a rich man walks into a room, his financial status gives him authority that a poor person in the same room doesn't have.

    C. The danger is that unless you are careful, you will begin to trust more in the power of money than you do in the power of God.

    D. The Lord is aware of this temptation, and that is why He said so many things about finances.

II. In one of His teachings, Jesus said,

> *Lay not up for yourselves treasures upon earth, where moth and rust doth corrupt, and where thieves break through and steal: But lay up for yourselves treasures in heaven, where neither moth nor rust doth corrupt, and where thieves do not break through nor steal: For where your treasure is, there will your heart be also.*
>
> MATTHEW 6:19-21

    A. You can tell where a person's heart is by where their money goes!

    B. This scripture illustrates the point Jesus was making with the rich man when He told the man to sell all of his goods: "If you really love and trust Me more than your money, then put your treasure in heaven."

    C. The man wouldn't do it because his treasure—and his heart—were in earthly riches.

    D. After the rich man walked away unwilling to part with his money, the Lord said,

> *How hardly shall they that have riches enter into the kingdom of God! And the disciples were astonished at his words. But Jesus answereth again, and saith unto them, Children, how hard is it for them that trust in riches to enter into the kingdom of God!*
>
> MARK 10:23-24

    E. You could say it this way: "How hard it is for rich people to be born again."

    F. That's quite a statement, which is why the disciples were astonished.

    G. But Jesus clarified His meaning by saying "how hard it is for them that *trust* in riches."

H. He wasn't saying that money itself makes it difficult to be saved; He was saying that having lots of money can trick people into putting faith in their money instead of in God.

I. You can say "Oh, yeah, I'm trusting in the Lord," but you have to do more than just say it.

J. As it says in the epistle of James, **"faith without works is dead"** (James 2:26).

K. Someone who is really trusting in the Lord will prove it by tithing and giving out of their resources.

III. Whatever you serve becomes your master (Rom. 6:16), and putting your trust in finances places you in bondage to money.

   A. While serving money enslaves you, the Bible is full of evidence that God freely blesses His servants:

      i. Isaac was so prosperous that a king asked him to leave the land because it couldn't sustain his wealth (Gen. 26:16).

      ii. Jacob was even more prosperous than Isaac or his father Abraham.

      iii. David started life as the runt of his family with the responsibility of tending his father's sheep, but God made him king of Israel, and he became so wealthy that he gave a six billion-dollar offering in one day toward the building of the temple.

      iv. His son Solomon was even more prosperous.

IV. The Lord knows how dependent we are upon money—He knows how fearful we can be about finances.

   A. God knows our frame (Ps. 103:14).

   B. He knows we are prone to fear in the area of finances, and that's the reason He made so many promises to prosper us when we trust in Him.

   C. Once we step out and begin trusting God, realizing that finances are the least use of our faith, we will start to see God's supernatural provision.

   D. It will increase our faith, and we will begin believing God for bigger and better things.

   E. On the other hand, if we never learn to trust God with our finances, we are always going to have a lack of confidence in Him.

   F. At some point, when we find ourselves in a tough situation, we'll try to stand on God's promises for a miracle, and it won't come to pass because we have lingering doubts.

G. Our own hearts will condemn us and say, "You never believed God's promises that say 'give and it will be given unto you.' How can you trust the words on this page about healing? What really makes you think that by Jesus' stripes, you are healed?"

    i. I didn't say God will condemn us—condemnation doesn't come from God.

    ii. God doesn't withhold His miracle-working power from us based on our works or history of giving.

H. The danger with money is that we can get to where we trust in what money can do for us more than we trust in God.

I. Then, when we come upon a problem that money can't solve, it will feel like the earth is crumbling beneath us.

J. God will still be there to help us, but we won't have learned to trust in His ability to deliver us.

V. This is a major reason giving is important: Learning to trust God starts with your finances.

A. Another word for trust is *reliance*.

B. To rely on something is to depend on it.

C. The dictionary defines reliance as "confident rest for support," as in, "We may have perfect *reliance* on the promises of God."[1]

D. Are you relying on your money, or are you relying on God?

E. Thinking *I want to give, but I can't—I need this money* means your confidence is in riches.

VI. After Jesus told His disciples that it is hard to enter the kingdom of God when your trust is in riches, He said,

> *It is easier for a camel to go through the eye of a needle, than for a rich man to enter into the kingdom of God. And they were astonished out of measure, saying among themselves, Who then can be saved?*
>
> MARK 10:25-26

A. The disciples were shocked before, but this statement put them over the top.

B. Jesus was stressing the importance of turning your finances over to God and trusting Him as your source, yet many people today are not acknowledging the emphasis that He put on trusting God with finances.

C. The disciples wondered if anyone could be saved.

D. In fact, Jesus specifically said it was impossible:

---

[1] *Century Dictionary Online.* "reliance"

And Jesus looking upon them saith, With men it is impossible, but not with God: for with God all things are possible.

VII. I believe that God has a plan for every one of you, and I believe His plans are bigger than your dreams.

    A. I don't think anyone has maxed out God's plans for them.

    B. God will do great things, but you have to rely on Him.

    C. One of the first steps in that direction is becoming a faithful steward of His resources.

    D. Once you begin trusting God for that which is seen—money—then you will be able to trust Him for that which is unseen: health, peace, joy, prosperity, and God's favor in your life.

VIII. I've mentioned the parable of the unjust steward a few times, but now I want to take a closer look at what Jesus was teaching.

    A. This parable is one of Jesus' hardest teachings to understand.

    B. I think understanding this parable will make a big difference in the way you view and use money.

    C. A wealthy man had someone managing his money and thought that the steward was stealing from him, or somehow mismanaging his funds, so he told the steward to get his books in order (Luke 16:1-2).

Then the steward said within himself, What shall I do? for my lord taketh away from me the stewardship: I cannot dig; to beg I am ashamed.

    D. You can tell from the steward's reaction that he was guilty.

    E. He didn't try to prove his innocence or defend himself in any way.

    F. He knew that when his master took a look at the books, he was going to get fired.

    G. So, the steward said, "What am I going to do? I can't dig."

    H. It is probably more accurate to say he *wouldn't* dig.

    I. This raises a good point: Not everyone who has financial problems is lazy, but lazy people usually have financial problems.

        i. They're looking for a quick fix: to win the lottery or something.

        ii. That's not how God's system works.

        iii. If you are looking to prosper through winning the lottery, then you have the wrong attitude toward finances.

    iv. The lottery isn't sinful necessarily, but it is a compromise.

    v. Even if you were to defy the odds and strike it rich, Scripture says that wealth obtained through vanity doesn't last (Prov. 13:11).

    vi. Prosperity isn't about getting money any way you can—there is a right and a wrong way to do it.

J. I'm sure the steward could have found a job if he wanted to, but that isn't the way he thought.

K. He didn't want to work to get his money; he wanted to steal it, inherit it, or come by it effortlessly somehow.

L. He was always looking for some scheme instead of simply believing that God would bless his work.

M. After concluding that he didn't want to look for work, he said, "I am ashamed to beg."

N. It's too bad he wasn't ashamed to *steal*—he might have still had a job!

O. Having ruled out working and begging, the steward struck upon a scheme he liked:

> *I am resolved what to do, that, when I am put out of the stewardship, they may receive me into their houses. So he called every one of his lord's debtors unto him, and said unto the first, How much owest thou unto my lord? And he said, An hundred measures of oil. And he said unto him, Take thy bill, and sit down quickly, and write fifty. Then said he to another, And how much owest thou? And he said, An hundred measures of wheat. And he said unto him, Take thy bill, and write fourscore.*
>
> LUKE 16:4-7

P. These examples show that the steward called in all of his master's debtors and cut their debts by huge margins.

Q. He was too lazy to work and too proud to beg, so he kept on stealing money—but instead of putting the money into his own pocket, he put the money in the pockets of people who owed his master money.

R. There could have been dozens or even hundreds of people who saved thousands of dollars because of the steward's discounts.

S. The logic behind this was that when the steward got fired, he could go back to all of those debtors and say, "Hey, remember how I saved you thousands of dollars? Well, I'm out of work now. Can you give me a hand?"

T. All of those people would feel indebted to him, or responsible for his unemployment, and he could mooch off them instead of getting a job.

U. People steal money from their employers all of the time, so nothing so far is all that strange.

IX.   What is unusual about this story is the master's response:

    And the lord commended the unjust steward, because he had done wisely.
                                                  LUKE 16:8A

    A.   The simple fact that the master found something to commend the steward on says a lot about the master's attitude toward money.

    B.   If you came home one night and discovered a thief standing in your living room, would you compliment the thief for bypassing your security system and nabbing your most valuable goods?

    C.   The master's reaction to catching a thief is not what you'd expect.

    D.   But if he didn't care about his money, he wouldn't have called the steward to account in the first place.

    E.   I think this master understood that money is just a tool.

    F.   Wealth is just a byproduct of God's favor.

    G.   The master had a revelation that his true wealth was the favor of God, not the money the steward was stealing.

    H.   This goes back to the first point I made about being a steward and recognizing that everything you have comes from God.

    I.   God gives you resources, but the resources aren't your real asset.

    J.   It's like the old children's fable about the goose that lays golden eggs:

        i.   The golden eggs are not as valuable as the goose that produces them!

        ii. When you have the goose, you get all of the golden eggs that come with it.

    K.   In the same way, money isn't your true asset; the true treasure is the blessing and favor of God that *produces* riches.

X.   Once you realize that God is the source of prosperity, you understand how pointless it is to chase after riches.

    A.   This is one reason Scripture reminds you that the power to get wealth comes from God:

    *But thou shalt remember the LORD thy God: for it is he that giveth thee
    power to get wealth, that he may establish his covenant which he sware
    unto thy fathers, as it is this day.*
                                      DEUTERONOMY 8:18

    B.   Notice the scripture doesn't say God *gives* you wealth; He gives you the power to *get* wealth.

C. He releases an anointing on whatever you do and causes it to prosper—and the blessing of God is so powerful that it cannot be reversed.

D. Balaam is the infamous prophet who was hired by a foreign king to curse the children of Israel, but he said,

Behold, I have received commandment to bless: and [God] hath blessed; and I cannot reverse it.

NUMBERS 23:20, BRACKETS MINE

E. Once the favor of God is on your life, it cannot be stopped!

F. The only thing that can derail the blessing of God is your own unbelief and negativity.

G. As long as you keep believing, the blessings of God will keep coming.

XI. Understanding the true value of God's favor on your life will cause you to have the same attitude that the rich master had toward his steward.

A. Riches can be stolen and property can be taken away, but no one can rob you of God's favor.

B. Once you get that same mindset, you could catch a thief robbing you blind and not feel fear or panic.

C. You can become so secure in your relationship with God and so certain of His favor in your life that you could actually find something to compliment a thief about.

D. The focus of your life should be your relationship with God, which is what causes wealth to accumulate.

XII. Money isn't that significant—on the other hand, God's favor in your life is priceless.

A. Pastor Bob Nichols pastors Calvary Cathedral in Fort Worth, Texas.

B. In April 2000, a tornado hit the area and destroyed his church.

C. It was an eighteen million-dollar facility, not including the building's contents, and in less than sixty seconds, it was completely obliterated.

D. Within one hour of the storm, CNN was standing in front of the wreckage interviewing Pastor Bob.

E. He was saying "God didn't do this. This is nothing but an attack of the devil" and that God was going to work it together for good, and they were going to end up with a facility twice as nice as the one that was destroyed.

F. Pastor Bob was expressing the same attitude that the rich master had.

G. The storm had taken his property, but God's blessing was still on his life.

  H. In the end, Pastor Bob did end up with a facility twice as nice as the one destroyed by the tornado.

  I. His confidence was in the Lord, and the Lord restored everything that was taken from him—and then some.

XIII. You can only have that kind of confidence when you quit basing your life on physical things and rely on God.

  A. When your trust is in what money can do for you, then your security is in your bank account—and when your bank account gets low, you are going to feel frightened and insecure.

  B. But when you know God is your source, you won't cling to assets.

  C. This mindset will help you sleep at night!

  D. It will completely transform your life to learn to rely on God instead of trusting in assets or other people.

  E. You can actually live your life without being tied to, or a servant of, your money.

XIV. The other important point to understand from this parable is why the steward was commended.

  A. You wouldn't think there is anything commendable about stealing money and giving it to other people, but here's the reason the rich master did it: The steward finally realized that the true power of money is in using it to affect the future.

  B. Instead of pocketing the stolen money, the steward was using it to bribe people and prepare for his future.

  C. It's easy to see that prior to this, the steward had just been blowing the money on "things."

  D. It doesn't matter what country it is, or how much money is in the bank; most people make the critical mistake of using money only for temporary, short-term things.

  E. They spend their money on things that give a little bit of momentary reward, and they ignore the power money has to shape their future.

XV. To a degree, lost people are better stewards of their assets than Christians are.

  A. That's not always the case, but often it is.

  B. I believe this is what Jesus was getting at when He said, **"The children of this world are in their generation wiser than the children of light"** (Luke 16:8b).

  C. Part of the reason is that Christians know this life isn't all there is.

  D. Lost people are planning for retirement and thinking death is the end, whereas Christians aren't as short-term in their thinking.

E. Christians don't have the same fear of death that unbelievers have, and they look beyond this life, into eternity.

F. As a result, Christians often don't prepare for their later years in life or gather an inheritance to leave for their children.

G. But money doesn't just give you power to shape your future on earth—it also influences eternity.

XVI. When Jesus was done teaching about the rich master who commended the unjust steward, He said,

> *And I say unto you, Make to yourselves friends of the mammon of unrighteousness; that, when ye fail, they may receive you into everlasting habitations.*
>
> LUKE 16:9

A. The Greek word translated as "fail" here also means death.

B. This scripture is telling you to use money to make friends who will receive you into everlasting habitations when you die.

C. In other words, you can touch people's lives through giving, and when you die, those people will be lined up in heaven to thank you for the way you used your resources to help them.

D. You can do it by giving to people directly or by giving to support the preaching of the Gospel, which saves, heals, and delivers.

E. Money doesn't exist in heaven, and you can't take it with you when you die—that's why you'll never see a hearse pulling a trailer.

F. But by investing money in the lives of others, you can take something that is destined for destruction and turn it into something eternal.

G. You can transform money into something that will never pass away by investing it in the Gospel and by using it to touch other people's lives.

XVII. The number one use of your money is to touch people's lives.

A. I believe that there are Christians who won't have much treasure waiting in heaven.

B. They'll still be blessed and overwhelmed by the love of God, because they weren't saved according to their works, but there won't be anybody waiting to welcome them into heaven, because they never used their money to spread the Gospel and change lives.

C. Other people who were not highly esteemed in this life will have people lined up by the thousands waiting to welcome them.

D. They might not have lived in the nicest house on the block, but they will have given from their resources to bless others—their giving will have transformed into eternal treasure.

E. You won't know how many lives you have touched by giving to support the preaching of the Gospel until you get to heaven and see everyone lined up to greet you.

XVIII. Yes, God wants you to take care of your needs.

A. You aren't a good steward if your family is sleeping under a tree because you keep giving all of your money away.

B. What I'm saying is that your attitude about money will change when you really get a revelation on prosperity.

C. You'll be thinking, *How little money do I need to take care of my family, and how much can I invest in eternity?*

D. A million years from now, people will still be stopping by your mansion in glory to thank you for the investment you made in the Gospel and for the way it touched their lives.

E. No saint will be saying, "Oh, I sure wish I'd spent my money on a nicer car, or a third flat-screen television."

XIX. God is in the people business!

A. All material things are going to fade away, and the only thing that will matter is how much you invested in people.

B. One day you will thank me for getting money out of your pocket and putting it into the Gospel.

C. Everything you hold on to, you end up losing.

D. It's only what you give away that you get to keep, and you are not a fool to give away something you can't keep in order to get something you can never lose.

XX. Most people take care of themselves first and tip God from the remains.

A. At least in the United States, a lot of people have swung clear over to gratifying every whim and thinking only about the moment.

B. People are mortgaging their futures so they can enjoy everything right now.

C. They are indulging themselves by grabbing everything they can, and they aren't planning for the future at all.

D. Like the unjust steward, they would do well to recognize that money is best spent on the future.

XXI. The two main points we learn from the parable of the dishonest steward are that money is not our greatest asset, and wise people invest their money in the future.

A. The blessing of God is what makes us rich, not money.

B. As long as we have God's blessing, wealth will find us.

C. The key is learning not to blow all of our money on short-lived pleasures but to use some of it to help shape our futures.

D. Money is not for treasures on earth but for the lives of multitudes of people, who will be waiting to welcome us into heaven.

TEACHER'S
GUIDE

1. Looking at the world around you, you can see that money has power. It obviously enables you to do things you otherwise can't do, and it gives you a certain level of respect. For instance, when a rich man walks into a room, his financial status gives him authority that a poor person in the same room doesn't have. The danger is that unless you are careful, you will begin to trust more in the power of money than you do in the power of God. The Lord is aware of this temptation, and that is why He said so many things about finances.

    1a. Where does money have power?
        In the world
    1b. The power of money comes with what temptation?
        To trust in it more than the power of God

2. In one of His teachings, Jesus said,

> *Lay not up for yourselves treasures upon earth, where moth and rust doth corrupt, and where thieves break through and steal: But lay up for yourselves treasures in heaven, where neither moth nor rust doth corrupt, and where thieves do not break through nor steal: For where your treasure is, there will your heart be also.*
>
> MATTHEW 6:19-21

You can tell where a person's heart is by where their money goes! This scripture illustrates the point Jesus was making with the rich man when He told the man to sell all of his goods: "If you really love and trust Me more than your money, then put your treasure in heaven." The man wouldn't do it because his treasure—and his heart—were in earthly riches. After the rich man walked away unwilling to part with his money, the Lord said,

> *How hardly shall they that have riches enter into the kingdom of God! And the disciples were astonished at his words. But Jesus answereth again, and saith unto them, Children, how hard is it for them that trust in riches to enter into the kingdom of God!*
>
> MARK 10:23-24

You could say it this way: "How hard it is for rich people to be born again." That's quite a statement, which is why the disciples were astonished. But Jesus clarified His meaning by saying "how hard it is for them that *trust* in riches." He wasn't saying that money itself makes it difficult to be saved; He was saying that having lots of money can trick people into putting faith in their money instead of in God. You can say "Oh, yeah, I'm trusting in the Lord," but you have to do more than just say it. As it says in the epistle of James, **"faith without works is dead"** (James 2:26). Someone who is really trusting in the Lord will prove it by tithing and giving out of their resources.

2a. Read Matthew 6:19-21. How can you tell where a person's heart is?
   A. By how much money they receive
   B. By where their money goes
   C. By using a stethoscope
   D. All of the above
   E. None of the above
2b. According to Mark 10:23-24, why is it hard for people who are rich to be born again?
   Because they tend to trust in their riches more than in God
2c. Read James 2:26. It's easy to say you're trusting in the Lord, but what accompanies true faith?
   Works

3. Whatever you serve becomes your master (Rom. 6:16), and putting your trust in finances places you in bondage to money. While serving money enslaves you, the Bible is full of evidence that God freely blesses His servants: Isaac was so prosperous that a king asked him to leave the land because it couldn't sustain his wealth (Gen. 26:16); Jacob was even more prosperous than Isaac or his father Abraham; David started life as the runt of his family with the responsibility of tending his father's sheep, but God made him king of Israel, and he became so wealthy that he gave a six billion-dollar offering in one day toward the building of the temple; and his son Solomon was even more prosperous.

    3a. Read Romans 6:16. What does serving money do to you?
        A. Enslaves you
        B. Rewards you
        C. Protects you
        D. Changes you
        E. Learns you
    3b. What evidence is the Bible full of?
    That God freely blesses His servants

4. The Lord knows how dependent we are upon money—He knows how fearful we can be about finances. God knows our frame (Ps. 103:14). He knows we are prone to fear in the area of finances, and that's the reason He made so many promises to prosper us when we trust in Him. Once we step out and begin trusting God, realizing that finances are the least use of our faith, we will start to see God's supernatural provision. It will increase our faith, and we will begin believing God for bigger and better things. On the other hand, if we never learn to trust God with our finances, we are always going to have a lack of confidence in Him. At some point, when we find ourselves in a tough situation, we'll try to stand on God's promises for a miracle, and it won't come to pass because we have lingering doubts. Our own hearts will condemn us and say, "You never believed God's promises that say 'give and it will be given unto you.' How can you trust the words on this page about healing? What really makes you think that by Jesus' stripes, you are healed?" I didn't say God will condemn us—condemnation doesn't come from God. God doesn't withhold His miracle-working power from us based on our works or history of giving. The danger with money is that we can get to where we trust in what money can do for us more than we trust in God. Then, when we come upon a problem that money can't solve, it will feel like the earth is crumbling beneath us. God will still be there to help us, but we won't have learned to trust in His ability to deliver us.

    4a. Why did God make so many promises to prosper you when you trust in Him?
    Because He knows you are prone to fear in the area of finances
    4b. You will always have a lack of confidence in God if you never what?
    Never learn to trust God with your finances
    4c. True or false: God doesn't withhold His miracle-working power from you based on your performance or history of giving.
    True

5. This is a major reason giving is important: Learning to trust God starts with your finances. Another word for trust is *reliance*. To rely on something is to depend on it. The dictionary defines reliance as "confident rest for support," as in, "We may have perfect *reliance* on the promises of God."[1] Are you relying on your money, or are you relying on God? Thinking *I want to give, but I can't—I need this money* means your confidence is in riches.

   5a. What is a major reason giving is important?
   Learning to trust God starts with your finances

6. After Jesus told His disciples that it is hard to enter the kingdom of God when your trust is in riches, He said,

> *It is easier for a camel to go through the eye of a needle, than for a rich man to enter into the kingdom of God. And they were astonished out of measure, saying among themselves, Who then can be saved?*
>
> MARK 10:25-26

The disciples were shocked before, but this statement put them over the top. Jesus was stressing the importance of turning your finances over to God and trusting Him as your source, yet many people today are not acknowledging the emphasis that He put on trusting God with finances. The disciples wondered if anyone could be saved. In fact, Jesus specifically said it was impossible:

> *And Jesus looking upon them saith, With men it is impossible, but not with God: for with God all things are possible.*
>
> MARK 10:27

   6a. Read Mark 10:26-27. How is it possible for the rich to be saved?
   With God

7. I believe that God has a plan for every one of you, and I believe His plans are bigger than your dreams. I don't think anyone has maxed out God's plans for them. God will do great things, but you have to rely on Him. One of the first steps in that direction is becoming a faithful steward of His resources. Once you begin trusting God for that which is seen—money—then you will be able to trust Him for that which is unseen: health, peace, joy, prosperity, and God's favor in your life.

   7a. Once you begin trusting God for that which is seen—money—what will you be able to trust Him for?
   That which is unseen: health, peace, joy, prosperity, and God's favor in your life

8. I've mentioned the parable of the unjust steward a few times, but now I want to take a closer look at what Jesus was teaching. This parable is one of Jesus' hardest teachings to understand. I think understanding this parable will make a big difference in the way you view and use money. A wealthy man had someone managing his money and thought that the steward was stealing from him, or somehow mismanaging his funds, so he told the steward to get his books in order (Luke 16:1-2).

> *Then the steward said within himself, What shall I do? for my lord taketh away from me the stewardship: I cannot dig; to beg I am ashamed.*
>
> LUKE 16:3

You can tell from the steward's reaction that he was guilty. He didn't try to prove his innocence or defend himself in any way. He knew that when his master took a look at the books, he was going to get fired. So, the steward said, "What am I going to do? I can't dig." It is probably more accurate to say he *wouldn't* dig. This raises a good point: Not everyone who has financial problems is lazy, but lazy people usually have financial problems. They're looking for a quick fix: to win the lottery or something. That's not how God's system works. If you are looking to prosper through winning the lottery, then you have the wrong attitude toward finances. The lottery isn't sinful necessarily, but it is a compromise. Even if you were to defy the odds and strike it rich, Scripture says that wealth obtained through vanity doesn't last (Prov. 13:11). Prosperity isn't about getting money any way you can—there is a right and a wrong way to do it. I'm sure the steward could have found a job if he wanted to, but that isn't the way he thought. He didn't want to work to get his money; he wanted to steal it, inherit it, or come by it effortlessly somehow. He was always looking for some scheme instead of simply believing that God would bless his work. After concluding that he didn't want to look for work, he said, "I am ashamed to beg." It's too bad he wasn't ashamed to *steal*—he might have still had a job! Having ruled out working and begging, the steward struck upon a scheme he liked:

> *I am resolved what to do, that, when I am put out of the stewardship, they may receive me into their houses. So he called every one of his lord's debtors unto him, and said unto the first, How much owest thou unto my lord? And he said, An hundred measures of oil. And he said unto him, Take thy bill, and sit down quickly, and write fifty. Then said he to another, And how much owest thou? And he said, An hundred measures of wheat. And he said unto him, Take thy bill, and write fourscore.*
>
> LUKE 16:4-7

These examples show that the steward called in all of his master's debtors and cut their debts by huge margins. He was too lazy to work and too proud to beg, so he kept on stealing money—but instead of putting the money into his own pocket, he put the money in the pockets of people who owed his master money. There could have been dozens or even hundreds of people who saved thousands of dollars because of the steward's discounts. The logic behind this was that when the steward got fired, he could go back to all of those debtors and say, "Hey, remember how I saved you thousands of dollars? Well, I'm out of work now. Can you give me a hand?" All of those people would feel indebted to him, or responsible for his unemployment, and he could mooch off them instead of getting a job. People steal money from their employers all of the time, so nothing so far is all that strange.

8a. What do lazy people usually have?
    A. Personal servants
    B. Big comfy couches
    C. Financial problems
    D. All of the above
    E. None of the above
8b. According to Proverbs 13:11, wealth obtained through_____doesn't last.
    Vanity
8c. In the parable of the unjust steward, how did the steward want to come by money?
    Effortlessly
8d. Why did the steward cut what his master's debtors owed?
    So the debtors would feel indebted to him, or responsible for his unemployment,
    and he could mooch off them instead of getting a job

9. What is unusual about this story is the master's response:

> *And the lord commended the unjust steward, because he had done wisely.*
> LUKE 16:8A

The simple fact that the master found something to commend the steward on says a lot about the master's attitude toward money. If you came home one night and discovered a thief standing in your living room, would you compliment the thief for bypassing your security system and nabbing your most valuable goods? The master's reaction to catching a thief is not what you'd expect. But if he didn't care about his money, he wouldn't have called the steward to account in the first place. I think this master understood that money is just a tool. Wealth is just a byproduct of God's favor. The master had a revelation that his true wealth was the favor of God, not the money the steward was stealing. This goes back to the first point I made about being a steward and recognizing that everything you have comes from God. God gives you resources, but the resources aren't your real asset. It's like the old children's fable about the goose that lays golden eggs: The golden eggs are not as valuable as the goose that produces them! When you have the goose, you get all of the golden eggs that come with it. In the same way, money isn't your true asset; the real treasure is the blessing and favor of God that *produces* riches.

    9a. Read Luke 16:8a. Why was the master's response to the steward unusual?
        Because he commended the steward for the way the steward stole from him
    9b. Why aren't riches the true treasure?
        Because the real treasure is the blessing and favor of God that produces riches

10. Once you realize that God is the source of prosperity, you understand how pointless it is to chase after riches. This is one reason Scripture reminds you that the power to get wealth comes from God:

> *But thou shalt remember the LORD thy God: for it is he that giveth thee power to get wealth, that he may establish his covenant which he sware unto thy fathers, as it is this day.*
>
> DEUTERONOMY 8:18

Notice the scripture doesn't say God *gives* you wealth; He gives you the power to *get* wealth. He releases an anointing on whatever you do and causes it to prosper—and the blessing of God is so powerful that it cannot be reversed. Balaam is the infamous prophet who was hired by a foreign king to curse the children of Israel, but he said,

> *Behold, I have received commandment to bless: and* [God] *hath blessed; and I cannot reverse it.*
>
> NUMBERS 23:20, BRACKETS MINE

Once the favor of God is on your life, it cannot be stopped! The only thing that can derail the blessing of God is your own unbelief and negativity. As long as you keep believing, the blessings of God will keep coming.

10a.   What is the one thing that can derail the blessing of God on your life?
Your own unbelief and negativity

11. Understanding the true value of God's favor on your life will cause you to have the same attitude that the rich master had toward his steward. Riches can be stolen and property can be taken away, but no one can rob you of God's favor. Once you get that same mindset, you could catch a thief robbing you blind and not feel fear or panic. You can become so secure in your relationship with God and so certain of His favor in your life that you could actually find something to compliment a thief about. The focus of your life should be your relationship with God, which is what causes wealth to accumulate.

11a.   What causes wealth to accumulate?
Your relationship with God

12. Money isn't that significant—on the other hand, God's favor in your life is priceless. Pastor Bob Nichols pastors Calvary Cathedral in Fort Worth, Texas. In April 2000, a tornado hit the area and destroyed his church. It was an eighteen million-dollar facility, not including the building's contents, and in less than sixty seconds, it was completely obliterated. Within one hour of the storm, CNN was standing in front of the wreckage interviewing Pastor Bob. He was saying "God didn't do this. This is nothing but an attack of the devil" and that God was going to work it together for good, and they were going to end up with a facility twice as nice as the one that was destroyed. Pastor Bob was expressing the same attitude that the rich master had. The storm had taken his property, but God's blessing was still on his life. In the end, Pastor Bob did end up with a facility twice as nice as the one destroyed by the tornado. His confidence was in the Lord, and the Lord restored everything that was taken from him— and then some.

12a.   When you've got the favor of God, which is priceless, money isn't that _____.
        Significant

13. You can only have that kind of confidence when you quit basing your life on physical things, and rely on God. When your trust is in what money can do for you, then your security is in your bank account—and when your bank account gets low, you are going to feel frightened and insecure. But when you know God is your source, you won't cling to assets. This mindset will help you sleep at night! It will completely transform your life to learn to rely on God instead of trusting in assets or other people. You can actually live your life without being tied to, or a servant of, your money.

13a.   When will you have the same confidence Pastor Bob Nichols had before he received a church facility that was twice as nice as the one destroyed by the tornado?
        When you quit basing your life on physical things, and rely on God

14. The other important point to understand from this parable is why the steward was commended. You wouldn't think there is anything commendable about stealing money and giving it to other people, but here's the reason the rich master did it: The steward finally realized that the true power of money is in using it to affect the future. Instead of pocketing the stolen money, the steward was using it to bribe people and prepare for his future. It's easy to see that prior to this, the steward had just been blowing the money on "things." It doesn't matter what country it is, or how much money is in the bank; most people make the critical mistake of using money only for temporary, short-term things. They spend their money on things that give a little bit of momentary reward, and they ignore the power money has to shape their future.

14a.   What is the true power of money?
        A.   To give it to your pastor
        B.   To buy whatever you want
        C.   To buy your way out of trouble
        D.   To affect the past
        E.   To affect the future

15. To a degree, lost people are better stewards of their assets than Christians are. That's not always the case, but often it is. I believe this is what Jesus was getting at when He said, **"The children of this world are in their generation wiser than the children of light"** (Luke 16:8b). Part of the reason is that Christians know this life isn't all there is. Lost people are planning for retirement and thinking death is the end, whereas Christians aren't as short-term in their thinking. Christians don't have the same fear of death that unbelievers have, and they look beyond this life, into eternity. As a result, Christians often don't prepare for their later years in life or gather an inheritance to leave for their children. But money doesn't just give you power to shape your future on earth—it also influences eternity.

    15a. Why are lost people often better stewards than Christians?
         Because they manage their money to affect their earthly futures

16. When Jesus was done teaching about the rich master who commended the unjust steward, He said,

> *And I say unto you, Make to yourselves friends of the mammon of unrighteousness; that, when ye fail, they may receive you into everlasting habitations.*
>
> LUKE 16:9

The Greek word translated as "fail" here also means death. This scripture is telling you to use money to make friends who will receive you into everlasting habitations when you die. In other words, you can touch people's lives through giving, and when you die, those people will be lined up in heaven to thank you for the way you used your resources to help them. You can do it by giving to people directly or by giving to support the preaching of the Gospel, which saves, heals, and delivers. Money doesn't exist in heaven, and you can't take it with you when you die—that's why you'll never see a hearse pulling a trailer. But by investing money in the lives of others, you can take something that is destined for destruction and turn it into something eternal. You can transform money into something that will never pass away by investing it in the Gospel and by using it to touch other people's lives.

    16a. True or false: According to Luke 16:9, you should use your money to make friends who will receive you in heaven when you die.
         True
    16b. What can you do by investing money in the lives of others?
         You can take something that is destined for destruction (money) and positively affect people's lives for eternity

17. The number one use of your money is to touch people's lives. I believe that there are Christians who won't have much treasure waiting in heaven. They'll still be blessed and overwhelmed by the love of God, because they weren't saved according to their works, but there won't be anybody waiting to welcome them into heaven, because they never used their money to spread the Gospel and change lives. Other people who were not highly esteemed in this life will have people lined up by the thousands waiting to welcome them. They might not have lived in the nicest house on the block, but they will have given from their resources to bless others—their giving will have transformed into eternal treasure. You won't know how many lives you have touched by giving to support the preaching of the Gospel until you get to heaven and see everyone lined up to greet you.

17a. True or false: Touching people's lives is the only use of money.
False

18. Yes, God wants you to take care of your needs. You aren't a good steward if your family is sleeping under a tree because you keep giving all of your money away. What I'm saying is that your attitude about money will change when you really get a revelation on prosperity. You'll be thinking, *How little money do I need to take care of my family, and how much can I invest in eternity?* A million years from now, people will still be stopping by your mansion in glory to thank you for the investment you made in the Gospel and for the way it touched their lives. No saint will be saying, "Oh, I sure wish I'd spent my money on a nicer car, or a third flat-screen television."

18a. What will change when you get a revelation on prosperity?
A. Your attitude about money
B. The number of zeroes on your paycheck
C. What you think of others
D. All of the above
E. None of the above
18b. What will you think then?
How little money do I need to take care of my family, and how much can I invest on eternity?

19. God is in the people business! All material things are going to fade away, and the only thing that will matter is how much you invested in people. One day you will thank me for getting money out of your pocket and putting it into the Gospel. Everything you hold on to, you end up losing. It's only what you give away that you get to keep, and you are not a fool to give away something you can't keep in order to get something you can never lose.

19a. You are not a fool to give away something you can't_____in order to get something you can never_____.
Keep, lose

20. Most people take care of themselves first and tip God from the remains. At least in the United States, a lot of people have swung clear over to gratifying every whim and thinking only about the moment. People are mortgaging their futures so they can enjoy everything right now. They are indulging themselves by grabbing everything they can, and they aren't planning for the future at all. Like the unjust steward, they would do well to recognize that money is best spent on the future.

    20a. You will do well to learn that money is best spent on_____.
         The future

21. The two main points we learn from the parable of the dishonest steward are that money is not our greatest asset, and wise people invest their money in the future. The blessing of God is what makes us rich, not money. As long as we have God's blessing, wealth will find us. The key is learning not to blow all of our money on short-lived pleasures but to use some of it to help shape our futures. Money is not for treasures on earth but for the lives of multitudes of people, who will be waiting to welcome us into heaven.

    21a. As long as you have God's blessing, what will wealth do?
         Find you

DISCIPLESHIP
—— QUESTIONS ——

1. Where does money have power?

2. The power of money comes with what temptation?

3. Read Matthew 6:19-21. How can you tell where a person's heart is?
   A. By how much money they receive
   B. By where their money goes
   C. By using a stethoscope
   D. All of the above
   E. None of the above

4. According to Mark 10:23-24, why is it hard for people who are rich to be born again?

5. Read James 2:26. It's easy to say you're trusting in the Lord, but what accompanies true faith?

6. Read Romans 6:16. What does serving money do to you?
   A. Enslaves you
   B. Rewards you
   C. Protects you
   D. Changes you
   E. Learns you

7. What evidence is the Bible full of?

8. Why did God make so many promises to prosper you when you trust in Him?

_____
_____
_____

9. You will always have a lack of confidence in God if you never what?

_____
_____
_____

10. True or false: God doesn't withhold His miracle-working power from you based on your performance or history of giving.

11. What is a major reason giving is important?

_____
_____
_____

12. Read Mark 10:26-27. How is it possible for the rich to be saved?

_____
_____
_____

13. Once you begin trusting God for that which is seen—money—what will you be able to trust Him for?

_____
_____
_____

14. What do lazy people usually have?
    A. Personal servants
    B. Big comfy couches
    C. Financial problems
    D. All of the above
    E. None of the above

15. According to Proverbs 13:11, wealth obtained through_____doesn't last.

16. In the parable of the unjust steward, how did the steward want to come by money?

_____
_____
_____

17. Why did the steward cut what his master's debtors owed?

_____

_____

_____

18. Read Luke 16:8a. Why was the master's response to the steward unusual?

_____

_____

_____

19. Why aren't riches the true treasure?

_____

_____

_____

20. What is the one thing that can derail the blessing of God on your life?

_____

_____

_____

21. What causes wealth to accumulate?

_____

_____

_____

22. When you've got the favor of God, which is priceless, money isn't that

_____.

23. When will you have the same confidence Pastor Bob Nichols had before he received a church facility that was twice as nice as the one destroyed by the tornado?

_____

_____

_____

24. What is the true power of money?
    A. To give it to your pastor
    B. To buy whatever you want
    C. To buy your way out of trouble
    D. To affect the past
    E. To affect the future

25. Why are lost people often better stewards than Christians?

_____
_____
_____

26. True or false: According to Luke 16:9, you should use your money to make friends who will receive you in heaven when you die.

27. What can you do by investing money in the lives of others?

_____
_____
_____

28. True or false: Touching people's lives is the only use of money.

29. What will change when you get a revelation on prosperity?
    A. Your attitude about money
    B. The number of zeroes on your paycheck
    C. What you think of others
    D. All of the above
    E. None of the above

30. What will you think then?

_____
_____
_____

31. You are not a fool to give away something you can't_____in order to get something you can never_____.

32. You will do well to learn that money is best spent on_____.

33. As long as you have God's blessing, what will wealth do?

_____
_____
_____

ANSWER
—KEY—

1. In the world

2. To trust in it more than the power of God

3. B. By where their money goes

4. Because they tend to trust in their riches more than in God

5. Works

6. A. Enslaves you

7. That God freely blesses His servants

8. Because He knows you are prone to fear in the area of finances

9. Never learn to trust God with your finances

10. True

11. Learning to trust God starts with your finances

12. With God

13. That which is unseen: health, peace, joy, prosperity, and God's favor in your life

14. C. Financial problems

15. Vanity

16. Effortlessly

17. So the debtors would feel indebted to him, or responsible for his unemployment, and he could mooch off them instead of getting a job

18. Because he commended the steward for the way the steward stole from him

19. Because the real treasure is the blessing and favor of God that *produces* riches

20. Your own unbelief and negativity

21. Your relationship with God

22. Significant

23. When you quit basing your life on physical things and rely on God

24. E. To affect the future

25. Because they manage their money to affect their earthly futures

26. True

27. You can take something that is destined for destruction (money) and positively affect people's lives for eternity

28. False

29. A. Your attitude about money

30. *How little money do I need to take care of my family, and how much can I invest on eternity?*

31. Keep, lose

32. The future

33. Find you

──SCRIPTURES──

MATTHEW 6:19-21

Lay not up for yourselves treasures upon earth, where moth and rust doth corrupt, and where thieves break through and steal: **[20]** But lay up for yourselves treasures in heaven, where neither moth nor rust doth corrupt, and where thieves do not break through nor steal: **[21]** For where your treasure is, there will your heart be also.

MARK 10:23-27

And Jesus looked round about, and saith unto his disciples, How hardly shall they that have riches enter into the kingdom of God! **[24]** And the disciples were astonished at his words. But Jesus answereth again, and saith unto them, Children, how hard is it for them that trust in riches to enter into the kingdom of God! **[25]** It is easier for a camel to go through the eye of a needle, than for a rich man to enter into the kingdom of God. **[26]** And they were astonished out of measure, saying among themselves, Who then can be saved? **[27]** And Jesus looking upon them saith, With men it is impossible, but not with God: for with God all things are possible.

JAMES 2:26

For as the body without the spirit is dead, so faith without works is dead also.

ROMANS 6:16

Know ye not, that to whom ye yield yourselves servants to obey, his servants ye are to whom ye obey; whether of sin unto death, or of obedience unto righteousness?

GENESIS 26:16

And Abimelech said unto Isaac, Go from us; for thou art much mightier than we.

PSALM 103:14

For he knoweth our frame; he remembereth that we are dust.

LUKE 16:1-9

And he said also unto his disciples, There was a certain rich man, which had a steward; and the same was accused unto him that he had wasted his goods. **[2]** And he called him, and said unto him, How is it that I hear this of thee? give an account of thy stewardship; for thou mayest be no longer steward. **[3]** Then the steward said within himself, What shall I do? for my lord taketh away from me the stewardship: I cannot dig; to beg I am ashamed. **[4]** I am resolved what to do, that, when I am put out of the stewardship, they may receive me into their houses. **[5]** So he called every one of his lord's debtors unto him, and said unto the first, How much owest thou unto my lord? **[6]** And he said, An hundred measures of oil. And he said unto him, Take thy bill, and sit down quickly, and write fifty. **[7]** Then said he to another, And how much owest thou? And he said, An hundred measures of wheat. And he said unto him, Take thy bill, and write fourscore. **[8]** And the lord commended the unjust steward, because he had done wisely: for the children of this world are in their generation wiser than the children of light. **[9]** And I say unto you, Make to yourselves friends of the mammon of unrighteousness; that, when ye fail, they may receive you into everlasting habitations.

PROVERBS 13:11

Wealth gotten by vanity shall be diminished: but he that gathereth by labour shall increase.

——SCRIPTURES——

GENESIS 12:2

And I will make of thee a great nation, and I will bless thee, and make thy name great; and thou shalt be a blessing.

DEUTERONOMY 8:18

But thou shalt remember the LORD thy God: for it is he that giveth thee power to get wealth, that he may establish his covenant which he sware unto thy fathers, as it is this day.

NUMBERS 23:20

Behold, I have received commandment to bless: and he hath blessed; and I cannot reverse it.

SEEK FIRST THE KINGDOM

It's important to have the right attitude about finances before you start focusing on God's desire to bring money your way. Scripture says that if your eye is single, then your whole body will be flooded with light, but if your eye is evil, then your body is full of darkness (Matt. 6:22-23). It also says that anyone who hastens to be rich has an evil eye (Prov. 28:22). In other words, if your focus is divided between the things of God and getting rich, then your whole body will be full of darkness.

This is a very important concept. The Lord is saying that He wants you to be single in your focus upon Him. At first, you might think it is impossible to be totally committed to and focused upon God in everything you do, and if it took relying on human strength, I would agree. But you don't live the Christian life in your own strength. The Apostle Paul wrote,

> *(For the weapons of our warfare are not carnal, but mighty through God to the pulling down of strong holds;) Casting down imaginations, and every high thing that exalteth itself against the knowledge of God, and bringing into captivity every thought to the obedience of Christ.*
> 2 CORINTHIANS 10:4-5

God has given you weapons so strong that they can bring every thought into obedience to Christ. You can work, raise a family, do all of the things you need to do in life, and still keep your attention 100 percent upon God. *But you can't be focused on God when you think you are the one who is responsible for producing the financial blessing in your life!* If you think that supporting your family and earning money is strictly up to you, then you are going to have a divided heart—and a divided heart is going to allow darkness to enter your life and hinder you in your relationship with God.

The Apostle Paul said, **"This one thing I do"** (Phil. 3:13). The reason he accomplished everything he did was because he did one thing: He sought first the kingdom of God. The quickest way to destroy a man's vision is to give him two. You can't accomplish your goals when your attention and resources are divided. If you really want to prosper, then you need to forget everything else and press toward this one goal of putting the kingdom first.

I know some people might hear that and think, *You're living in la-la land. Out in the real world, you have to work to pay bills. Life is all about working to get ahead.* It's true that we are supposed to work. Scripture says that lazy people who don't work shouldn't expect to eat (2 Thess. 3:10), but God's plan for our financial freedom doesn't rely on the natural results of hard work. We have to change the way we think about money and prosperity. The Apostle Paul encouraged the Ephesians to think differently about the goal of work when he said,

> *Let him that stole steal no more: but rather let him labour, working with his hands the thing which is good, that he may have to give to him that needeth.*
> EPHESIANS 4:28

He didn't tell them to labor so they could pay their bills and keep a roof over their heads. Nor did he tell them to labor so they could feed and clothe their children. He said "work so you'll have money to give to those in need." He was echoing Jesus' teaching that the most important use of money is not satisfying self's temporary needs. By satisfying *other* people's temporal needs, the Apostle Paul was saying, they could demonstrate the love of God and touch people's lives.

Every dollar you get has the potential to influence a person's life for the better. Of course, you have needs, too, and God knows that. The natural inclination is to think, *If I start taking care of everybody else, then who is going to take care of me?* God! God will take care of you, and He'll do a better job than you ever have. This is where you see that finances are a matter of faith. You can't dissect what I'm saying and see exactly how it works. I can't write out a contract and say that if you do these things, you are going to have more money than you ever dreamed. But the Word teaches that when you put the kingdom of God first, then all of your financial needs will be taken care of. Prosperity is a *byproduct* of seeking God; it shouldn't be the goal.

What I'm talking about here is a matter of the heart. You can't create some kind of formula from what I'm saying, where you put effort in on one end and prosperity comes out the other. God's financial system doesn't work the same way that the world's system works. God's kind of prosperity results from faith. When you work so you can have money to give, God takes care of you. It's a mindset and a heart condition, not a get-rich-quick scheme.

> **PROSPERITY IS A BYPRODUCT OF SEEKING GOD; IT SHOULDN'T BE THE GOAL.**

God's kind of prosperity comes when we shift our focus from getting and maintaining stuff, to living to give. Most people say, "I want to give…and if I ever get any extra, I will." We saw earlier that what they mean is that as soon as they get everything they want, they'll toss a tip God's way. As long as their needs get met first, then God can have the leftovers. That isn't seeking first the kingdom of God. The Lord says we should work so we will have money to bless other people.

The highest form of giving is to help share the Gospel. When you start helping the Good News to be shared, demonstrating the love of God in word and deed, there is a divine flow that takes place. God starts supernaturally supplying your needs. This is why Scripture says to give God the first fruits (Prov. 3:9)—not the leftover fruit. The first thing you should do when you get money is give back to God. When you do that, God takes better care of you accidentally than you have ever done through striving and grasping at your resources.

The reason some Christians preach about financial prosperity and believe for it so hard is because they want the new houses, cars, and things they see people in the world enjoying. They are preaching about prosperity, but it's all about them. They wear huge jewelry and flash their money around just like unbelievers. Again, there's nothing wrong with being prosperous. God wants you to have nice things, but your heart attitude should be that prosperity isn't about you—it's really about how much is flowing through you.

God gave you two hands: one hand to receive and one hand to give. If God can get the money *through* you to other people, then He will get it *to* you—and as the money flows *through*, there will be plenty left over for *you*. You are not supposed to live in poverty; it's just that your first priority should be helping other people, rather than trying to grab everything you can for yourself. It's the same attitude taught in Scripture:

> *And God is able to make all grace abound toward you; that ye, always*
> *having all sufficiency in all things, may abound to every good work.*
> 2 CORINTHIANS 9:8

The context of this scripture is money. The Apostle Paul was writing to the Corinthians about being good stewards. It's not just about spiritual blessings. This is saying that the reason God makes all financial blessings abound toward you is so you'll have the resources to do good things for others—because true prosperity isn't defined by how nice your house is or by what kind of car you drive. God evaluates prosperity by how much of a blessing you are to others. This is all easy to say, but it's a lot harder to live.

The average high school graduate in the United States earns more than a million dollars in their lifetime, and college graduates earn twice that. Many people will have had one or two million dollars pass through their hands in this life, but they won't have anything to show for it in eternity. They will have spent all of their money on cars, clothes, and food. Right now, we have the privilege of taking something that will eventually be completely destroyed and converting it into something that will never pass away. Once we understand this truth, we realize what an incredible blessing it is to be able to give. It's the investment opportunity of a lifetime.

PROSPERITY ISN'T ABOUT YOU— IT'S REALLY ABOUT HOW MUCH MONEY IS FLOWING THROUGH YOU.

My wife and I had virtually nothing when we started out in ministry. We've been through a lot of hard financial times. Most of it was because of religious bondage and wrong doctrine I believed, keeping me from experiencing God's blessing. But we always put God first, and He has blessed us as a result. We put our focus on seeking God and giving to others, and the side effect for us has been prosperity—that's how God's financial system works.

Your carnal mind thinks *If I don't take care of myself, no one else will either*, and I guess that's true if you don't have faith in God. But when you trust God and begin honoring Him with your first fruits, then God will make your **"barns be filled with plenty, and thy presses shall burst out with new wine"** (Prov. 3:10). He causes a supernatural flow of finances toward you. God's promise is this:

But seek ye first the kingdom of God, and his righteousness; and all these things shall be added unto you.

MATTHEW 6:33

What "things" will be added unto you? In context, Jesus was talking about where you sleep, what you eat, and the clothes you wear. He was saying that finances will be added unto you. So, when you put the kingdom of God first, God takes care of your physical needs. In other words, when your first priority is seeking God, then He assumes the responsibility of taking care of you—and God will do a lot better job than you can.

In the Old Testament, Elijah prophesied to King Ahab that a drought was coming, and then Elijah fled into the desert to hide. King Ahab was persecuting God's prophets, so Elijah had to run for his life. Initially, God sent ravens to feed him at a brook. When the brook dried up, God told Elijah to go to the city of Zarephath where He had commanded a widow woman to sustain him. So, Elijah went to the city and found the woman. The first thing he said to her was, "Go get me some water, and while you're at it, bring me something to eat." The widow turned to him and said,

As the LORD thy God liveth, I have not a cake, but an handful of meal in a barrel, and a little oil in a cruse: and, behold, I am gathering two sticks, that I may go in and dress it for me and my son, that we may eat it, and die.

1 KINGS 17:12

Water is obviously a precious commodity during a drought, yet the widow was still willing to go get Elijah some water. But she drew the line when he asked for food. This widow was down to her very last meal. She and her son were going to die of starvation after they ate it because they had absolutely nothing left. Elijah told her to go make his meal first and bring it to him. *Then*, he said, she could go cook for herself and her son. Elijah said,

For thus saith the LORD God of Israel, The barrel of meal shall not waste, neither shall the cruse of oil fail, until the day that the LORD sendeth rain upon the earth.

1 KINGS 17:14

The widow only had enough oil and flour for one tiny meal, but she believed what Elijah told her, so she made his meal first. As a result, the Lord supernaturally maintained the tiny amount of oil and flour in her containers, and it fed Elijah, the widow, and her son for three years. Can you imagine what bystanders would have thought if they had heard Elijah telling a widow to give him her last meal? They would have accused him of stealing from her. *The Jerusalem Post* headline would have been, "Man of God Takes Widow's Last Meal." But Elijah wasn't taking from the widow—he was giving to her.

If the widow hadn't given him that meal, then the Lord wouldn't have supernaturally multiplied the food, and the widow and her son would have died of starvation within days. The step of faith she took by feeding God's prophet first, before taking care of herself, resulted in a supply that supported her and her son for three years. Later on, Elijah also raised her son from the dead, which wouldn't have happened if she hadn't formed a relationship with Elijah through feeding him for three years. So, her giving of the little bit she had was the way to multiple miracles in her life.

I remember ministering on these same passages years ago at a church in Texas. At the end of the service, a woman came up to me, asking for prayer. She asked me if I remembered who she was and I said no. She went on to tell me how I had prayed for her the year before. At the time, she had been in a mental institution and wanted God to restore her mind. I had prayed for her, and she had been completely healed—praise God! She was eventually released from the institution, but she didn't have anywhere to go, so the institution had given her a place to live and a job as a custodian.

But she wanted to be totally free from that place, and to do that, she needed a financial miracle. She needed a new job and a new place to live. Well, I had just finished preaching about Elijah telling the widow to give to him first and how the widow's step of faith opened up God's supernatural provision. So, I told the woman that she needed to give.

"What do you have?" I asked.

She got her purse and took out a little coin pouch. She emptied the coin pouch into my hand, and it was something like eighty-seven dollars and change.

"Give it to me," I said.

"All of it?" she asked.

"All of it," I said.

She gave me every last penny. She said she wouldn't have any money until she got paid again, and she hadn't even bought groceries yet. To top it off, it was going to be more than a week until her next payday. But I took all of her money and gave it to the pastor of the church, and then I prayed for her financial miracle.

> **GOD ASSUMES THE RESPONSIBILITY OF TAKING CARE OF YOU WHEN YOU PUT SEEKING HIS KINGDOM FIRST. AND GOD CAN TAKE FAR BETTER CARE OF YOU THAN YOU CAN.**

The pastor of that church called me the next week to tell me what had happened. The Monday after I prayed with her, someone who didn't even go to their church gave her a car. It wasn't anyone who knew that she needed a car. It was just God's supernatural provision. A day or two after that, the woman's mother called. Previously, her mother had been embarrassed by her mental condition and had severed all relations with her when she entered the mental institution. The mother asked forgiveness for the way she had treated her and asked her to move back home. And by the end of the week, the woman had a new job that paid twice as much as working as a custodian at the mental institute had.

Someone who didn't have faith in God might have thought I was being cruel to ask for that woman's last penny, but I wasn't taking from her. I was giving her an opportunity to activate God's supernatural flow, and her step of faith got her a car, a place to live, a restored relationship with her mother, and a new job that paid twice what her old job did! That's awesome. It shows God's concern for every aspect of our lives. He wants us to prosper in every way: physically, emotionally, financially, and in our relationships. When we put the kingdom of God first, He takes care of our needs supernaturally. So, if we want God to assume all of our financial liabilities, then we need to put the kingdom of God first in our finances.

It might seem like a radical concept, but it works. It has worked in my life, and I've seen it work in the lives of hundreds of others. You are going to wind up frustrated if you think that work is all about getting money so you can pay your bills. It's discouraging to get up every morning and go to work just so you can make your house payment and buy food and clothes. There is a better way to live! Matthew 6:19-33 reveals God's plan for your earthly provision.

> *Lay not up for yourselves treasures upon earth, where moth and rust doth corrupt, and where thieves break through and steal.*
>
> MATTHEW 6:19

It would be a mistake to interpret this verse to mean that you can't ever have any money. Other scriptures say you should leave an inheritance for your children's children (Prov. 13:22), and you need to save up quite a bit of money to do that. I think what Jesus is getting at here is your motives. It's wrong to build up savings out of fear, or so you can sit back and say to yourself, "Eat, drink, and be merry, for I have goods laid up for many days ahead" (Luke 12:19). That's the wrong attitude. But it's good to build up savings so you always have resources to abound unto every good work and to leave an inheritance to your grandchildren. That's using money to bless others.

When Jesus said these things, He knew people would be asking "How do you seek first the kingdom of God and build up an inheritance at the same time? If I do everything for the sake of the Lord, who is going to pay my rent, buy my clothes, and provide food for me to eat?" so, He said,

> *No man can serve two masters: for either he will hate the one, and love the other; or else he will hold to the one, and despise the other. Ye cannot serve God and mammon. Therefore I say unto you, Take no thought for your life, what ye shall eat, or what ye shall drink; nor yet for your body, what ye shall put on. Is not the life more than meat, and the body than raiment?*
>
> MATTHEW 6:24-25

This clearly says that you can't serve God and money, but that doesn't mean you'll never have money when you serve God. It's obvious that you should choose to serve God, so Jesus goes on to explain how God takes care of your needs. He said that life is about more than eating and deciding which clothes to wear. Besides, worrying about your finances won't help anyway.

> *Behold the fowls of the air: for they sow not, neither do they reap, nor gather into barns; yet your heavenly Father feedeth them. Are ye not much better than they? Which of you by taking thought can add one cubit unto his stature?*
>
> MATTHEW 6:26-27

Have you ever read a headline about millions of birds dying of starvation? No. And you never will. They don't plant or harvest or store food away—yet God feeds them. If God cares that much for a tiny little bird, think how much better care will He take of a person who has been made in His image! Jesus is encouraging you that you can have much more confidence in God to take care of you. This is a radical statement. You might feel like it's your duty to worry about things, but God is telling you to rely on Him with your whole heart (1 Pet. 5:7).

> *Therefore take no thought, saying, What shall we eat? or, What shall we drink? or, Wherewithal shall we be clothed? (For after all these things do the Gentiles seek:) for your heavenly Father knoweth that ye have need of all these things.*
>
> MATTHEW 6:31-32

In modern language, we'd say that those are things lost people seek after. There should be a difference between Christians and unbelievers—between people who have a covenant with God and people who are trying to do it all on their own. The world should be able to see a difference in every area of our lives, including finances. We shouldn't be out in the world chasing money and struggling to survive the same way that unbelievers are. God wants us to prosper, and we have a covenant that includes financial prosperity. God is pleased when we prosper (Ps. 35:27)! He wants to see us succeed.

After giving all of this reassurance, Jesus tells you to seek first the kingdom of God and **"all of these things shall be added unto you"** (Matt. 6:33). What things? The same things He was talking about earlier: what you eat, where you sleep, the clothes you wear, and all of your physical needs. When you put the kingdom of God first, God takes care of everything else.

Most of us work our fingers to the bone trying to get ahead: we have garage sales, we scrimp and save, we work two jobs, we get more fuel-efficient cars, we do anything we can to save a little money. But all of that is really about meeting our own needs and taking care of our responsibilities. At the end of the day, if we have any spare money lying around, then we give to God to promote the Gospel.

The scriptural way to live is to seek first the kingdom of God—even with your finances. You should be working to give. When your heart is transformed and you start working so that you can be a blessing to other people, then God starts taking better care of you than you ever took of yourself. God is El Shaddai, not El Cheapo. When you seek first the kingdom of God, even in your giving and finances, then God prospers you.

This is a truth you need to open up your heart to and allow the Holy Spirit to reveal. I can explain it, but it's going to take a supernatural revelation to really get what I'm talking about here. You can't just go through the motions of giving and think that God is going to return your giving one hundred times over. You have to rely on God and trust that He is your source. It has to be a heart-level revelation, not just a conclusion you arrive at mentally. But once you grab a hold of this, it will revolutionize your life. You will be completely transformed once you believe that by putting God first, He will begin to supernaturally take care of you. It will bring you a tremendous amount of peace and confidence.

— OUTLINE —

I.   It's important to have the right attitude about finances before you start focusing on God's desire to bring money your way.

    A.   Scripture says that if your eye is single, then your whole body will be flooded with light, but if your eye is evil, then your body is full of darkness (Matt. 6:22-23).

    B.   It also says that anyone who hastens to be rich has an evil eye (Prov. 28:22).

    C.   In other words, if your focus is divided between the things of God and getting rich, then your whole body will be full of darkness.

    D.   At first, you might think it is impossible to be totally committed to and focused upon God in everything you do, and if it took relying on human strength, I would agree.

    E.   But you don't live the Christian life in your own strength.

    F.   God has given you weapons so strong that they can bring every thought into obedience to Christ (2 Cor. 10:4-5).

    G.   You can work, raise a family, do all of the things you need to do in life, and still keep your attention 100 percent upon God.

    H.   *But you can't be focused on God when you think you are the one who is responsible for producing the financial blessing in your life!*

II. The Apostle Paul said, **"This one thing I do"** (Phil. 3:13).

    A.   The reason he accomplished everything he did was because he did one thing: He sought first the kingdom of God.

    B.   The quickest way to destroy a man's vision is to give him two.

    C.   You can't accomplish your goals when your attention and resources are divided.

    D.   If you really want to prosper, then you need to forget everything else and press toward this one goal of putting the kingdom first.

    E.   It's true that you are supposed to work.

    F.   Scripture says that lazy people who don't work shouldn't expect to eat (2 Thess. 3:10), but God's plan for your financial freedom doesn't rely on the natural results of hard work.

III. The Apostle Paul encouraged the Ephesians to think differently about the goal of work when he said,

*Let him that stole steal no more: but rather let him labour, working with his
hands the thing which is good, that he may have to give to him that needeth.*
EPHESIANS 4:28

A. He was echoing Jesus' teaching that the most important use of money is not satisfying self's temporary needs.

B. By satisfying *other* people's temporal needs, the Apostle Paul was saying, they could demonstrate the love of God and touch people's lives.

C. Every dollar you get has the potential to influence a person's life for the better.

D. God will take care of you, and He'll do a better job than you ever have.

E. This is where you see that finances are a matter of faith.

F. The Word teaches that when you put the kingdom of God first, then all of your financial needs will be taken care of.

G. Prosperity is a *byproduct* of seeking God; it shouldn't be the goal.

IV. What I'm talking about here is a matter of the heart.

A. You can't create some kind of formula from what I'm saying, where you put effort in on one end and prosperity comes out the other.

B. When you work so you can have money to give, God takes care of you.

C. It's a mindset and a heart condition, not a get-rich-quick scheme.

D. God's kind of prosperity comes when you shift your focus from getting and maintaining stuff, to living to give.

E. When you start helping the Good News to be shared, demonstrating the love of God in word and deed, there is a divine flow that takes place.

F. God starts supernaturally supplying your needs.

G. This is why Scripture says to give God the first fruits (Prov. 3:9)—not the leftover fruit.

H. The first thing you should do when you get money is give back to God.

V. The reason some Christians preach about financial prosperity and believe for it so hard is because they want the new houses, cars, and things they see people in the world enjoying.

A. Again, there's nothing wrong with being prosperous, but your heart attitude should be that prosperity isn't about you—it's really about how much is flowing through you.

B. God gave you two hands: one hand to receive and one hand to give.

C. If God can get the money *through* you to other people, then He will get it *to* you—and as the money flows *through*, there will be plenty left over for *you*.

D. It's the same attitude taught in Scripture:

And God is able to make all grace abound toward you; that ye, always having all sufficiency in all things, may abound to every good work.
2 CORINTHIANS 9:8

E. The context of this scripture is money.

F. This is saying that the reason God makes all financial blessings abound toward you is so you'll have the resources to do good things for others.

G. God evaluates prosperity by how much of a blessing you are to others.

H. This is all easy to say, but it's a lot harder to live.

I. Once you understand this truth, you realize what an incredible blessing it is to be able to give.

J. It's the investment opportunity of a lifetime.

VI. My wife and I had virtually nothing when we started out in ministry.

A. Most of it was because of religious bondage and wrong doctrine I believed, keeping me from experiencing God's blessing—but we always put God first, and He has blessed us as a result.

B. We put our focus on seeking God and giving to others, and the side effect for us has been prosperity—that's how God's financial system works.

C. The carnal mind thinks *If I don't take care of myself, no one else will either*, and I guess that's true if you don't have faith in God.

D. But when you trust God and begin honoring Him with your first fruits, then God will make your **"barns be filled with plenty, and thy presses shall burst out with new wine"** (Prov. 3:10).

E. God's promise is this:

But seek ye first the kingdom of God, and his righteousness; and all these things shall be added unto you.
MATTHEW 6:33

F. In context, Jesus was talking about where you sleep, what you eat, and the clothes you wear.

G. In other words, when your first priority is seeking God, then He assumes the responsibility of taking care of you.

VII. In the Old Testament, Elijah prophesied to King Ahab that a drought was coming, and then Elijah fled into the desert to hide.

    A. Initially, God sent ravens to feed him at a brook.

    B. When the brook dried up, God told Elijah to go to the city of Zarephath where He had commanded a widow woman to sustain him.

    C. The first thing Elijah said to her was, "Go get me some water, and while you're at it, bring me something to eat."

    D. The widow turned to him and said,

> *As the LORD thy God liveth, I have not a cake, but an handful of meal in a barrel, and a little oil in a cruse: and, behold, I am gathering two sticks, that I may go in and dress it for me and my son, that we may eat it, and die.*
>
> 1 KINGS 17:12

    E. Water is obviously a precious commodity during a drought, yet the widow was still willing to go get Elijah some water.

    F. But she drew the line when he asked for food.

    G. She and her son were going to die of starvation after they ate this last meal because they had absolutely nothing left.

    H. Elijah told her to go make his meal first and bring it to him—*then*, he said, she could go cook for herself and her son.

    I. Then he gave her a prophecy:

> *For thus saith the LORD God of Israel, The barrel of meal shall not waste, neither shall the cruse of oil fail, until the day that the LORD sendeth rain upon the earth.*
>
> 1 KINGS 17:14

    J. The widow believed what Elijah told her, so she made his meal first.

    K. Can you imagine what bystanders would have thought if they had heard Elijah telling a widow to give him her last meal?

    L. They would have accused him of stealing from her.

    M. But Elijah wasn't taking from the widow—he was giving to her.

    N. If the widow hadn't given him that meal, then the Lord wouldn't have supernaturally multiplied the food.

    O. The step of faith she took by feeding God's prophet first, before taking care of herself, resulted in a supply that supported her and her son for three years.

P.   Later on, Elijah also raised her son from the dead, which wouldn't have happened if she hadn't formed a relationship with Elijah through feeding him.

Q.   So, her giving of the little bit she had was the way to multiple miracles in her life.

VIII. I remember ministering on these same passages years ago at a church in Texas.

A.   At the end of the service, a woman came up to me, asking for prayer.

B.   She told me how I had prayed for her the year before and how, at the time, she had been in a mental institution and wanted God to restore her mind.

C.   I had prayed for her, and she had been completely healed—praise God!

D.   Now she needed a new job and a new place to live.

E.   So, I told the woman that she needed to give.

F.   She emptied her coin pouch into my hand.

G.   She said she wouldn't have any money until she got paid again, and she hadn't even bought groceries yet.

H.   But I took all of her money and gave it to the pastor of the church, and then I prayed for her financial miracle.

I.   The Monday after I prayed for her, someone gave her a car.

J.   A day or two after that, the woman's mother called, who had been embarrassed by her mental condition and had severed all relations with her when she entered the mental institution.

K.   The mother asked forgiveness for the way she had treated her and asked her to move back home.

L.   Someone who didn't have faith in God might have thought I was being cruel to ask for that woman's last penny, but I was giving her an opportunity to activate God's supernatural flow, and her step of faith got her a car, a place to live, a restored relationship with her mother, and a new job that paid twice what her old job did!

M.   God wants us to prosper in every way: physically, emotionally, financially, and in our relationships.

N.   When we put the kingdom of God first, He takes care of our needs supernaturally.

O.   So, if we want God to assume all of our financial liabilities, then we need to put the kingdom of God first in our finances.

P.   It might seem like a radical concept, but it works.

Q. It has worked in my life, and I've seen it work in the lives of hundreds of others.

R. We are going to wind up frustrated if we think that work is all about getting money so we can pay our bills.

S. It's discouraging to get up every morning and go to work just so we can make our house payments and buy food and clothes.

T. There is a better way to live!

IX. Matthew 6:19-33 reveals God's plan for your earthly provision.

Lay not up for yourselves treasures upon earth, where moth and rust doth corrupt, and where thieves break through and steal.
MATTHEW 6:19

A. It would be a mistake to interpret this verse to mean that you can't ever have any money.

B. Other scriptures say you should leave an inheritance for your children's children (Prov. 13:22), and you need to save up quite a bit of money to do that.

C. I think what Jesus is getting at here is your motives.

D. It's wrong to build up savings out of fear, or so you can sit back and say to yourself, "Eat, drink, and be merry, for I have goods laid up for many days ahead" (Luke 12:19).

E. But it's good to build up savings so you always have resources to abound unto every good work and to leave an inheritance to your grandchildren.

F. That's using money to bless others.

G. When Jesus said these things, He knew people would be asking "How do you seek first the kingdom of God and build up an inheritance at the same time?" so, He said,

No man can serve two masters: for either he will hate the one, and love the other; or else he will hold to the one, and despise the other. Ye cannot serve God and mammon. Therefore I say unto you, Take no thought for your life, what ye shall eat, or what ye shall drink; nor yet for your body, what ye shall put on. Is not the life more than meat, and the body than raiment?
MATTHEW 6:24-25

H. This clearly says that you can't serve God and money, but that doesn't mean you'll never have money when you serve God.

I. It's obvious that you should choose to serve God, so Jesus goes on to explain how God takes care of your needs.

Behold the fowls of the air: for they sow not, neither do they reap, nor gather into barns; yet your heavenly Father feedeth them. Are ye not much better than they? Which of you by taking thought can add one cubit unto his stature?

MATTHEW 6:26-27

J. You've never read a headline about millions of birds dying of starvation and you never will—God feeds them.

K. Think how much better care He will take of a person who has been made in His image!

L. Jesus is encouraging you that you can have much more confidence in God to take care of you.

M. Then Jesus said,

Therefore take no thought, saying, What shall we eat? or, What shall we drink? or, Wherewithal shall we be clothed? (For after all these things do the Gentiles seek:) for your heavenly Father knoweth that ye have need of all these things.

MATTHEW 6:31-32

N. In modern language, it could be said that those are things lost people seek after.

O. There should be a difference between Christians and unbelievers—between people who have a covenant with God and people who are trying to do it all on their own.

P. The world should be able to see a difference in every area of your life, including finances.

Q. God is pleased when you prosper (Ps. 35:27)!

R. The scriptural way to live is to seek first the kingdom of God—even with your finances.

X. This is a truth you need to open up your heart to and allow the Holy Spirit to reveal.

A. I can explain it, but it's going to take a supernatural revelation to really get what I'm talking about here.

B. You can't just go through the motions of giving and think that God is going to return your giving one hundred times over.

C. You have to rely on God and trust that He is your source.

D. It has to be a heart-level revelation, not just a conclusion you arrive at mentally.

E. But once you grab a hold of this, it will revolutionize your life.

F. You will be completely transformed once you believe that by putting God first, He will begin to supernaturally take care of you.

G. It will bring you a tremendous amount of peace and confidence.

TEACHER'S
——— GUIDE ———

1. It's important to have the right attitude about finances before you start focusing on God's desire to bring money your way. Scripture says that if your eye is single, then your whole body will be flooded with light, but if your eye is evil, then your body is full of darkness (Matt. 6:22-23). It also says that anyone who hastens to be rich has an evil eye (Prov. 28:22). In other words, if your focus is divided between the things of God and getting rich, then your whole body will be full of darkness. At first, you might think it is impossible to be totally committed to and focused upon God in everything you do, and if it took relying on human strength, I would agree. But you don't live the Christian life in your own strength. God has given you weapons so strong that they can bring every thought into obedience to Christ (2 Cor. 10:4-5). You can work, raise a family, do all of the things you need to do in life, and still keep your attention 100 percent upon God. *But you can't be focused on God when you think you are the one who is responsible for producing the financial blessing in your life!*

    1a. Why is it important to have the right attitude about finances before you start focusing on God's desire to bring money your way?
       Because if you have the wrong attitude about finances, your focus will be divided getting rich and the things of God

    1b. Read Matthew 6:22-23. What has to be single in order for your whole body to be full of light?
       Your eye

    1c. Read Proverbs 28:22. Anyone who hastens to be rich has a what?
       An evil eye

2. The Apostle Paul said, **"This one thing I do"** (Phil. 3:13). The reason he accomplished everything he did was because he did one thing: He sought first the kingdom of God. The quickest way to destroy a man's vision is to give him two. You can't accomplish your goals when your attention and resources are divided. If you really want to prosper, then you need to forget everything else and press toward this one goal of putting the kingdom first. It's true that you are supposed to work. Scripture says that lazy people who don't work shouldn't expect to eat (2 Thess. 3:10), but God's plan for your financial freedom doesn't rely on the natural results of hard work.

    2a. What's the quickest way to destroy a man's vision?
       A. Poke him in the eyes
       B. Give him the wrong prescription
       C. Give him two visions
       D. Don't help him with his vision
       E. Ridicule his vision

3. The Apostle Paul encouraged the Ephesians to think differently about the goal of work when he said,

> *Let him that stole steal no more: but rather let him labour, working with his hands the thing which is good, that he may have to give to him that needeth.*
>
> EPHESIANS 4:28

He was echoing Jesus' teaching that the most important use of money is not satisfying self's temporary needs. By satisfying *other* people's temporal needs, the Apostle Paul was saying, they could demonstrate the love of God and touch people's lives. Every dollar you get has the potential to influence a person's life for the better. God will take care of you, and He'll do a better job than you ever have. This is where you see that finances are a matter of faith. The Word teaches that when you put the kingdom of God first, then all of your financial needs will be taken care of. Prosperity is a *byproduct* of seeking God; it shouldn't be the goal.

   3a. Every dollar you get has what potential?
   To influence a person's life for the better

4. What I'm talking about here is a matter of the heart. You can't create some kind of formula from what I'm saying, where you put effort in on one end and prosperity comes out the other. When you work so you can have money to give, God takes care of you. It's a mindset and a heart condition, not a get-rich-quick scheme. God's kind of prosperity comes when you shift your focus from getting and maintaining stuff, to living to give. When you start helping the Good News to be shared, demonstrating the love of God in word and deed, there is a divine flow that takes place. God starts supernaturally supplying your needs. This is why Scripture says to give God the first fruits (Prov. 3:9)—not the leftover fruit. The first thing you should do when you get money is give back to God.

   4a. When you start helping the Good News to be shared, demonstrating the love of God in word and deed, what is the divine flow that takes place?
   God starts supernaturally supplying your needs
   4b. What is the first thing you should do when you get money?
   A. Pay for your living expenses
   B. Give back to God
   C. Give a tenth of your tithe
   D. All of the above
   E. None of the above

5. The reason some Christians preach about financial prosperity and believe for it so hard is because they want the new houses, cars, and things they see people in the world enjoying. Again, there's nothing wrong with being prosperous, but your heart attitude should be that prosperity isn't about you—it's really about how much is flowing through you. God gave you two hands: one hand to receive and one hand to give. If God can get the money *through* you to other people, then He will get it *to* you—and as the money flows *through*, there will be plenty left over for *you*. It's the same attitude taught in Scripture:

> *And God is able to make all grace abound toward you; that ye, always having all sufficiency in all things, may abound to every good work.*
> 2 CORINTHIANS 9:8

The context of this scripture is money. This is saying that the reason God makes all financial blessings abound toward you is so you'll have the resources to do good things for others. God evaluates prosperity by how much of a blessing you are to others. This is all easy to say, but it's a lot harder to live. Once you understand this truth, you realize what an incredible blessing it is to be able to give. It's the investment opportunity of a lifetime.

    5a. If God can get the money_____ you to other people, then He will get it _____ you.
    Through, to
    5b. Read 2 Corinthians 9:8. Why does God make all financial blessings abound toward you?
    So you'll have the resources to do good things for others

6. My wife and I had virtually nothing when we started out in ministry. Most of it was because of religious bondage and wrong doctrine I believed, keeping me from experiencing God's blessing—but we always put God first, and He has blessed us as a result. We put our focus on seeking God and giving to others, and the side effect for us has been prosperity—that's how God's financial system works. The carnal mind thinks *If I don't take care of myself, no one else will either*, and I guess that's true if you don't have faith in God. But when you trust God and begin honoring Him with your first fruits, then God will make your **"barns be filled with plenty, and thy presses shall burst out with new wine"** (Prov. 3:10). God's promise is this:

> *But seek ye first the kingdom of God, and his righteousness; and all these things shall be added unto you.*
> MATTHEW 6:33

In context, Jesus was talking about where you sleep, what you eat, and the clothes you wear. In other words, when your first priority is seeking God, then He assumes the responsibility of taking care of you.

    6a. How is this statement true: "If I don't take care of myself, no one else will either"?
    If you don't have faith in God, it's true
    6b. According to Matthew 6:33, when does God assume the responsibility of taking care of you?
    When your first priority is seeking Him

7. In the Old Testament, Elijah prophesied to King Ahab that a drought was coming, and then Elijah fled into the desert to hide. Initially, God sent ravens to feed him at a brook. When the brook dried up, God told Elijah to go to the city of Zarephath where He had commanded a widow woman to sustain him. The first thing Elijah said to her was, "Go get me some water, and while you're at it, bring me something to eat." The widow turned to him and said,

> *As the LORD thy God liveth, I have not a cake, but an handful of meal in*
> *a barrel, and a little oil in a cruse: and, behold, I am gathering two sticks,*
> *that I may go in and dress it for me and my son, that we may eat it,*
> *and die.*
>
> 1 KINGS 17:12

Water is obviously a precious commodity during a drought, yet the widow was still willing to go get Elijah some water. But she drew the line when he asked for food. She and her son were going to die of starvation after they ate this last meal because they had absolutely nothing left. Elijah told her to go make his meal first and bring it to him—*then*, he said, she could go cook for herself and her son. Then he gave her a prophecy:

> *For thus saith the LORD God of Israel, The barrel of meal shall not waste,*
> *neither shall the cruse of oil fail, until the day that the LORD sendeth rain*
> *upon the earth.*
>
> 1 KINGS 17:14

The widow believed what Elijah told her, so she made his meal first. Can you imagine what bystanders would have thought if they had heard Elijah telling a widow to give him her last meal? They would have accused him of stealing from her. But Elijah wasn't taking from the widow—he was giving to her. If the widow hadn't given him that meal, then the Lord wouldn't have supernaturally multiplied the food. The step of faith she took by feeding God's prophet first, before taking care of herself, resulted in a supply that supported her and her son for three years. Later on, Elijah also raised her son from the dead, which wouldn't have happened if she hadn't formed a relationship with Elijah through feeding him. So, her giving of the little bit she had was the way to multiple miracles in her life.

7a. Why did Elijah ask the widow woman for her last meal?
<u>Because he knew that if she did, God would supply her needs</u>

8. I remember ministering on these same passages years ago at a church in Texas. At the end of the service, a woman came up to me, asking for prayer. She told me how I had prayed for her the year before and how, at the time, she had been in a mental institution and wanted God to restore her mind. I had prayed for her, and she had been completely healed—praise God! Now she needed a new job and a new place to live. So, I told the woman that she needed to give. She emptied her coin pouch into my hand. She said she wouldn't have any money until she got paid again, and she hadn't even bought groceries yet. But I took all of her money and gave it to the pastor of the church, and then I prayed for her financial miracle. The Monday after I prayed for her, someone gave her a car. A day or two after that, the woman's mother called, who had been embarrassed by her mental condition and had severed all relations with her when she entered the mental institution. The mother asked forgiveness for the way she had treated her and asked her to move back home. Someone who didn't have faith in God might have thought I was being cruel to ask for that woman's last penny, but I was giving her an opportunity to activate God's supernatural flow, and her step of faith got her a car, a place to live, a restored relationship with her mother, and a new job that paid twice what her old job did! God wants us to prosper in every way: physically, emotionally, financially, and in our relationships. When we put the kingdom of God first, He takes care of our needs supernaturally. So, if we want God to assume all of our financial liabilities, then we need to put the kingdom of God first in our finances. It might seem like a radical concept, but it works. It has worked in my life, and I've seen it work in the lives of hundreds of others. We are going to wind up frustrated if we think that work is all about getting money so we can pay our bills. It's discouraging to get up every morning and go to work just so we can make our house payments and buy food and clothes. There is a better way to live!

8a. It's_____ to get up every morning and go to work just so you can make your house payment and buy food and clothes.
Discouraging

9. Matthew 6:19-33 reveals God's plan for your earthly provision.

> *Lay not up for yourselves treasures upon earth, where moth and rust doth*
> *corrupt, and where thieves break through and steal.*
>
> MATTHEW 6:19

It would be a mistake to interpret this verse to mean that you can't ever have any money. Other scriptures say you should leave an inheritance for your children's children (Prov. 13:22), and you need to save up quite a bit of money to do that. I think what Jesus is getting at here is your motives. It's wrong to build up savings out of fear, or so you can sit back and say to yourself, "Eat, drink, and be merry, for I have goods laid up for many days ahead" (Luke 12:19). But it's good to build up savings so you always have resources to abound unto every good work and to leave an inheritance to your grandchildren. That's using money to bless others. When Jesus said these things, He knew people would be asking "How do you seek first the kingdom of God and build up an inheritance at the same time?" so, He said,

> *No man can serve two masters: for either he will hate the one, and love the*
> *other; or else he will hold to the one, and despise the other. Ye cannot serve*
> *God and mammon. Therefore I say unto you, Take no thought for your life,*
> *what ye shall eat, or what ye shall drink; nor yet for your body, what ye*
> *shall put on. Is not the life more than meat, and the body than raiment?*
>
> MATTHEW 6:24-25

This clearly says that you can't serve God and money, but that doesn't mean you'll never have money when you serve God. It's obvious that you should choose to serve God, so Jesus goes on to explain how God takes care of your needs.

> *Behold the fowls of the air: for they sow not, neither do they reap, nor*
> *gather into barns; yet your heavenly Father feedeth them. Are ye not much*
> *better than they? Which of you by taking thought can add one cubit unto*
> *his stature?*
>
> MATTHEW 6:26-27

You've never read a headline about millions of birds dying of starvation and you never will—God feeds them. Think how much better care He will take of a person who has been made in His image!

Jesus is encouraging you that you can have much more confidence in God to take care of you. Then Jesus said,

> *Therefore take no thought, saying, What shall we eat? or, What shall we*
> *drink? or, Wherewithal shall we be clothed? (For after all these things do*
> *the Gentiles seek:) for your heavenly Father knoweth that ye have need of*
> *all these things.*
>
> MATTHEW 6:31-32

In modern language, it could be said that those are things lost people seek after. There should be a difference between Christians and unbelievers—between people who have a covenant with God and people who are trying to do it all on their own. The world should be able to see a difference in every area of your life, including finances. God is pleased when you prosper (Ps. 35:27)! The scriptural way to live is to seek first the kingdom of God—even with your finances.

9a. How can you know God's plan for your earthly provision?
By reading Matthew 6:19-33
9b. How do you seek first the kingdom of God and build up an inheritance at the same time?
When you serve God, you'll have money
9c. Read Matthew 6:26. How do you know God will take care of you?
Because He takes care of the birds
9d. To seek after food, drink, and clothing is to be like who?
Lost people
9e. Read Psalm 35:27. True or false: God is pleased when you prosper.
True

10. This is a truth you need to open up your heart to and allow the Holy Spirit to reveal. I can explain it, but it's going to take a supernatural revelation to really get what I'm talking about here. You can't just go through the motions of giving and think that God is going to return your giving one hundred times over. You have to rely on God and trust that He is your source. It has to be a heart-level revelation, not just a conclusion you arrive at mentally. But once you grab a hold of this, it will revolutionize your life. You will be completely transformed once you believe that by putting God first, He will begin to supernaturally take care of you. It will bring you a tremendous amount of peace and confidence.

10a. What does it take to understand what Andrew is saying?
A revelation from the Holy Spirit

10b. Why can't you just go through the motions of giving and think that God is going to return your giving one hundred times over?
Because you have to rely on God and trust that He is your source, and it has to be a heart-level revelation, not just a conclusion you arrive at mentally

DISCIPLESHIP
—— QUESTIONS ——

1. Why is it important to have the right attitude about finances before you start focusing on God's desire to bring money your way?

   _____
   _____
   _____

2. Read Matthew 6:22-23. What has to be single in order for your whole body to be full of light?

   _____
   _____
   _____

3. Read Proverbs 28:22. Anyone who hastens to be rich has a what?

   _____
   _____
   _____

4. What's the quickest way to destroy a man's vision?
   A. Poke him in the eyes
   B. Give him the wrong prescription
   C. Give him two visions
   D. Don't help him with his vision
   E. Ridicule his vision

5. Every dollar you get has what potential?

   _____
   _____
   _____

6. When you start helping the Good News to be shared, demonstrating the love of God in word and deed, what is the divine flow that takes place?

   _____
   _____
   _____

7. What is the first thing you should do when you get money?
   A. Pay for your living expenses
   B. Give back to God
   C. Give a tenth of your tithe
   D. All of the above
   E. None of the above

8. If God can get the money_____ you to other people, then He will get it
    _____ you.

9. Read 2 Corinthians 9:8. Why does God makes all financial blessings abound toward you?
    _____
    _____
    _____

10. How is this statement true: "If I don't take care of myself, no one else will either"?
    _____
    _____
    _____

11. According to Matthew 6:33, when does God assume the responsibility of taking care of you?
    _____
    _____
    _____

12. Why did Elijah ask the widow woman for her last meal?
    _____
    _____
    _____

13. It's_____ to get up every morning and go to work just so you can make
    your house payment and buy food and clothes.

14. How can you know God's plan for your earthly provision?
    _____
    _____
    _____

15. How do you seek first the kingdom of God and build up an inheritance at the same time?
    _____
    _____
    _____

16. Read Matthew 6:26. How do you know God will take care of you?
    _____
    _____
    _____

17. To seek after food, drink, and clothing is to be like who?

_____
_____
_____

18. Read Psalm 35:27. True or false: God is pleased when you prosper.

19. What does it take to understand what Andrew is saying?

_____
_____
_____

20. Why can't you just go through the motions of giving and think that God is going to return your giving one hundred times over?

_____
_____
_____

ANSWER
—KEY—

1. Because if you have the wrong attitude about finances, your focus will be divided getting rich and the things of God

2. Your eye

3. An evil eye

4. C. Give him two visions

5. To influence a person's life for the better

6. God starts supernaturally supplying your needs

7. B. Give back to God

8. Through, to

9. So you'll have the resources to do good things for others

10. If you don't have faith in God, it's true

11. When your first priority is seeking Him

12. Because he knew that if she did, God would supply her needs

13. Discouraging

14. By reading Matthew 6:19-33

15. When you serve God, you'll have money

16. Because He takes care of the birds

17. Lost people

18. True

19. A revelation from the Holy Spirit

20. Because you have to rely on God and trust that He is your source, and it has to be a heart-level revelation, not just a conclusion you arrive at mentally

—— SCRIPTURES ——

MATTHEW 6:19-25

Lay not up for yourselves treasures upon earth, where moth and rust doth corrupt, and where thieves break through and steal: [20] But lay up for yourselves treasures in heaven, where neither moth nor rust doth corrupt, and where thieves do not break through nor steal: [21] For where your treasure is, there will your heart be also. [22] The light of the body is the eye: if therefore thine eye be single, thy whole body shall be full of light. [23] But if thine eye be evil, thy whole body shall be full of darkness. If therefore the light that is in thee be darkness, how great is that darkness! [24] No man can serve two masters: for either he will hate the one, and love the other; or else he will hold to the one, and despise the other. Ye cannot serve God and mammon. [25] Therefore I say unto you, Take no thought for your life, what ye shall eat, or what ye shall drink; nor yet for your body, what ye shall put on. Is not the life more than meat, and the body than raiment?

MATTHEW 6:26-33

Behold the fowls of the air: for they sow not, neither do they reap, nor gather into barns; yet your heavenly Father feedeth them. Are ye not much better than they? [27] Which of you by taking thought can add one cubit unto his stature? [28] And why take ye thought for raiment? Consider the lilies of the field, how they grow; they toil not, neither do they spin: [29] And yet I say unto you, That even Solomon in all his glory was not arrayed like one of these. [30] Wherefore, if God so clothe the grass of the field, which to day is, and to morrow is cast into the oven, shall he not much more clothe you, O ye of little faith? [31] Therefore take no thought, saying, What shall we eat? or, What shall we drink? or, Wherewithal shall we be clothed? [32] (For after all these things do the Gentiles seek:) for your heavenly Father knoweth that ye have need of all these things. [33] But seek ye first the kingdom of God, and his righteousness; and all these things shall be added unto you.

PROVERBS 28:22

He that hasteth to be rich hath an evil eye, and considereth not that poverty shall come upon him.

2 CORINTHIANS 10:4-5

(For the weapons of our warfare are not carnal, but mighty through God to the pulling down of strong holds;) [5] Casting down imaginations, and every high thing that exalteth itself against the knowledge of God, and bringing into captivity every thought to the obedience of Christ.

PHILIPPIANS 3:13

Brethren, I count not myself to have apprehended: but this one thing I do, forgetting those things which are behind, and reaching forth unto those things which are before.

2 THESSALONIANS 3:10

For even when we were with you, this we commanded you, that if any would not work, neither should he eat.

EPHESIANS 4:28

Let him that stole steal no more: but rather let him labour, working with his hands the thing which is good, that he may have to give to him that needeth.

──SCRIPTURES──

PROVERBS 3:9-10

Honour the LORD with thy substance, and with the firstfruits of all thine increase: [10] So shall thy barns be filled with plenty, and thy presses shall burst out with new wine.

2 CORINTHIANS 9:8

And God is able to make all grace abound toward you; that ye, always having all sufficiency in all things, may abound to every good work.

1 KINGS 17:12

And she said, As the LORD thy God liveth, I have not a cake, but an handful of meal in a barrel, and a little oil in a cruse: and, behold, I am gathering two sticks, that I may go in and dress it for me and my son, that we may eat it, and die.

1 KINGS 17:14

For thus saith the LORD God of Israel, The barrel of meal shall not waste, neither shall the cruse of oil fail, until the day that the LORD sendeth rain upon the earth.

PROVERBS 13:22

A good man leaveth an inheritance to his children's children: and the wealth of the sinner is laid up for the just.

LUKE 12:19

And I will say to my soul, Soul, thou hast much goods laid up for many years; take thine ease, eat, drink, and be merry.

1 PETER 5:7

Casting all your care upon him; for he careth for you.

PSALM 35:27

Let them shout for joy, and be glad, that favour my righteous cause: yea, let them say continually, Let the LORD be magnified, which hath pleasure in the prosperity of his servant.

PROSPERITY ISN'T SELFISH

The book of Matthew gives a lengthy description of stewardship in its final chapters. It starts with the story of ten virgins, some of whom didn't manage the oil in their lamps well. Then we are given the parable about three servants who were entrusted with money by their master. The master gave one servant five talents; another, two talents; and the last servant, one talent (a *talent* was a specific weight of money in coins). The servant with five talents took what his master had given him and made another five talents. Likewise, the servant with two talents made an additional two talents. But the man who received one talent just buried it for safekeeping.

Later, the master returned and asked the servants what they had done with his money. The servant who made five talents was commended by the master, and so was the servant who made two talents. When the servant who received one talent came before the master, he said **"Lord, I knew thee that thou art an hard man, reaping where thou hast not sown, and gathering where thou hast not strawed: And I was afraid, and went and hid thy talent in the earth"** (Matt. 25:24-25), and then he gave back the one talent he had received. The master was furious. He rebuked the servant for not at least having put the money in the bank to earn interest, and then he said,

> **THE MOTIVE BEHIND WHAT YOU DO IS MORE IMPORTANT THAN THE ACTION ITSELF.**

Take therefore the talent from him, and give it unto him which hath ten talents. For unto every one that hath shall be given, and he shall have abundance: but from him that hath not shall be taken away even that which he hath. And cast ye the unprofitable servant into outer darkness: there shall be weeping and gnashing of teeth.

MATTHEW 25:28-30

This passage says that because the poorer servant didn't invest what he was given, even the little he had was taken away, and he was cast into outer darkness. It clearly reveals that the Lord expects us to take what He has given us and do something with it, not just hide it in the earth. Our God is a God of multiplication. He wants us to increase the resources we are given, not just spend our money on carnal appetites.

Right after giving this parable, Jesus talked about coming back in glory and separating the sheep from the goats. To some, He will say, **"Come, ye blessed of my Father, inherit the kingdom prepared for you from the foundation of the world"** (Matt. 25:34). Those are the people who clothed the naked, fed the sick, gave water to the thirsty, and visited inmates in prison. This is all still related to stewardship. Jesus is talking about taking the resources God has blessed us with and using them to touch others. It takes money to visit people in prison. If nothing else, it's going to cost gas and transportation. All ministry costs money.

Jesus said that those who never clothe the naked, care for the sick, or feed the hungry don't really know Him, and they will be cast into everlasting fire (Matt. 25:41-46). That's strong, and a lot of people don't like to hear it, because it makes stewardship an integral part of what God expects them to do. Many people aren't willing to give up control of their finances like that. In fact, the word "talent" in those verses is spiritualized by some who say it is talking about the spiritual gifts you have been given. I'm not saying you can't make that application, but Jesus was literally talking about money, which again shows that stewardship is far more important than how it is typically taught today.

Another problem some people have is thinking that prosperity is selfish. I've had lots of people tell me they are satisfied with what they have, and they don't want any more. I agree that being content with what one has is godly, but it's also selfish to say they don't want more resources. What most of those people are really saying is, "As long as my needs are met, then I'm satisfied. I don't need any more." What about everyone else? If they have excess money, they can be a blessing to those in need. Without extra finances, they are limited in their ability to give. It would be better for them to prosper and increase their finances, not for themselves, but so they can be a blessing to someone else.

Prosperity isn't all about you. God entrusts you with resources so you can be a blessing to other people, so it isn't selfish to desire prosperity. When you see God as your source, and treat the money He gives you as a resource to be stewarded, then it is very godly to want to prosper so that you can give and help establish God's covenant on earth.

On the other hand, there are people teaching prosperity from a selfish standpoint. Some preachers present prosperity like it's all about getting more. It's selfish, and the driving motive for that kind of prosperity is covetousness. But you aren't going to see a supernatural return on your giving when you do it with the wrong motive. It has to come from a humble heart that desires to bless other people. Since the motive behind what you do is more important than the action itself, giving with a wrong heart is of no benefit. Scripture says,

> *And though I bestow all my goods to feed the poor, and though I give my*
> *body to be burned, and have not charity, it profiteth me nothing.*
> 1 CORINTHIANS 13:3

This says you can go so far as to make the ultimate sacrifice of laying down your life, but it will be of no benefit to you whatsoever if it isn't done out of a motivation of love. It will bless the person you sacrifice yourself for, but it isn't going to result in a supernatural return for you. Likewise, going out and playing the role of a good steward isn't going to help you at all if you aren't doing it with the right motivation. If your only reason for giving is so that God will give back to you, it isn't going to work. Yes, God wants you to prosper—but having faith in God's provision is different from lusting after money and hoping for a supernatural flow of finances. Faith works, but carnal appetites are going to profit you nothing.

Some Christians have the wrong attitude about prosperity. When I talk about God's desire for them to prosper through stewardship, immediately their greed and selfishness kick in. They start thinking, *Man, here is scriptural justification for me to get as much stuff as I can, then can all I get, and sit on my can. This is awesome!* Not really. It's true that God wants you to increase, but the motive behind your actions is super important.

Having the right motivations behind financial stewardship doesn't come naturally. Society today is so focused on self-fulfillment and self-gratification that living for God is a totally foreign concept. It doesn't make sense to the natural mind. Think of how the Apostle Paul reacted to slavery. In his time, slavery was a very common practice. Paul was probably the most influential man in the body of Christ at the time, and he was in a position to change how Christians behaved. If he had spoken out against the unjust practice of slavery, then he probably would have set tens of thousands of slaves free, but he didn't do that.

For instance, Paul wrote a letter to Philemon to talk about his slave, Onesimus, who had run away and escaped to Rome. Once in Rome, Onesimus encountered Paul, who led him to the Lord and then told him to go back to his master and submit to his position as a slave! God doesn't approve of slavery and Paul knew that. Paul was just saying that there is no difference between slave and free: slaves are free in Christ, and the free are slaves to Christ. When your total life is in Christ, you have so much victory and contentment in the Lord that it doesn't matter whether you are living freely or as a slave.

We are more humanistic today than people were in Paul's time, so we might find this attitude hard to stomach. Our society is all about personal freedoms and self-interest. I'd say that freedom is nearly a god to some people. Yet here Paul was telling people not to despise Christian slave masters. A lot of people today would get bitter and say that a Christian should treat a slave differently—in fact, a Christian should set them all free—but Paul told them to serve their Christian slave masters even harder because they were brothers. When Paul was finished talking about slaves submitting to their masters, he said,

> *If any man teach otherwise, and consent not to wholesome words, even*
> *the words of our Lord Jesus Christ, and to the doctrine which is according*
> *to godliness; He is proud, knowing nothing, but doting about questions*
> *and strifes of words, whereof cometh envy, strife, railings, evil surmisings,*
> *Perverse disputings of men of corrupt minds, and destitute of the truth,*
> *supposing that gain is godliness: from such withdraw thyself.*
>   1 TIMOTHY 6:3-5

Paul's words are a reminder that personal freedom isn't everything. Life isn't supposed to be all about taking care of yourself and seeking your own gain. Yet there is an entire generation in the United States that has been called the "me generation." Most people are living very self-centered lives. Everything is all about "me." The truth is, when you're all wrapped up in yourself, you make a very small package.

In the United States, a lot has been made of the sacrifices carried out by the people who fought in World War II. A relative of mine was a Marine who fought at Iwo Jima. He was in one of the first waves of soldiers in the amphibious assault. Before they invaded, he was told that the first few waves of soldiers would never make it. They were basically being used to draw all of the enemy fire and expend their ammunition, but they were willing to make that sacrifice so that the waves of soldiers behind them would have a chance to survive and win the fight. They believed in making a sacrifice to win the war. They were committed to principle more than to self-interest, and they realized there was something more important than their individual freedom or existence.

Selfishness is the most prevalent attitude today. A lot of people are making their decisions based purely upon whatever is best for them. If something promotes their personal well-being, then it's good—if not, then it's bad. They don't have any reference larger than their own needs. That kind of attitude is going to affect how they handle their finances. Paul made that application when he was finished talking about slavery:

> *But godliness with contentment is great gain. For we brought nothing into this world, and it is certain we can carry nothing out. And having food and raiment let us be therewith content. But they that will be rich fall into temptation and a snare, and into many foolish and hurtful lusts, which drown men in destruction and perdition. For the love of money is the root of all evil: which while some coveted after, they have erred from the faith, and pierced themselves through with many sorrows. But thou, O man of God, flee these things; and follow after righteousness, godliness, faith, love, patience, meekness. Fight the good fight of faith.*
>
> 1 TIMOTHY 6:6-12A

Some people have taken these verses to mean that money itself is evil, but the word **"contentment"** in this passage is talking about having your needs met. It isn't saying that a godly attitude means you can't have riches. You can have both if your motive is right. Loving God doesn't mean you have to be poor, and having money doesn't mean you are ungodly. For one thing, wealth is relative. Some of the people preaching that you can't have money and still be a servant of God are extremely wealthy by the rest of the world's standards. Many are super rich compared to the people Paul wrote this passage to. Today there are conveniences that they couldn't have dreamed of: running hot water, air conditioning, indoor plumbing, microwaves, automobiles, and homes fit for kings. We are living in a period of unparalleled prosperity.

This passage of Scripture isn't saying you can't have money; it says *the love* of money is the root of all evil—not money itself. Money isn't the problem; it's the attitude that people have toward money. It's putting your trust in money and finding your fulfillment in it. If you just put your trust in God, then He will give you money to accomplish His

PROSPERITY IS HAVING ENOUGH SO THAT YOU CAN ABOUND UNTO EVERY GOOD WORK.

instructions and the call He has placed on your life. The problem comes when you love money and what it will produce more than you love God, and when you rely on it instead of looking to God as your source.

It's amazing to me how religion has perverted this passage, with Christians promoting poverty in the name of the Lord. It isn't godly to be poor any more than it is godly to be rich. Money has nothing to do with godliness. God doesn't want you to always be dependent upon others because you are poor. He wants you to be able to help others out financially. He wants Christians to be part of the answer, not part of the problem, and to do that, you have to have financial increase. I know a lot has been taught about money being evil, but if you want to be a blessing to others, then you have to drop your prejudices against having money.

This might sound strange. You might be thinking, *Who could have a prejudice against having money?* Well, I did! I was raised in a pretty affluent home compared to the other kids I grew up with, but I had been taught that it was ungodly for people who serve God to have money. I remember a missionary couple coming to speak at my church when I was young, and instead of getting a hotel or something, they slept in the back of their station wagon. They didn't want to spend any money on a hotel. The wife only had two dresses—she washed one every night and wore the other the next day. I'm telling you, our pastor set that couple on a pedestal and promoted them as an ideal example of how true Christians should live. They were "suffering for Jesus."

I look back on that now and realize what a completely backward model of poverty that was. God doesn't want you sleeping in the back of your car or without enough clothes to wear. What a terrible witness! It makes it look like God can't even take care of His own children.

Part of the cause for my financial problems when I first got started in ministry was that I was embarrassed to have things. I thought that ministers were supposed to do without. Have you ever seen someone go into a store and ask for a discount because they are a minister? I don't like seeing things like that. It's like announcing to the world that Christians can't compete or prosper. It's a kind of begging and telling the world that we need help. Yet Scripture says, "[I have never] **seen the righteous forsaken, nor his seed begging bread**" (Ps. 37:25, brackets mine). Poverty does not glorify God, and saying that it does is a perversion of Scripture.

Biblical prosperity isn't selfish, because it isn't about meeting personal needs. The Christian motivation for prosperity is about desiring to have the resources to bless others and accomplish what God has called you to do. Prosperity isn't about indulging your flesh—that's not it at all. Prosperity is about giving. When you get that attitude, God will get money to you—and there will be plenty left over for you.

It's also important to remember that prosperity is relative. It isn't limited to those living in developed nations. Prosperity for a farmer in a small village might mean having ten goats instead of one. It might mean living in the nicest hut in the community and having six chickens instead of two. You don't have to live in a multi-million dollar home in Beverly Hills in order to be prosperous. The standard of prosperity is relative, but these truths about prosperity will work in any situation, anywhere in the world. The key is having the right motivation and seeking God first. When you do that, you put yourself in position to receive God's supernatural flow. Scripture says,

> *And God is able to make all grace abound toward you; that ye, always having all sufficiency in all things, may abound to every good work.*
>
> 2 CORINTHIANS 9:8

The reason God causes His grace to abound toward us is so that we will be able to abound unto every good work. Real prosperity is defined by how much we give away, not by how much we keep for ourselves. A lot of people look good on paper. They have huge houses, fancy things, and a ton of money in the stock market and all kinds of investments—but all of their money is tied up. I've had lots of "wealthy" people tell me they'd like to give finances to my ministry, but they can't, because they don't have any "liquid assets." Those people aren't truly prosperous. If we are using all of our money for ourselves, then we aren't prosperous. True prosperity is about giving and the ability to **"abound to every good work."** It isn't determined by the size of our houses, by the cars that we drive, or by jewels and expensive clothing. In fact, we can be prosperous without having any of those things.

The Old Testament tells the story of Joseph, who was sold into slavery as a young man. Slaves up for sale used to be stripped naked so that prospective buyers could see the physical condition of the slave they were buying. As Joseph was standing naked on an auction block, without a single possession to his name, the Bible says he was a prosperous man (Gen. 39:1-2). How? It's because prosperity isn't measured by how many assets you have. Joseph was a naked slave, but God was still with him, and it was just a matter of time before money started flowing his way.

God's blessing on Joseph's life caused him to prosper in everything he did. Potiphar, the man who purchased Joseph as a slave, soon recognized the anointing on Joseph and put him in charge of his entire estate. Potiphar's wife was even drawn to the anointing on Joseph, but when he refused to sleep with her, she lied about him and had him thrown in prison. But God was with Joseph even in prison. Before long, the head jailer turned the entire prison operation over to Joseph and let him run it.

While he was in prison, Joseph interpreted the dreams of two of Pharaoh's servants who had been confined with him. Two years later, Pharaoh had a couple of dreams that no one could interpret for him, and one of the servants told Pharaoh about Joseph. Joseph was brought before

GOD GIVES SEED TO SOWERS.

Pharaoh, who said, "I hear you can interpret dreams." "Not I," Joseph answered, "but God will interpret the dream for you." This reveals where Joseph's heart was: He always put God first. Sure enough, God interpreted the dream through Joseph, and Pharaoh made him second in command over all of Egypt. Joseph saved Egypt from famine, and he made Pharaoh even richer.

Joseph prospered every life that he came into contact with. He was a super blessing. He helped other people and eventually became rich himself, but it was never all about him. Joseph was first a blessing to the people around him, and it was by blessing others that he was promoted and eventually became prosperous himself. But even when Joseph became rich and powerful, he didn't use it just to satisfy his every whim. He used his position to save his brothers and their families—the very people who sold him into slavery in the first place.

Joseph was a giver, and he always put God first—that's the same attitude we need to have. Today, if recession hits, the first thing most of us as Christians cut back on is our giving, which is the absolute worst thing we can do. Like Joseph, we need to put God first regardless of our circumstances. In fact, when hard times come, we should increase our giving so that we can increase our harvest.

The Bible records that Isaac, Joseph's grandfather, sowed in a year of famine and reaped a hundredfold return (Gen. 26:12). Almost everyone else had fled to Egypt from Canaan in search of food, but Isaac stayed. He decided to sow crops in the fields that had been abandoned by those who went looking for prosperity in the world, and he reaped a huge harvest. He became tremendously wealthy because he planted seed at a time when everyone else was holding back in fear of poverty.

These two stories are good illustrations of what I've been talking about: The reason God wants to bless you is so that you can be a blessing. If you come into a recession, cut back on your personal spending but never cut back on what you are giving to God. If God can get money through you, He will get it to you. Prosperity means having such an abundant supply that you are able to abound unto every good work, which means that blessings will flow your way when you are living to give. Scripture says,

> *Now he that ministereth seed to the sower both minister bread for your food, and multiply your seed sown, and increase the fruits of your righteousness.*
>
> 2 CORINTHIANS 9:10

This isn't really about farming; it's an illustration of a spiritual principle. A single kernel of corn planted in the ground will sprout up a plant that bears thousands of kernels of corn. When you give money, it's like planting a seed. In the same way that planting a seed gives rise to a new plant that bears many more seeds, giving money away causes finances to grow in your life.

This scripture is saying that God gives seed to the sower—just like God gave Isaac a hundredfold return on the crop he planted during a drought. The people who abandoned their fields and ran off to Egypt in search of prosperity didn't receive anything. God gave the return to Isaac because he sowed. As I just said, when we give money, it's like planting a seed. God gives money to people if they are givers. We are told,

> *For the eyes of the LORD run to and fro throughout the whole earth, to shew himself strong in the behalf of them whose heart is perfect toward him.*
> 2 CHRONICLES 16:9

The word **"perfect"** here means complete, whole, or at peace. It isn't talking about being sinless; it's talking about having a mature heart with a right attitude toward God. The Lord is searching the earth, looking for people who will believe His promises and put first the kingdom of God. He is looking for people who will give genuinely, from the heart, not as a form of manipulation, not giving just to get. God is literally searching the world for people He can give finances to—people who are givers.

You could turn this around and say that if you are consistently short on money, if you always have more month than you have money, then maybe God doesn't see you as a giver. That's not the only reason for being poor. I've already shared how I was poor because of wrong teaching I believed, so other things could be going on, but it's also possible that your heart isn't right.

There are two dominant heart conditions when it comes to money: eaters and sowers. Eaters are the ones who are all about getting their own needs met. They are seeking to establish their own kingdoms. They use their resources to buy everything they want, and they only give when there is something left over. Sowers, on the other hand, are all about putting other people first. Sowers need to eat, too, so it's not like they don't buy things for themselves, but their hearts' desire is to give and seek God's kingdom first. Sowers are the people God is searching the world to find.

I saw a great example of this when I was ministering at a church a long time ago. The pastor told his people that he believed God had laid it on his heart for their church to give a fifty thousand-dollar donation to my ministry that week. At the time, I was believing for extra finances to finish out a new building, and fifty thousand dollars would have been a huge gift. The pastor stood in front of his church and read this verse that says God **"ministereth seed to the sower."** Then he asked, "How many of you would give a thousand dollars in this offering if God gave you the money?" About fifty people stood up to say they would give if God gave them the money, and the pastor then prayed for finances to come to them.

IF GOD CAN GET MONEY THROUGH YOU, HE'LL GET IT TO YOU—AND IT WON'T BE LONG BEFORE YOU HAVE PLENTY LEFT OVER FOR YOURSELF.

Within a couple of days, some of those people started sharing testimonies of how God was supernaturally providing money. There wasn't a single person who only got a thousand dollars either. God was giving people two and three thousand dollars, so after they gave a thousand dollars in the offering, they still had plenty of money left over. It was awesome! God doesn't just give you enough money to bless others; He always blesses you with extra.

The pastor collected the offering on a Monday night. One of the men who stood up and wanted to give a thousand dollars was going to give the money from his savings, but when he went into work on Monday morning, he got a promotion. I forget all the details, but his income jumped by like four thousand dollars a month! He wanted to give a one-time offering of one thousand dollars, and God multiplied his income for every month of the year.

As the testimonies came rolling in, other people began to realize that the givers weren't losing money by giving—they were actually making money. All of a sudden, other people started popping up and saying, "I want to pledge to give a thousand dollars too." From what I understood later, not many of those people who gave after they heard the testimonies saw God give them finances. I think it's because their hearts were wrong. They weren't trying to put God's kingdom first by giving; they just wanted to make some extra money. It was selfish. Going back to the scripture in Paul's letter to the Corinthians: Giving profits you nothing if you don't do it motivated by love—even if you give all of your goods to feed the poor.

When you understand finances properly, you realize that prosperity isn't about you. It's about being able to bless other people. When you get that attitude, you'll experience the reality that God gives seed to the sower. Selfishness short-circuits your prosperity because it causes you to consume all of your resources. It turns you into a vacuum cleaner that sucks up everything in sight. You ought to be just the opposite. Christians should be like leaf blowers, giving money left and right. You should be imitating God by searching for opportunities to give and asking Him to show you how you can be a blessing.

Another thing to keep in mind is that prosperity doesn't happen overnight. There are a couple of reasons that you don't go from being selfish to becoming a generous millionaire instantly. First, there is a time between planting seed and harvesting. Fruit doesn't show up the next day. Second, money has power, and you might not be able to handle the power of prosperity right away.

God knows you have needs, and He wants you to be taken care of. Remember, He doesn't mind if you live in a nice house and drive a nice car, as long as you aren't consuming all of your finances on yourself. When you get the attitude of a giver and walk it out over time, God will increase your finances. If God can get money through you, He'll get it to you—and it won't be long before you have plenty left over for yourself.

— OUTLINE —

I. The book of Matthew gives a lengthy description of stewardship in its final chapters.

    A. We are given the parable about three servants who were entrusted with money by their master.

    B. The master gave one servant five talents; another, two talents; and the last servant, one talent (a *talent* was a specific weight of money in coins).

    C. The servant with five talents took what his master had given him and made another five talents.

    D. Likewise, the servant with two talents made an additional two talents.

    E. But the man who received one talent just buried it for safekeeping.

    F. The servant who made five talents was commended by the master, and so was the servant who made two talents.

    G. When the servant who received one talent came before the master, he said **"Lord, I knew thee that thou art an hard man, reaping where thou hast not sown, and gathering where thou hast not strawed: And I was afraid, and went and hid thy talent in the earth"** (Matt. 25:24-25), and then he gave back the one talent he had received.

    H. The master was furious, and he rebuked the servant for not at least having put the money in the bank to earn interest.

    I. Then he said,

> *Take therefore the talent from him, and give it unto him which hath ten talents. For unto every one that hath shall be given, and he shall have abundance: but from him that hath not shall be taken away even that which he hath. And cast ye the unprofitable servant into outer darkness: there shall be weeping and gnashing of teeth.*
>
> MATTHEW 25:28-30

    J. This passage clearly reveals that the Lord expects us to take what He has given us and do something with it, not just hide it in the earth.

    K. Our God is a God of multiplication.

II. Right after giving this parable, Jesus talked about coming back in glory and separating the sheep from the goats.

    A. To some, He will say, **"Come, ye blessed of my Father, inherit the kingdom prepared for you from the foundation of the world"** (Matt. 25:34).

B. Those are the people who clothed the naked, fed the sick, gave water to the thirsty, and visited inmates in prison.

C. This is all still related to stewardship.

D. Jesus is talking about taking the resources God has blessed us with and using them to touch others.

E. Jesus said that those who never clothe the naked, care for the sick, or feed the hungry don't really know Him, and they will be cast into everlasting fire (Matt. 25:41-46).

F. That's strong, and a lot of people don't like to hear it, because it makes stewardship an integral part of what God expects them to do.

G. Stewardship is far more important than how it is typically taught today.

III. Another problem some people have is thinking that prosperity is selfish.

A. I've had lots of people tell me they are satisfied with what they have, and they don't want any more.

B. What most of those people are really saying is, "As long as my needs are met, then I'm satisfied. I don't need any more."

C. What about everyone else?

D. Without extra finances, they are limited in their ability to give.

E. It would be better for them to prosper and increase their finances, not for themselves, but so they can be a blessing to someone else.

F. God entrusts you with resources so you can be a blessing to other people, so it isn't selfish to desire prosperity.

G. When you see God as your source, and treat the money He gives you as a resource to be stewarded, then it is very godly to want to prosper so that you can give and help establish God's covenant on earth.

IV. On the other hand, there are people teaching prosperity from a selfish standpoint.

A. The driving motive for that kind of prosperity is covetousness.

B. You aren't going to see a supernatural return on your giving when you do it with the wrong motive.

C. It has to come from a humble heart that desires to bless other people.

D. Since the motive behind what you do is more important than the action itself, giving with a wrong heart is of no benefit.

E. Scripture says,

And though I bestow all my goods to feed the poor, and though I give my body to be burned, and have not charity, it profiteth me nothing.
1 CORINTHIANS 13:3

F. This says you can go so far as to make the ultimate sacrifice of laying down your life, but it will be of no benefit to you whatsoever if it isn't done out of a motivation of love.

G. It will bless the person you sacrifice yourself for, but it isn't going to result in a supernatural return for you.

H. If your only reason for giving is so that God will give back to you, it isn't going to work.

I. Carnal appetites are going to profit you nothing.

J. Society today is so focused on self-fulfillment and self-gratification that living for God is a totally foreign concept.

K. It doesn't make sense to the natural mind.

L. The truth is, when you're all wrapped up in yourself, you make a very small package.

V. In the United States, a lot has been made of the sacrifices carried out by the people who fought in World War II.

A. A relative of mine was a Marine who fought at Iwo Jima.

B. He was in one of the first waves of soldiers in the amphibious assault.

C. Before they invaded, he was told that the first few waves of soldiers would never make it.

D. They were basically being used to draw all of the enemy fire and expend their ammunition, but they were willing to make that sacrifice so that the waves of soldiers behind them would have a chance to survive and win the fight.

E. They believed in making a sacrifice to win the war.

F. They were committed to principle more than to self-interest, and they realized there was something more important than their individual freedom or existence.

VI. Selfishness is the most prevalent attitude today.

A. A lot of people are making their decisions based purely upon whatever is best for them.

B. If something promotes their personal well-being, then it's good—if not, then it's bad.

C. They don't have any reference larger than their own needs.

D. That kind of attitude is going to affect how they handle their finances.

E. Paul made that application:

But godliness with contentment is great gain. For we brought nothing into this world, and it is certain we can carry nothing out. And having food and raiment let us be therewith content. But they that will be rich fall into temptation and a snare, and into many foolish and hurtful lusts, which drown men in destruction and perdition. For the love of money is the root of all evil: which while some coveted after, they have erred from the faith, and pierced themselves through with many sorrows. But thou, O man of God, flee these things; and follow after righteousness, godliness, faith, love, patience, meekness. Fight the good fight of faith.

1 TIMOTHY 6:6-12A

F. Some people have taken these verses to mean that money itself is evil, but the word **"contentment"** in this passage is talking about having your needs met.

G. It isn't saying that a godly attitude means you can't have riches.

H. Loving God doesn't mean you have to be poor, and having money doesn't mean you are ungodly.

I. This passage of Scripture says *the love* of money is the root of all evil—not money itself.

J. Money isn't the problem; it's putting your trust in money and finding your fulfillment in it.

K. If you just put your trust in God, then He will give you money to accomplish His instructions and the call He has placed on your life.

L. The problem comes when you love money and what it will produce more than you love God, and when you rely on it instead of looking to God as your source.

M. It's amazing to me how religion has perverted this passage, with Christians promoting poverty in the name of the Lord.

N. It isn't godly to be poor any more than it is godly to be rich.

VII. God doesn't want you to always be dependent upon others because you are poor.

A. He wants you to be able to help others out financially.

B. He wants Christians to be part of the answer, not part of the problem, and to do that, you have to have financial increase.

C. I know a lot has been taught about money being evil, but if you want to be a blessing to others, then you have to drop your prejudices against having money.

D. I was raised in a pretty affluent home compared to the other kids I grew up with, but I had been taught that it was ungodly for people who serve God to have money.

E. I remember a missionary couple coming to speak at my church when I was young, and instead of getting a hotel or something, they slept in the back of their station wagon.

F. They didn't want to spend any money on a hotel.

G. The wife only had two dresses—she washed one every night and wore the other the next day.

H. Our pastor set that couple on a pedestal and promoted them as an ideal example of how true Christians should live.

I. They were "suffering for Jesus."

J. I look back on that now and realize what a completely backward model of poverty that was.

K. What a terrible witness!

L. It makes it look like God can't even take care of His own children.

M. Part of the cause for my financial problems when I first got started in ministry was that I was embarrassed to have things.

N. I thought that ministers were supposed to do without.

VIII. Have you ever seen someone go into a store and ask for a discount because they are a minister?

A. I don't like seeing things like that.

B. It's like announcing to the world that Christians can't compete or prosper.

C. It's a kind of begging and telling the world that we need help.

D. Yet Scripture says, "[I have never] **seen the righteous forsaken, nor his seed begging bread**" (Ps. 37:25, brackets mine).

E. Poverty does not glorify God, and saying that it does is a perversion of Scripture.

IX. Biblical prosperity isn't selfish, because it isn't about meeting personal needs.

A. The Christian motivation for prosperity is about desiring to have the resources to bless others and accomplish what God has called you to do.

B. Prosperity is about giving.

C. When you get that attitude, God will get money to you—and there will be plenty left over for you.

D. It's also important to remember that prosperity is relative—it isn't limited to those living in developed nations.

        i.   Prosperity for a farmer in a small village might mean having ten goats instead of one.

       ii.   It might mean living in the nicest hut in the community and having six chickens instead of two.

   E.   These truths about prosperity will work in any situation, anywhere in the world.

   F.   The key is having the right motivation and seeking God first.

X.   Real prosperity is defined by how much we give away, not by how much we keep for ourselves.

   A.   A lot of people have huge houses, fancy things, and a ton of money in the stock market and all kinds of investments—but all of their money is tied up.

   B.   I've had lots of "wealthy" people tell me they'd like to give finances to my ministry, but they can't, because they don't have any "liquid assets."

   C.   Those people aren't truly prosperous.

   D.   True prosperity is about giving and the ability to **"abound to every good work."**

XI. The Old Testament tells the story of Joseph, who was sold into slavery as a young man.

   A.   As Joseph was standing naked on an auction block, without a single possession to his name, the Bible says he was a prosperous man (Gen. 39:1-2).

   B.   It's because prosperity isn't measured by how many assets we have.

   C.   God was still with him, and it was just a matter of time before money started flowing his way.

   D.   God's blessing on Joseph's life caused him to prosper in everything he did.

   E.   Potiphar, the man who purchased Joseph as a slave, soon recognized the anointing on Joseph and put him in charge of his entire estate.

   F.   Potiphar's wife was even drawn to the anointing on Joseph, but when he refused to sleep with her, she lied about him and had him thrown in prison.

   G.   But God was with Joseph even in prison.

   H.   Before long, the head jailer turned the entire prison operation over to Joseph and let him run it.

   I.   While he was in prison, Joseph interpreted the dreams of two of Pharaoh's servants who had been confined with him.

   J.   Two years later, Pharaoh had a couple of dreams that no one could interpret for him, and one of the servants told Pharaoh about Joseph.

K. God interpreted the dream through Joseph, and Pharaoh made him second in command over all of Egypt.

L. Joseph saved Egypt from famine, and he made Pharaoh even richer.

M. Joseph was first a blessing to the people around him, and it was by blessing others that he was promoted and eventually became prosperous himself.

N. But even when Joseph became rich and powerful, he didn't use it just to satisfy his every whim.

O. He used his position to save his brothers and their families—the very people who sold him into slavery in the first place.

P. Joseph was a giver, and he always put God first—that's the same attitude we need to have.

Q. Today, when recession hits, the first thing most of us as Christians cut back on is our giving, which is the absolute worst thing we can do.

R. Like Joseph, we need to put God first regardless of our circumstances.

S. In fact, when hard times come, we should increase our giving so that we can increase our harvest.

XII. The Bible records that Isaac, Joseph's grandfather, sowed in a year of famine and reaped a hundredfold return (Gen. 26:12).

A. Almost everyone else had fled to Egypt in search of food, but Isaac stayed.

B. He decided to sow crops in the fields that had been abandoned by those who went looking for prosperity in the world, and he reaped a huge harvest.

C. He became tremendously wealthy because he planted seed at a time when everyone else was holding back in fear of poverty.

D. Joseph's and Isaac's stories are good illustrations of what I've been talking about: The reason God wants to bless you is so that you can be a blessing.

E. If you come into a recession, cut back on your personal spending but never cut back on what you are giving to God.

F. Scripture says,

Now he that ministereth seed to the sower both minister bread for your food, and multiply your seed sown, and increase the fruits of your righteousness.
2 CORINTHIANS 9:10

G. This isn't really about farming; it's an illustration of a spiritual principle.

H. When you give money, it's like planting a seed.

177

I. In the same way that planting a seed gives rise to a new plant that bears many more seeds, giving money away causes finances to grow in your life.

J. This scripture is saying that God gives seed to the sower—just like God gave Isaac a hundredfold return on the crop he planted during a drought.

K. The people who abandoned their fields and ran off to Egypt in search of prosperity didn't receive anything.

L. God gave the return to Isaac because he sowed.

M. God gives money to people if they are givers.

XIII. Second Chronicles 16:9 is talking about having a mature heart with a right attitude toward God.

A. The Lord is searching the earth, looking for people who will believe His promises and put first the kingdom of God.

B. He is looking for people who will give genuinely, from the heart, not as a form of manipulation, not giving just to get.

C. God is literally searching the world for people He can give finances to—people who are givers.

D. You could turn this around and say that if you are consistently short on money, if you always have more month than you have money, then maybe God doesn't see you as a giver.

E. That's not the only reason for being poor, but it's also possible that your heart isn't right.

XIV. There are two dominant heart conditions when it comes to money: eaters and sowers.

A. Eaters are the ones who are all about getting their own needs met.

B. They are seeking to establish their own kingdoms.

C. They use their resources to buy everything they want, and they only give when there is something left over.

D. Sowers, on the other hand, are all about putting other people first.

E. Sowers need to eat, too, so it's not like they don't buy things for themselves, but their hearts' desire is to give and seek God's kingdom first.

F. Sowers are the people God is searching the world to find.

G. I saw a great example of this when I was ministering at a church a long time ago.

H. The pastor told his people that he believed God had laid it on his heart for their church to give a fifty thousand-dollar donation to my ministry that week.

I. At the time, I was believing for extra finances to finish out a new building.

J. The pastor stood in front of his church and read this verse that says God **"ministereth seed to the sower."**

K. Then he asked, "How many of you would give a thousand dollars in this offering if God gave you the money?"

L. About fifty people stood up to say they would give if God gave them the money, and the pastor then prayed for finances to come to them.

M. Within a couple of days, some of those people started sharing testimonies of how God was supernaturally providing money.

N. God was giving people two and three thousand dollars, so after they gave a thousand dollars in the offering, they still had plenty of money left over.

O. As the testimonies came rolling in, other people began to realize that the givers weren't losing money by giving—they were actually making money.

P. All of a sudden, other people started popping up and saying, "I want to pledge to give a thousand dollars too."

Q. From what I understood later, not many of those people who gave after they heard the testimonies saw God give them finances.

R. I think it's because their hearts were wrong.

S. They weren't trying to put God's kingdom first by giving; they just wanted to make some extra money.

T. It was selfish.

U. Going back to the scripture in Paul's letter to the Corinthians: Giving profits you nothing if you don't do it motivated by love—even if you give all of your goods to feed the poor.

V. Selfishness short-circuits your prosperity because it causes you to consume all of your resources.

W. You should be imitating God by searching for opportunities to give and asking Him to show you how you can be a blessing.

XV. Another thing to keep in mind is that prosperity doesn't happen overnight.

A. There are a couple of reasons that you don't go from being selfish to becoming a generous millionaire instantly.

B. First, there is a time between planting seed and harvesting.

C. Fruit doesn't show up the next day.

D. Second, money has power, and you might not be able to handle the power of prosperity right away.

XVI. God knows you have needs, and He wants you to be taken care of.

A. Remember, He doesn't mind if you live in a nice house and drive a nice car, as long as you aren't consuming all of your finances on yourself.

B. When you get the attitude of a giver and walk it out over time, God will increase your finances.

C. If God can get money through you, He'll get it to you—and it won't be long before you have plenty left over for yourself.

TEACHER'S
—— GUIDE ——

1. The book of Matthew gives a lengthy description of stewardship in its final chapters. We are given the parable about three servants who were entrusted with money by their master. The master gave one servant five talents; another, two talents; and the last servant, one talent (a *talent* was a specific weight of money in coins). The servant with five talents took what his master had given him and made another five talents. Likewise, the servant with two talents made an additional two talents. But the man who received one talent just buried it for safekeeping. The servant who made five talents was commended by the master, and so was the servant who made two talents. When the servant who received one talent came before the master, he said **"Lord, I knew thee that thou art an hard man, reaping where thou hast not sown, and gathering where thou hast not strawed: And I was afraid, and went and hid thy talent in the earth"** (Matt. 25:24-25), and then he gave back the one talent he had received. The master was furious, and he rebuked the servant for not at least having put the money in the bank to earn interest. Then he said,

> *Take therefore the talent from him, and give it unto him which hath ten talents. For unto every one that hath shall be given, and he shall have abundance: but from him that hath not shall be taken away even that which he hath. And cast ye the unprofitable servant into outer darkness: there shall be weeping and gnashing of teeth.*
>
> MATTHEW 25:28-30

This passage clearly reveals that the Lord expects us to take what He has given us and do something with it, not just hide it in the earth. Our God is a God of multiplication.

1a. Read Matthew 25:24-25 and 28-30. What is the message in the parable of the talents?
That the Lord expects you to take what He has given you and do something with it, not just hide it in the earth

2. Right after giving this parable, Jesus talked about coming back in glory and separating the sheep from the goats. To some, He will say, **"Come, ye blessed of my Father, inherit the kingdom prepared for you from the foundation of the world"** (Matt. 25:34). Those are the people who clothed the naked, fed the sick, gave water to the thirsty, and visited inmates in prison. This is all still related to stewardship. Jesus is talking about taking the resources God has blessed us with and using them to touch others. Jesus said that those who never clothe the naked, care for the sick, or feed the hungry don't really know Him, and they will be cast into everlasting fire (Matt. 25:41-46). That's strong, and a lot of people don't like to hear it, because it makes stewardship an integral part of what God expects them to do. Stewardship is far more important than how it is typically taught today.

2a. Read Matthew 25:34 and 41-46. What lesson can be learned from the parable of the sheep and the goats?
Stewardship—taking the resources God has blessed you with and using them to touch others

2b. What makes stewardship far more important than how it is typically taught today?
The emphasis that Jesus placed on it

3. Another problem some people have is thinking that prosperity is selfish. I've had lots of people tell me they are satisfied with what they have, and they don't want any more. What most of those people are really saying is, "As long as my needs are met, then I'm satisfied. I don't need any more." What about everyone else? Without extra finances, they are limited in their ability to give. It would be better for them to prosper and increase their finances, not for themselves, but so they can be a blessing to someone else. God entrusts you with resources so you can be a blessing to other people, so it isn't selfish to desire prosperity. When you see God as your source, and treat the money He gives you as a resource to be stewarded, then it is very godly to want to prosper so that you can give and help establish God's covenant on earth.

    3a. What's the reason some people think prosperity is selfish?
       A. Because people who are wealthy only want money for themselves
       B. Because they only want enough money for their needs to be met
       C. Because selfishness is what they typically see in prosperous people
       D. All of the above
       E. None of the above

4. On the other hand, there are people teaching prosperity from a selfish standpoint. The driving motive for that kind of prosperity is covetousness. You aren't going to see a supernatural return on your giving when you do it with the wrong motive. It has to come from a humble heart that desires to bless other people. Since the motive behind what you do is more important than the action itself, giving with a wrong heart is of no benefit. Scripture says,

> *And though I bestow all my goods to feed the poor, and though I give my body to be burned, and have not charity, it profiteth me nothing.*
> 1 CORINTHIANS 13:3

This says you can go so far as to make the ultimate sacrifice of laying down your life, but it will be of no benefit to you whatsoever if it isn't done out of a motivation of love. It will bless the person you sacrifice yourself for, but it isn't going to result in a supernatural return for you. If your only reason for giving is so that God will give back to you, it isn't going to work. Carnal appetites are going to profit you nothing. Society today is so focused on self-fulfillment and self-gratification that living for God is a totally foreign concept. It doesn't make sense to the natural mind. The truth is, when you're all wrapped up in yourself, you make a very small package.

4a. Without extra finances, you are _____ in your ability to give.
   Limited
4b. From a selfish standpoint, what's the driving motive for prosperity?
   Covetousness
4c. Read 1 Corinthians 13:3. The gift you give is not more important than the what?
   Motive behind it
4d. What is a totally foreign concept in today's society?
   A. Living for another
   B. Living for self
   C. Living for the moment
   D. Living for money
   E. Living for God
4e. You make a very small package when you're wrapped up in what?
   A. Yourself
   B. Christmas wrapping
   C. Work
   D. All of the above
   E. None of the above

5. In the United States, a lot has been made of the sacrifices carried out by the people who fought in World War II. A relative of mine was a Marine who fought at Iwo Jima. He was in one of the first waves of soldiers in the amphibious assault. Before they invaded, he was told that the first few waves of soldiers would never make it. They were basically being used to draw all of the enemy fire and expend their ammunition, but they were willing to make that sacrifice so that the waves of soldiers behind them would have a chance to survive and win the fight. They believed in making a sacrifice to win the war. They were committed to principle more than to self-interest, and they realized there was something more important than their individual freedom or existence.

6. Selfishness is the most prevalent attitude today. A lot of people are making their decisions based purely upon whatever is best for them. If something promotes their personal well-being, then it's good—if not, then it's bad. They don't have any reference larger than their own needs. That kind of attitude is going to affect how they handle their finances. Paul made that application:

> *But godliness with contentment is great gain. For we brought nothing into this world, and it is certain we can carry nothing out. And having food and raiment let us be therewith content. But they that will be rich fall into temptation and a snare, and into many foolish and hurtful lusts, which drown men in destruction and perdition. For the love of money is the root of all evil: which while some coveted after, they have erred from the faith, and pierced themselves through with many sorrows. But thou, O man of God, flee these things; and follow after righteousness, godliness, faith, love, patience, meekness. Fight the good fight of faith.*
>
> 1 TIMOTHY 6:6-12A

Some people have taken these verses to mean that money itself is evil, but the word **"contentment"** in this passage is talking about having your needs met. It isn't saying that a godly attitude means you can't have riches. Loving God doesn't mean you have to be poor, and having money doesn't mean you are ungodly. This passage of Scripture says *the love* of money is the root of all evil—not money itself. Money isn't the problem; it's putting your trust in money and finding your fulfillment in it. If you just put your trust in God, then He will give you money to accomplish His instructions and the call He has placed on your life. The problem comes when you love money and what it will produce more than you love God, and when you rely on it instead of looking to God as your source. It's amazing to me how religion has perverted this passage, with Christians promoting poverty in the name of the Lord. It isn't godly to be poor any more than it is godly to be rich.

6a. What is the most prevalent attitude today?
   Selfishness
6b. True or false: A lot of people are making their decisions based purely upon whatever is best for them.
   True
6c. Read 1 Timothy 6:6-12a. Loving God doesn't mean you have to be _____ , and having money doesn't mean you are _____.
   Poor, ungodly
6d. What is the root of all evil?
   A. Money itself
   B. Giving to live
   C. The love of money
   D. Hatred
   E. Lack of faith
6e. People use this passage to promote what?
   Poverty in the name of the Lord

7. God doesn't want you to always be dependent upon others because you are poor. He wants you to be able to help others out financially. He wants Christians to be part of the answer, not part of the problem, and to do that, you have to have financial increase. I know a lot has been taught about money being evil, but if you want to be a blessing to others, then you have to drop your prejudices against having money. I was raised in a pretty affluent home compared to the other kids I grew up with, but I had been taught that it was ungodly for people who serve God to have money. I remember a missionary couple coming to speak at my church when I was young, and instead of getting a hotel or something, they slept in the back of their station wagon. They didn't want to spend any money on a hotel. The wife only had two dresses—she washed one every night and wore the other the next day. Our pastor set that couple on a pedestal and promoted them as an ideal example of how true Christians should live. They were "suffering for Jesus." I look back on that now and realize what a completely backward model of poverty that was. What a terrible witness! It makes it look like God can't even take care of His own children. Part of the cause for my financial problems when I first got started in ministry was that I was embarrassed to have things. I thought that ministers were supposed to do without.

  7a. God doesn't want you to always be dependent upon others because you are poor; He wants you to be able to what?
      Help others out financially
  7b. Choosing to live in poverty as a Christian is what kind of witness?
      A. A reasonable one
      B. A terrible one
      C. A great one
      D. All of the above
      E. None of the above

8. Have you ever seen someone go into a store and ask for a discount because they are a minister? I don't like seeing things like that. It's like announcing to the world that Christians can't compete or prosper. It's a kind of begging and telling the world that we need help. Yet Scripture says, "[I have never] **seen the righteous forsaken, nor his seed begging bread**" (Ps. 37:25, brackets mine). Poverty does not glorify God, and saying that it does is a perversion of Scripture.

  8a. Read Psalm 37:25. The righteous should never have to _____ in order to get their needs met.
      Beg

9. Biblical prosperity isn't selfish, because it isn't about meeting personal needs. The Christian motivation for prosperity is about desiring to have the resources to bless others and accomplish what God has called you to do. Prosperity is about giving. When you get that attitude, God will get money to you—and there will be plenty left over for you. It's also important to remember that prosperity is relative—it isn't limited to those living in developed nations. Prosperity for a farmer in a small village might mean having ten goats instead of one. It might mean living in the nicest hut in the community and having six chickens instead of two. These truths about prosperity will work in any situation, anywhere in the world. The key is having the right motivation and seeking God first.

  9a. True or false: Prosperity is limited to those living in developed nations.
      False

10. Real prosperity is defined by how much we give away, not by how much we keep for ourselves. A lot of people have huge houses, fancy things, and a ton of money in the stock market and all kinds of investments—but all of their money is tied up. I've had lots of "wealthy" people tell me they'd like to give finances to my ministry, but they can't, because they don't have any "liquid assets." Those people aren't truly prosperous. True prosperity is about giving and the ability to **"abound to every good work."**

   10a.   What is true prosperity?
          Giving and the ability to "abound to every good work"

11. The Old Testament tells the story of Joseph, who was sold into slavery as a young man. As Joseph was standing naked on an auction block, without a single possession to his name, the Bible says he was a prosperous man (Gen. 39:1-2). It's because prosperity isn't measured by how many assets we have. God was still with him, and it was just a matter of time before money started flowing his way. God's blessing on Joseph's life caused him to prosper in everything he did. Potiphar, the man who purchased Joseph as a slave, soon recognized the anointing on Joseph and put him in charge of his entire estate. Potiphar's wife was even drawn to the anointing on Joseph, but when he refused to sleep with her, she lied about him and had him thrown in prison. But God was with Joseph even in prison. Before long, the head jailer turned the entire prison operation over to Joseph and let him run it. While he was in prison, Joseph interpreted the dreams of two of Pharaoh's servants who had been confined with him. Two years later, Pharaoh had a couple of dreams that no one could interpret for him, and one of the servants told Pharaoh about Joseph. God interpreted the dream through Joseph, and Pharaoh made him second in command over all of Egypt. Joseph saved Egypt from famine, and he made Pharaoh even richer. Joseph was first a blessing to the people around him, and it was by blessing others that he was promoted and eventually became prosperous himself. But even when Joseph became rich and powerful, he didn't use it just to satisfy his every whim. He used his position to save his brothers and their families—the very people who sold him into slavery in the first place. Joseph was a giver, and he always put God first—that's the same attitude we need to have. Today, if recession hits, the first thing most of us as Christians cut back on is our giving, which is the absolute worst thing we can do. Like Joseph, we need to put God first regardless of our circumstances. In fact, when hard times come, we should increase our giving so that we can increase our harvest.

   11a.   Read Genesis 39:1-2. Why does the Bible say Joseph was a prosperous man even though he was being sold into slavery?
          Because God was with him
   11b.   How was Joseph promoted?
          By being a blessing to others
   11c.   If recession hits, what is the worst thing you can do as a Christian?
          Cut back on giving

12. The Bible records that Isaac, Joseph's grandfather, sowed in a year of famine and reaped a hundredfold return (Gen. 26:12). Almost everyone else had fled to Egypt in search of food, but Isaac stayed. He decided to sow crops in the fields that had been abandoned by those who went looking for prosperity in the world, and he reaped a huge harvest. He became tremendously wealthy because he planted seed at a time when everyone else was holding back in fear of poverty. Joseph's and Isaac's stories are good illustrations of what I've been talking about: The reason God wants to bless you is so that you can be a blessing. If you come into a recession, cut back on your personal spending but never cut back on what you are giving to God. Scripture says,

> *Now he that ministereth seed to the sower both minister bread for your*
> *food, and multiply your seed sown, and increase the fruits of your*
> *righteousness.*
>
> 2 CORINTHIANS 9:10

This isn't really about farming; it's an illustration of a spiritual principle. When you give money, it's like planting a seed. In the same way that planting a seed gives rise to a new plant that bears many more seeds, giving money away causes finances to grow in your life. This scripture is saying that God gives seed to the sower—just like God gave Isaac a hundredfold return on the crop he planted during a drought. The people who abandoned their fields and ran off to Egypt in search of prosperity didn't receive anything. God gave the return to Isaac because he sowed. God gives money to people if they are givers.

12a.   Before you cut back on what you're giving to God, you should cut back on what?
   A.   Watching television
   B.   Eating out
   C.   Buying stuff
   D.   Sowing seed
   E.   Personal spending
12b.   Read 2 Corinthians 9:10. When you give money, what is it like?
   Planting a seed
12c.   To whom does God give seed?
   Sowers
12d.   That means God gives _____ to people if they are _____ .
   Money, givers

13. Second Chronicles 16:9 is talking about having a mature heart with a right attitude toward God. The Lord is searching the earth, looking for people who will believe His promises and put first the kingdom of God. He is looking for people who will give genuinely, from the heart, not as a form of manipulation, not giving just to get. God is literally searching the world for people He can give finances to—people who are givers. You could turn this around and say that if you are consistently short on money, if you always have more month than you have money, then maybe God doesn't see you as a giver. That's not the only reason for being poor, but it's also possible that your heart isn't right.

13a.   Read 2 Chronicles 16:9. True or false: This verse proves God is looking for perfect people.
   False
13b.   What's one reason you might have more month than money?
   God doesn't see you as a giver; i.e., your heart isn't right

14. There are two dominant heart conditions when it comes to money: eaters and sowers. Eaters are the ones who are all about getting their own needs met. They are seeking to establish their own kingdoms. They use their resources to buy everything they want, and they only give when there is something left over. Sowers, on the other hand, are all about putting other people first. Sowers need to eat, too, so it's not like they don't buy things for themselves, but their hearts' desire is to give and seek God's kingdom first. Sowers are the people God is searching the world to find. I saw a great example of this when I was ministering at a church a long time ago. The pastor told his people that he believed God had laid it on his heart for their church to give a fifty thousand-dollar donation to my ministry that week. At the time, I was believing for extra finances to finish out a new building. The pastor stood in front of his church and read this verse that says God **"ministereth seed to the sower."** Then he asked, "How many of you would give a thousand dollars in this offering if God gave you the money?" About fifty people stood up to say they would give if God gave them the money, and the pastor then prayed for finances to come to them. Within a couple of days, some of those people started sharing testimonies of how God was supernaturally providing money. God was giving people two and three thousand dollars, so after they gave a thousand dollars in the offering, they still had plenty of money left over. As the testimonies came rolling in, other people began to realize that the givers weren't losing money by giving—they were actually making money. All of a sudden, other people started popping up and saying, "I want to pledge to give a thousand dollars too." From what I understood later, not many of those people who gave after they heard the testimonies saw God give them finances. I think it's because their hearts were wrong. They weren't trying to put God's kingdom first by giving; they just wanted to make some extra money. It was selfish. Going back to the scripture in Paul's letter to the Corinthians: Giving profits you nothing if you don't do it motivated by love—even if you give all of your goods to feed the poor. Selfishness short-circuits your prosperity because it causes you to consume all of your resources. You should be imitating God by searching for opportunities to give and asking Him to show you how you can be a blessing.

    14a. What is an eater?
        An eater is one who is all about getting their own needs met. They use their resources to buy everything they want, and they only give when there is something left over.
    14b. What is a sower?
        A sower is all about putting other people first
    14c. Giving profits you nothing if you don't do it motivated by _____.
        Love
    14d. Because it causes you to consume all of your resources, what short-circuits your prosperity?
        Selfishness

15. Another thing to keep in mind is that prosperity doesn't happen overnight. There are a couple of reasons that you don't go from being selfish to becoming a generous millionaire instantly. First, there is a time between planting seed and harvesting. Fruit doesn't show up the next day. Second, money has power, and you might not be able to handle the power of prosperity right away.

    15a. Why doesn't prosperity happen fast?
        Because there is a time between planting seed and harvesting, and you might not be able to handle the power of prosperity right away

16. God knows you have needs, and He wants you to be taken care of. Remember, He doesn't mind if you live in a nice house and drive a nice car, as long as you aren't consuming all of your finances on yourself. When you get the attitude of a giver and walk it out over time, God will increase your finances. If God can get money through you, He'll get it to you—and it won't be long before you have plenty left over for yourself.

DISCIPLESHIP
—— QUESTIONS ——

1. Read Matthew 25:24-25 and 28-30. What is the message in the parable of the talents?

    _____
    _____
    _____

2. Read Matthew 25:34 and 41-46. What lesson can be learned from the parable of the sheep and the goats?

    _____
    _____
    _____

3. What makes stewardship far more important than how it is typically taught today?

    _____
    _____
    _____

4. What's the reason some people think prosperity is selfish?
    A. Because people who are wealthy only want money for themselves
    B. Because they only want enough money for their needs to be met
    C. Because selfishness is what they typically see in prosperous people
    D. All of the above
    E. None of the above

5. Without extra finances, you are _____ in your ability to give.

6. From a selfish standpoint, what's the driving motive for prosperity?

    _____
    _____
    _____

7. Read 1 Corinthians 13:3. The gift you give is not more important than the what?

    _____
    _____
    _____

8. What is a totally foreign concept in today's society?
    A. Living for another
    B. Living for self
    C. Living for the moment
    D. Living for money
    E. Living for God

9. You make a very small package when you're wrapped up in what?
    A. Yourself
    B. Christmas wrapping
    C. Work
    D. All of the above
    E. None of the above

10. What is the most prevalent attitude today?
    _____
    _____
    _____

11. True or false: A lot of people are making their decisions based purely upon whatever is best for them.

12. Read 1 Timothy 6:6-12a. Loving God doesn't mean you have to be _____ , and having money doesn't mean you are _____.

13. What is the root of all evil?
    A. Money itself
    B. Giving to live
    C. The love of money
    D. Hatred
    E. Lack of faith

14. People use this passage to promote what?
    _____
    _____
    _____

15. God doesn't want you to always be dependent upon others because you are poor; He wants you to be able to what?
    _____
    _____
    _____

16. Choosing to live in poverty as a Christian is what kind of witness?
    A. A reasonable one
    B. A terrible one
    C. A great one
    D. All of the above
    E. None of the above

17. Read Psalm 37:25. The righteous should never have to _____ in order to get their needs met.

18. True or false: Prosperity is limited to those living in developed nations.

19. What is true prosperity?

_____

_____

_____

20. Read Genesis 39:1-2. Why does the Bible say Joseph was a prosperous man even though he was being sold into slavery?

_____

_____

_____

21. How was Joseph promoted?

_____

_____

_____

22. If recession hits, what is the worst thing you can do as a Christian?

_____

_____

_____

23. Before you cut back on what you're giving to God, you should cut back on what?
    A. Watching television
    B. Eating out
    C. Buying stuff
    D. Sowing seed
    E. Personal spending

24. Read 2 Corinthians 9:10. When you give money, what is it like?

_____
_____
_____

25. To whom does God give seed?

_____
_____
_____

26. That means God gives _____ to people if they are _____ .

27. Read 2 Chronicles 16:9. True or false: This verse proves God is looking for perfect people.

28. What's one reason you might have more month than money?

_____
_____
_____

29. What is an eater?

_____
_____
_____

30. What is a sower?

_____
_____
_____

31. Giving profits you nothing if you don't do it motivated by _____.

32. Because it causes you to consume all of your resources, what short-circuits your prosperity?

_____
_____
_____

33. Why doesn't prosperity happen fast?

_____
_____
_____

ANSWER
—KEY—

1. That the Lord expects you to take what He has given you and do something with it, not just hide it in the earth

2. Stewardship—taking the resources God has blessed you with and using them to touch others

3. The emphasis that Jesus placed on it

4. B. Because they only want enough money for their needs to be met

5. Limited

6. Covetousness

7. Motive behind it

8. E. Living for God

9. A. Yourself

10. Selfishness

11. True

12. Poor, ungodly

13. C. The love of money

14. Poverty in the name of the Lord

15. Help others out financially

16. B. A terrible one

17. Beg

18. False

19. Giving and the ability to **"abound to every good work"**

20. Because God was with him

21. By being a blessing to others

22. Cut back on giving

23. E. Personal spending

24. Planting a seed

25. Sowers

26. Money, givers

27. False

28. God doesn't see you as a giver; i.e., your heart isn't right

29. An eater is one who is all about getting their own needs met. They use their resources to buy everything they want, and they only give when there is something left over

30. A sower is all about putting other people first

31. Love

32. Selfishness

33. Because there is a time between planting seed and harvesting, and you might not be able to handle the power of prosperity right away

——SCRIPTURES——

MATTHEW 25:28-30

Take therefore the talent from him, and give it unto him which hath ten talents. [29] For unto every one that hath shall be given, and he shall have abundance: but from him that hath not shall be taken away even that which he hath. [30] And cast ye the unprofitable servant into outer darkness: there shall be weeping and gnashing of teeth.

MATTHEW 25:41-46

Then shall he say also unto them on the left hand, Depart from me, ye cursed, into everlasting fire, prepared for the devil and his angels: [42] For I was an hungred, and ye gave me no meat: I was thirsty, and ye gave me no drink: [43] I was a stranger, and ye took me not in: naked, and ye clothed me not: sick, and in prison, and ye visited me not. [44] Then shall they also answer him, saying, Lord, when saw we thee an hungred, or athirst, or a stranger, or naked, or sick, or in prison, and did not minister unto thee? [45] Then shall he answer them, saying, Verily I say unto you, Inasmuch as ye did it not to one of the least of these, ye did it not to me. [46] And these shall go away into everlasting punishment: but the righteous into life eternal.

1 CORINTHIANS 13:3

And though I bestow all my goods to feed the poor, and though I give my body to be burned, and have not charity, it profiteth me nothing.

1 TIMOTHY 6:3-12

If any man teach otherwise, and consent not to wholesome words, even the words of our Lord Jesus Christ, and to the doctrine which is according to godliness; [4] He is proud, knowing nothing, but doting about questions and strifes of words, whereof cometh envy, strife, railings, evil surmisings, [5] Perverse disputings of men of corrupt minds, and destitute of the truth, supposing that gain is godliness: from such withdraw thyself. [6] But godliness with contentment is great gain. [7] For we brought nothing into this world, and it is certain we can carry nothing out. [8] And having food and raiment let us be therewith content. [9] But they that will be rich fall into temptation and a snare, and into many foolish and hurtful lusts, which drown men in destruction and perdition. [10] For the love of money is the root of all evil: which while some coveted after, they have erred from the faith, and pierced themselves through with many sorrows. [11] But thou, O man of God, flee these things; and follow after righteousness, godliness, faith, love, patience, meekness. [12] Fight the good fight of faith, lay hold on eternal life, whereunto thou art also called, and hast professed a good profession before many witnesses.

PSALM 37:25

I have been young, and now am old; yet have I not seen the righteous forsaken, nor his seed begging bread.

2 CORINTHIANS 9:8

And God is able to make all grace abound toward you; that ye, always having all sufficiency in all things, may abound to every good work.

GENESIS 39:1-2

And Joseph was brought down to Egypt; and Potiphar, an officer of Pharaoh, captain of the guard, an Egyptian, bought him of the hands of the Ishmeelites, which had brought him down thither. [2] And the LORD was with Joseph, and he was a prosperous man; and he was in the house of his master the Egyptian.

——SCRIPTURES——

GENESIS 26:12

Then Isaac sowed in that land, and received in the same year an hundredfold: and the LORD blessed him.

1 CORINTHIANS 9:10

Now he that ministereth seed to the sower both minister bread for your food, and multiply your seed sown, and increase the fruits of your righteousness.

2 CHRONICLES 16:9

For the eyes of the LORD run to and fro throughout the whole earth, to shew himself strong in the behalf of them whose heart is perfect toward him. Herein thou hast done foolishly: therefore from henceforth thou shalt have wars.

THE
TITHE

I was taught to believe that the tithe is mandatory.[1] We were told that we owed God a tenth of our income, and if we didn't pay up, we'd be cursed. Not tithing, we were told, is the same as stealing from God. "You're robbing from God," they'd tell us, "and God is going to get you." Fortunately, none of that is true. God loves us independent of our works, which includes whether or not we tithe. New Testament giving isn't a debt or an obligation. Scripture says,

> *But this I say, He which soweth sparingly shall reap also sparingly; and he which soweth bountifully shall reap also bountifully. Every man according as he purposeth in his heart, so let him give; not grudgingly, or of necessity: for God loveth a cheerful giver.*
>
> 2 CORINTHIANS 9:6-7

I don't know how anyone can read these verses and still think you are obligated to tithe, or that you are cursed if you don't. It says you're not supposed to give **"grudgingly, or of necessity."** If the reason you pay a tithe is because you don't want to be under a curse, then you are paying out of necessity and it isn't cheerful. It's like paying hush money to God.

You've probably heard the stories about how the Mafia collects protection money from businesses. They come into a person's business and talk about how there has been a rash of break-ins or fires in the area, but they can make sure nothing happens to that person's business as long as they are paid every month. Of course, these guys are the ones doing all of the robberies and arson, but those who pay them won't be destroyed too. In a sense, that's what people are teaching when they say you are cursed if you don't pay the tithe. They are saying you have to tithe to keep the curse off your life. It's like paying the godfather, instead of God the Father.

If that is why you are giving, then you are totally violating the motive given in this scripture. The Word says not to give grudgingly or of necessity because God loves a cheerful giver. Under the New Covenant, you should be giving from a cheerful heart. You should be giving because you want to, not to pay God hush money. The Apostle Paul ended his teaching on giving by saying,

> *Thanks be unto God for his unspeakable gift.*
>
> 2 CORINTHIANS 9:15

This summarizes why we should give back to the Lord under the New Covenant: He has already given to us beyond measure. God has provided everything for us, and our giving is actually an expression of appreciation for all He has done for us. It goes back to the scripture that says nothing we do is of any benefit unless it is motivated by love (1 Cor. 13:3). Again, the motive behind the gift is more important than the gift itself.

---

[1] Tithe means *a tenth part,* and tithing is the act of giving a tenth of your income back to God.

Some people are vicious about the tithe. They harp on the curse of not tithing and talk about the wrath of God. I hate to disappoint those people, but Scripture says we have been redeemed from the curse of the Law. God isn't mad at us if we don't tithe—I think it's dumb not to tithe, but God will still love us if we don't. Some people, reacting against the curse of the tithe teaching, have swung in the completely opposite direction and say that the tithe was an Old Testament thing. They don't think it has any bearing on our lives today. I don't believe that is true. We're not cursed if we don't tithe, but tithing is still in our best interests.

YOU ARE NOT UNDER A CURSE IF YOU DON'T TITHE.

The very first time the tithe was mentioned in Scripture is when Abraham gave tithes to Melchizedek, the king of Salem. It was the same incident where Abraham refused to keep the king of Sodom's money because he didn't want anyone trying to say they made him rich. Abraham knew that he was rich only because God had blessed him. This incident happened more than 400 years before Moses gave the Law to Israel.

We have been redeemed from the curse of the Law and we aren't under the bondage of legalism to tithe, but we should also recognize that tithing was a biblical principle before the Law came along. Abraham wasn't living under the Law, yet he tithed. I believe that we are supposed to tithe too. Actually, I think the tithe is a starting place. Everything we have under the New Covenant is far superior to the Old Covenant, so I think we should be doing more than what was required under the Law. Let's look at the classic passage from Malachi that is used to teach on the tithe:

> *Will a man rob God? Yet ye have robbed me. But ye say, Wherein have we robbed thee? In tithes and offerings. Ye are cursed with a curse: for ye have robbed me, even this whole nation. Bring ye all the tithes into the storehouse, that there may be meat in mine house, and prove me now herewith, saith the LORD of hosts, if I will not open you the windows of heaven, and pour you out a blessing, that there shall not be room enough to receive it. And I will rebuke the devourer for your sakes, and he shall not destroy the fruits of your ground; neither shall your vine cast her fruit before the time in the field, saith the LORD of hosts.*
>
> MALACHI 3:8-11

Nearly everyone who teaches on the tithe cites this passage. Usually, this passage is used like a club to beat people into submission. But there is a huge difference between the punishment that came for disobeying the Law under the Old Covenant and the grace that we live under in the New Testament. The motivation for tithing today is out of appreciation for what God has done in our lives. It should come as a response of love from the heart, out of a desire to bless people. We don't tithe in an attempt to keep the Law. In fact, it would be a bad idea to even try.

For as many as are of the works of the law are under the curse: for it is
written, Cursed is every one that continueth not in all things which are
written in the book of the law to do them.
GALATIANS 3:10

You are cursed if you don't keep all of the Law, which includes all the commandments and sacrifices. You can't just keep some of the Law, or do the best you can and God will make up the difference. No, if you don't keep every letter of the Law, then you are cursed! This is why Jesus came—because you are absolutely incapable of keeping the Law. It's impossible. The people who are trying to say you are cursed if you don't tithe are missing this point. You either trust the grace of God, or you reject Jesus' sacrifice and put your trust in your own performance and forfeit God's grace. You have to be 100 percent perfect—never making a single mistake in thought, word, or deed for your entire life—or you have to humble yourself and receive the gift of God's grace. Trying to satisfy the Law by paying a tithe isn't going to help. Scripture says,

But that no man is justified by the law in the sight of God, it is evident: for,
The just shall live by faith. And the law is not of faith: but, The man that doeth
them shall live in them. Christ hath redeemed us from the curse of the law,
being made a curse for us: for it is written, Cursed is every one that hangeth on
a tree: That the blessing of Abraham might come on the Gentiles through Jesus
Christ; that we might receive the promise of the Spirit through faith.
GALATIANS 3:11-14

You have been redeemed from the curse of the Law! This passage couldn't be any clearer. The verse in Malachi says you **"are cursed with a curse"** if you don't tithe—this is exactly what you have been redeemed from. The whole attitude that God is going to punish you for not paying a tithe is completely unscriptural. The church I went to as a child used to say that if people didn't pay their tithes, God would take it from them in doctors' bills. Either that or He would make their cars break down or their dishwashers stop working or something like that.

I'm telling you, under the New Covenant, God doesn't relate to you that way. Christ freed you from the curse of the Law. God is not coming against you. He is not going to take money from you if you don't tithe. Trying to pay off God like He's some kind of mobster is the wrong motivation. You're not going to benefit from that kind of giving.

It's also worth mentioning that the passage in Malachi 3 says the curse comes for robbing God in tithes *and* offerings. The people who use this verse to teach about tithing from a Law perspective conveniently overlook that you also have to give offerings to keep the Law. I've never personally sat down and figured it out, but I've heard other ministers say that the offerings added up to way more than the tithe. There were so many offerings that all together, the mandatory giving totaled more like 33 percent. So, if you are trying to live by the Law, you are cursed unless you are giving at least 33 percent.

I've had a number of people criticize me over teaching that we aren't under the curse when we don't tithe, but they don't have anything to say when I point out that Malachi mentions tithes *and* offerings. I can guarantee that most of the people who are so adamant about the curse of the tithe are not giving 33 percent. But it's hypocritical to say we are cursed for not paying tithes and just leave out the offerings.

Christ has redeemed you from the curse of the Law, so you're not cursed under the New Covenant for not tithing. The motive for your giving has to be a cheerful heart, but you can see the natural reasons tithing is beneficial. It's just like a farmer who sows seeds to reap a crop. God gives you seed, and you have a choice about what to do with that seed. You can eat all of the seed that God gives you, or you can plant some of it and reap a crop that will ensure you have something to eat next year. Planting seeds ensures a future crop, and tithing moves money into your future—in addition to the eternal benefit. Money is like seed, and when you consume every dollar that comes your way, you aren't investing in your future.

God loves you if you eat all of your seed, but don't be surprised when the money runs out and you're crying out to Him about not meeting your needs. It's not His fault you ate all of your seed. You need to be disciplined enough to take a portion of what God has given you and sow it into your future. The tithe is a starting place; ultimately, you should desire to give even more than 10 percent. God is still going to love you, whether you give 9 percent, 11 percent, or nothing at all. Tithing has nothing to do with how God relates to you, but there is still a benefit to tithing.

WE DON'T TITHE TO PLEASE GOD; WE DO IT OUT OF A SENSE OF APPRECIATION FOR ALL THAT GOD HAS DONE FOR US.

God the Father put all of His wrath on Jesus, so He isn't mad at us for not tithing. He's not even in a bad mood. Jesus became a curse so that we wouldn't be cursed. We aren't living under the bondage of the Law anymore. We don't tithe to please God; we do it out of a sense of appreciation for all that God has done for us and because it's the smart thing to do. There is no longer a punishment associated with tithing, and it doesn't change how God sees us.

But just because the punishment for not tithing has been taken away, that doesn't mean we should stop giving. It's similar to how parents teach children to do the right thing by using punishment, or the threat of it, to keep them in line. I grew up on a busy road, and my mother used to threaten to beat me if I ever crossed the street without looking both ways. Actually, she had to whoop me a number of times! She did it because she loved me, and she didn't want me getting hit by a car. My mother isn't around to spank me anymore, but I still look both ways before crossing the street because it's the smart thing to do.

This is a lot like the difference between how God related to Israel under the Old Covenant and how He deals with Christians under the New Covenant. Old Testament believers didn't have the capacity to understand why they should or shouldn't do certain things, because the natural mind can't understand the things of God.

> *But the natural man receiveth not the things of the Spirit of God: for they are foolishness unto him: neither can he know them, because they are spiritually discerned.*
>
> 1 CORINTHIANS 2:14

The people under the Law were spiritually dead, as all people are until they are born again by believing in Jesus. God couldn't explain to them the spiritual benefits of godly behavior, so, in a sense, He treated them like children and threatened punishment to keep them from hurting themselves. You can't reason with a toddler, but you also can't wait until a child is twenty years old before you start teaching them the difference between right and wrong. So, you use punishment as a tool until he or she is old enough to understand reason. But punishment is only a temporary fix. You won't, or shouldn't, still be doing the right thing out of fear of punishment when you are fifty or sixty years old. Something would be seriously wrong if you were. As an adult, you do the right thing because you understand that actions have consequences.

This is the way it was with mankind. Prior to Jesus coming and bringing the new birth, people didn't have the right heart motives and couldn't understand spiritual things, so God just told them what to do and enforced it with punishment. That's why the book of Malachi said the people of Israel would be under a curse if they didn't tithe. Even a lost man could understand that it was in his best interests to tithe when the alternative was to be cursed.

Now that we are born again and God's Spirit lives in us, He has removed the curse. It's like we're adults now, and He is no longer trying to get us to behave by threatening punishment. Now we do what is right out of good hearts and because we understand spiritual things. I give tithes and offerings because it's a way of showing my faith and using the finances God gave me to help build His kingdom. I believe in tithing just like I still look both ways before crossing the street; I just give with a different motivation than they did under the Old Covenant.

A long time ago, a man heard me preach on how giving out of a sense of obligation profits nothing, and he decided to change how he was giving. He was the kind who wrote out his tithe check down to the penny. The bottom line was that he was tithing because he felt obligated to give God 10 percent of his income. At the time, he was making around three thousand dollars a month, which was a lot of money back then, but he still felt like he was always behind financially. So, after hearing me teach, he and his wife decided they were going to start giving as they purposed in their hearts. He stopped calculating his tithe exactly, and they just started giving whatever they wanted.

About six months later, he realized that they had more money in the bank than they'd ever had before. His first thought was, *I bet I've decreased my giving.* Prior to his change of heart, he paid his tithe like a bill. He put it in the same column as all of his other debts and paid it every month like clockwork. By his thinking, extra money in his account meant he must not have been paying his "tithing bill." So, he went back and added together his checks over the previous six months to see how much he had been giving. What he discovered surprised him: He had moved his giving up to 24 percent of his income. He was giving more than twice as much as he ever had, yet he was more prosperous than ever—because God was prospering him supernaturally.

When you give grudgingly or of necessity, or because you think God is going to break your kneecaps if you don't pay up, it profits you nothing. You get zero benefit from that kind of giving. The people you give to will benefit, but it isn't going to come back to you. That kind of giving won't influence your future. You have to come out from under the mindset of Old Testament obligation and start giving with a joyful heart if you want to see a return on your giving.

Scripture says **"Give, and it shall be given unto you; good measure, pressed down, and shaken together, and running over, shall men give into your bosom. For with the same measure that ye mete withal it shall be measured to you again"** (Luke 6:38), but if that was all there was to prosperity, then nearly every Christian would be prosperous. If all people had to do was give and—*boom*—it came back to them a hundredfold, then every church would be packed full of millionaires. You'd probably be surprised at the total if you were to take all that you have given in your lifetime and multiply it by a hundred; every ten grand you have given equals a million dollars in return. So, why hasn't every believer seen that kind of return? Because the motive behind the gift is more important than the gift itself.

Some people have been giving faithfully for a long time, but they've been doing it with the wrong motivation. They've been taught they should tithe out of obligation, and they've just been paying a bill or doing it to appease God. That kind of giving benefits the church you are writing your checks to, but it isn't going to benefit you in this life. You won't get a hundredfold return on that giving. You have to plant your financial seed with a cheerful heart, motivated by love, because your gift is ruined when you give with the wrong motive.

I think tithing is a godly thing, and I believe all Christians should tithe. In the Old Testament, they gave because they had to, but our giving should flow from a revelation of God's love for us. I don't want anyone to think I'm saying that Christians are free from the tithe, or that we shouldn't be giving back to the Lord. I'm just saying we need to purify our motives. Actually, I think that if Old Testament believers gave 10 percent, then New Testament saints should be giving at least that much. But we need to learn to give cheerfully.

Since the wrong motivation voids your giving, it's better to give God 1 percent or 2 percent cheerfully than to give 10 percent with the wrong attitude. Let's say you have a hundred seeds. Would it be better to plant ten of those seeds and have nothing grow or to plant one seed that actually produces a crop? It would be better to plant one seed that produces fruit than to plant ten seeds that don't produce anything. The same is true with your giving: It would be better to give a little with the right motivation than to give 10 percent without any benefit. It would also build your faith to see a return come from giving with the right motive. You saw earlier that the Lord talked about this, saying,

> *Bring ye all the tithes into the storehouse, that there may be meat in mine house, and prove me now herewith, saith the LORD of hosts, if I will not open you the windows of heaven, and pour you out a blessing, that there shall not be room enough to receive it.*
>
> MALACHI 3:10

As far as I know, this is the only instance in Scripture where the Lord says "prove Me." Basically, He's saying, "Try it, and see if it doesn't work!" Nearly everything else the Lord said was a command: thou shalt do this, or thou shalt *not* do that. But when it comes to tithing, He said "prove Me." I think He said it this way because He knows it is scary for people to take a portion of what they need to survive and give it away. When you are dependent upon money to pay bills and buy food, it's hard to move your trust over to a God you can't see. God knows that, so He said, "Try Me."

When you first start giving, it might be better for you to give 2 or 5 percent if that is what you can trust God with and do it with joy and peace. If that is what you can give cheerfully, then start there. It's better to give a small percentage cheerfully than to tithe in fear. Ultimately, I think you should be giving more than 10 percent, but you should start where you are comfortable—or where you "purpose in your heart."[2]

I'm not encouraging people who are giving 10 percent to drop down in their giving. I'm just saying that the motive behind your gift is more important than the quantity of the gift. So, if you need to drop back until your faith can build up and you can give 10 percent with a good heart, then do it. But eventually you want to get to where you are thinking, *God, this is Your money. What do You want me to do with it?* It all comes down to the motive of your heart.

Giving out of fear is the same thing as giving **"grudgingly,"** and giving out of manipulation and condemnation is the same as giving **"of necessity."** Giving with those motives profits you nothing. Unfortunately, you sometimes hear ministers at church or on television manipulating people into giving **"of necessity."** I actually heard someone on a television fundraiser say that if anyone gave one thousand dollars within the next ten minutes, then God was going to open up the heavens and pour out all kinds of blessings.

---

[2] See 2 Cor. 9:11

That's not fundraising; it's bribery! Besides, Jesus already opened the heavens for you, and nothing you do changes that. Sure enough, when the ten minutes were up, the television minister said, "I believe the Lord is extending the window another seven minutes." I'm telling you, it would be funny if it wasn't so pathetic how believers are regularly manipulated into giving.

The sad part is that ministers only do that kind of stuff because it works. On the whole, Christians are so immature in financial matters that they will fall for anything. Then the ministers look at the response they get and say, "It worked! Do it again!" They are making hundreds of millions of dollars because believers are giving toward manipulation and thinking they can buy the blessings of God. "You've got to get in on this opportunity to give," they say, "because after five minutes, God is going to cut off His blessings." But the blessings of God don't come with an expiration date.

Christians shouldn't fall for that kind of coercion. The only gift that is acceptable to God is that which you purpose in your own heart and give cheerfully—not grudgingly or of necessity. You aren't going to buy prosperity from God or force Him to bless you—just like you don't need to pay Him protection money to keep the curse of the Law out of your life. All of that stuff is manipulation and condemnation, and giving with those motivations profits you nothing.

When I was eighteen years old, I went to hear a man speak at a Baptist church in Texas. He said, "If you were going to a movie, you'd pay three dollars to get in. I don't want some people giving twenty or fifty dollars in this offering; I just want every person in here to give three dollars." *(Paying three dollars for a movie ticket tells you how long ago this was!)* He said, "I want everybody to get their three dollars and hold it up so I can see. If you don't have three dollars, then borrow it from your neighbor. We're going to wait until everybody has their three dollars up."

I had just gotten really fired up about the Lord at that time in my life, and I was sitting on the front row. I had three dollars in my wallet, too, but I wasn't about to give in response to an offering like that. So, I sat in the front row with my arms folded across my chest, looking the pastor in the eye and thinking, *I dare you to point me out and make an issue of it. Give me an opportunity, and I'll stand up in front of this crowd and rebuke you!* He never did look at me, but he continued to pressure people to hold up their three dollars.

Some people might think I had a bad attitude, but I didn't. I defied him because I think that kind of manipulation is wrong, and every time a person gives in, it's like voting for a politician. He or she gets into power and continues to do what got them there. Well, if people voted for them, then they've got no right to complain about how they operate. They're the ones who empowered them. If the body of Christ would quit giving to ministers who use manipulation, then those ministers would be out of business: they wouldn't be on television, and they wouldn't be in a position to continue manipulating people.

Some of the organizations that use those tactics receive hundreds of millions of dollars every year. They have learned how to influence people into giving them money. It's wrong, but it isn't going to change unless people learn to give with the right motivation. Scripture says that you should be motivated by love in your giving, not guilt. *God loves a cheerful giver!* I encourage you to give and to tithe, but don't do it out of fear or guilt. Do it because you love God, and you want to show your appreciation for all He has done for you. When you purify your motives for tithing and start doing it as you desire in your heart, then you'll begin to see the hundredfold return on your giving—and you'll probably find yourself wanting to give a lot more than 10 percent.

— OUTLINE —

I. I was taught to believe that the tithe is mandatory.[1]

    A. We were told that we owed God a tenth of our income, and if we didn't pay up, we'd be cursed.

    B. Not tithing, we were told, is the same as stealing from God.

    C. Fortunately, none of that is true—God loves us independent of our works, which includes whether or not we tithe.

II. New Testament giving isn't a debt or an obligation.

    A. Scripture says,

> *But this I say, He which soweth sparingly shall reap also sparingly; and he which soweth bountifully shall reap also bountifully. Every man according as he purposeth in his heart, so let him give; not grudgingly, or of necessity: for God loveth a cheerful giver.*
> 2 CORINTHIANS 9:6-7

    B. I don't know how anyone can read these verses and still think you are obligated to tithe.

    C. If the reason you pay a tithe is because you don't want to be under a curse, then you are paying out of necessity.

    D. Under the New Covenant, you should be giving from a cheerful heart.

    E. You should be giving because you want to, not to pay God hush money.

    F. The Apostle Paul ended his teaching on giving by saying,

> *Thanks be unto God for his unspeakable gift.*
> 2 CORINTHIANS 9:15

    G. This summarizes why you should give back to the Lord under the New Covenant: He has already given to you beyond measure.

    H. God has provided everything for you, and your giving is actually an expression of appreciation for all He has done for you.

    I. It goes back to the scripture that says nothing you do is of any benefit unless it is motivated by love (1 Cor. 13:3).

---

[1] Tithe means *a tenth part*, and tithing is the act of giving a tenth of your income back to God.

III. The very first time the tithe was mentioned in Scripture is when Abraham gave tithes to Melchizedek, the king of Salem.

    A. It was the same incident where Abraham refused to keep the king of Sodom's money because he didn't want anyone trying to say they made him rich.

    B. This incident happened more than 400 years before Moses gave the Law to Israel.

    C. We have been redeemed from the curse of the Law and we aren't under the bondage of legalism to tithe, but we should also recognize that tithing was a biblical principle before the Law came along.

    D. Abraham wasn't living under the Law, yet he tithed.

    E. I believe that we are supposed to tithe too.

    F. Actually, I think the tithe is a starting place.

    G. Everything we have under the New Covenant is far superior to the Old Covenant, so I think we should be doing more than what was required under the Law.

IV. Let's look at the classic passage from Malachi that is used to teach on the tithe:

> *Will a man rob God? Yet ye have robbed me. But ye say, Wherein have we robbed thee? In tithes and offerings. Ye are cursed with a curse: for ye have robbed me, even this whole nation. Bring ye all the tithes into the storehouse, that there may be meat in mine house, and prove me now herewith, saith the* Lord *of hosts, if I will not open you the windows of heaven, and pour you out a blessing, that there shall not be room enough to receive it. And I will rebuke the devourer for your sakes, and he shall not destroy the fruits of your ground; neither shall your vine cast her fruit before the time in the field, saith the* Lord *of hosts.*
>
> MALACHI 3:8-11

    A. Nearly everyone who teaches on the tithe cites this passage.

    B. Usually, this passage is used like a club to beat people into submission.

    C. But there is a huge difference between the punishment that came for disobeying the Law under the Old Covenant and the grace that we live under in the New Testament.

    D. We don't tithe in an attempt to keep the Law.

    E. In fact, it would be a bad idea to even try.

> *For as many as are of the works of the law are under the curse: for it is written, Cursed is every one that continueth not in all things which are written in the book of the law to do them.*
>
> GALATIANS 3:10

    F. We are cursed if we don't keep all of the Law, which includes all the commandments and sacrifices.

G. We can't just keep some of it, or do the best we can and God will make up the difference.

H. This is why Jesus came—because we are absolutely incapable of keeping the Law.

I. The people who are trying to say we are cursed if we don't tithe are missing this point.

J. We either trust the grace of God, or we reject Jesus' sacrifice and put our trust in our own works and forfeit God's grace.

K. We have to be 100 percent perfect—never making a single mistake in thought, word, or deed for our entire lives—or we have to humble ourselves and receive the gift of God's grace.

L. Scripture says,

But that no man is justified by the law in the sight of God, it is evident: for, The just shall live by faith. And the law is not of faith: but, The man that doeth them shall live in them. Christ hath redeemed us from the curse of the law, being made a curse for us: for it is written, Cursed is every one that hangeth on a tree: That the blessing of Abraham might come on the Gentiles through Jesus Christ; that we might receive the promise of the Spirit through faith.
GALATIANS 3:11-14

M. This passage couldn't be any clearer.

N. The verse in Malachi says we **"are cursed with a curse"** if we don't tithe—this is exactly what we have been redeemed from.

O. The whole attitude that God is going to punish us for not paying a tithe is completely unscriptural.

P. The church I went to as a child used to say that if people didn't pay their tithes, God would take it from them in doctors' bills.

Q. Under the New Covenant, God doesn't relate to us that way.

R. Trying to pay off God like He's some kind of mobster is the wrong motivation.

S. We're not going to benefit from that kind of giving.

V. It's also worth mentioning that the passage in Malachi 3 says the curse comes for robbing God in tithes *and* offerings.

A. The people who use this verse to teach about tithing from a Law perspective conveniently overlook that you also have to give offerings to keep the Law.

B. I've never personally sat down and figured it out, but I've heard other ministers say that there were so many offerings that all together, the mandatory giving totaled more like 33 percent.

C. So, if you are trying to live by the Law, you are cursed unless you are giving at least 33 percent.

D. It's hypocritical to say you are cursed for not paying tithes and just leave out the offerings.

VI. You can see the natural reasons tithing is beneficial.

   A. God gives you seed, and you have a choice about what to do with that seed.

   B. You can eat all of the seed that God gives you, or you can plant some of it and reap a crop.

   C. Planting seeds ensures a future crop, and tithing moves money into your future—in addition to the eternal benefit.

   D. Money is like seed, and when you consume every dollar that comes your way, you aren't investing in your future.

   E. God loves you if you eat all of your seed, but don't be surprised when the money runs out and you're crying out to Him about not meeting your needs.

   F. It's not His fault you ate all of your seed.

   G. You need to be disciplined enough to take a portion of what God has given you and sow it into your future.

VII. God the Father put all of His wrath on Jesus, so He isn't mad at us for not tithing.

   A. He's not even in a bad mood.

   B. But just because the punishment for not tithing has been taken away, that doesn't mean we should stop giving.

   C. It's similar to how parents teach children to do the right thing by using punishment, or the threat of it, to keep them in line.

   D. Old Testament believers didn't have the capacity to understand why they should or shouldn't do certain things, because the natural mind can't understand the things of God (1 Cor. 2:14).

   E. The people under the Law were spiritually dead, as all people are until they are born again by believing in Jesus.

   F. God couldn't explain to them the spiritual benefits of godly behavior, so, in a sense, He treated them like children and threatened punishment to keep them from hurting themselves.

   G. Even a lost man could understand that it was in his best interests to tithe when the alternative was to be cursed.

H. Now that we are born again and God's Spirit lives in us, He has removed the curse.

I. Now we do what is right out of good hearts and because we understand spiritual things.

J. I give tithes and offerings because it's a way of showing my faith and using the finances God gave me to help build His kingdom.

K. I believe in tithing just like I still look both ways before crossing the street; I just give with a different motivation than they did under the Old Covenant.

VIII. A long time ago, a man heard me preach on how giving out of a sense of obligation profits nothing, and he decided to change how he was giving.

A. He was tithing because he felt obligated to give God 10 percent of his income and still felt like he was always behind financially.

B. So, after hearing me teach, he and his wife decided they were going to start giving as they purposed in their hearts.

C. He stopped calculating his tithe exactly, and they just started giving whatever they wanted.

D. About six months later, he realized that they had more money in the bank than they'd ever had before.

E. His first thought was, *I bet I've decreased my giving.*

F. What he discovered surprised him: He had moved his giving up to 24 percent of his income.

G. He was giving more than twice as much as he ever had, yet he was more prosperous than ever—because God was prospering him supernaturally.

IX. When you give grudgingly or of necessity, you get zero benefit from that kind of giving.

A. It isn't going to come back to you or influence your future.

B. Scripture says **"Give, and it shall be given unto you; good measure, pressed down, and shaken together, and running over, shall men give into your bosom. For with the same measure that ye mete withal it shall be measured to you again"** (Luke 6:38), but if that was all there was to prosperity, then nearly every Christian would be prosperous.

C. If all people had to do was give and—*boom*—it came back to them a hundredfold, then every church would be packed full of millionaires.

D. So, why hasn't every believer seen that kind of return?

E. Because the motive behind the gift is more important than the gift itself.

F. You have to plant your financial seed with a cheerful heart, motivated by love, because your gift is ruined when you give with the wrong motive.

G. Let's say you have a hundred seeds.

H. It would be better to plant one seed that produces fruit than to plant ten seeds that don't produce anything.

I. The same is true with your giving: It would be better to give a little with the right motivation than to give 10 percent without any benefit.

J. It would also build your faith to see a return come from giving with the right motive.

X. Read what the Lord said in Malachi 3:10 again:

Bring ye all the tithes into the storehouse, that there may be meat in mine house, and prove me now herewith, saith the LORD of hosts, if I will not open you the windows of heaven, and pour you out a blessing, that there shall not be room enough to receive it.

A. As far as I know, this is the only instance in Scripture where the Lord says "prove Me."

B. Basically, He's saying, "Try it, and see if it doesn't work!"

C. I think He said it this way because He knows it is scary for people to take a portion of what they need to survive and give it away.

D. When you are dependent upon money to pay bills and buy food, it's hard to move your trust over to a God you can't see.

E. God knows that, so He said, "Try Me."

XI. When you first start giving, it might be better for you to give 2 or 5 percent if that is what you can trust God with and do it with joy and peace.

A. If that is what you can give cheerfully, then start there.

B. You should start where you are comfortable—or where you "purpose in your heart."

C. I'm not encouraging people who are giving 10 percent to drop down in their giving.

D. If you need to drop back until your faith can build up and you can give 10 percent with a good heart, then do it.

E. But eventually you want to get to where you are thinking, *God, this is Your money. What do You want me to do with it?*

XII. Giving out of fear is the same thing as giving **"grudgingly,"** and giving out of manipulation and condemnation is the same as giving **"of necessity."**

A. Unfortunately, you sometimes hear ministers at church or on television manipulating people into giving **"of necessity."**

B. I actually heard someone on a television fundraiser say that if anyone gave one thousand dollars within the next ten minutes, then God was going to open up the heavens and pour out all kinds of blessings.

C. When the ten minutes were up, the television minister said, "I believe the Lord is extending the window another seven minutes."

D. I'm telling you, it would be funny if it wasn't so pathetic how believers are regularly manipulated into giving.

E. The sad part is that ministers only do that kind of stuff because it works.

F. "You've got to get in on this opportunity to give," they say, "because after five minutes, God is going to cut off His blessings."

G. But the blessings of God don't come with an expiration date.

H. The only gift that is acceptable to God is that which you purpose in your own heart and give cheerfully—not grudgingly or of necessity.

I. You aren't going to buy prosperity from God or force Him to bless you.

J. All of that stuff is manipulation and condemnation, and giving with those motivations profits you nothing.

XIII. When I was eighteen years old, I went to hear a man speak at a Baptist church in Texas.

A. He said, "If you were going to a movie, you'd pay three dollars to get in. I don't want some people giving twenty or fifty dollars in this offering; I just want every person in here to get three dollars and hold it up so I can see. If you don't have three dollars, then borrow it from your neighbor."

B. I had just gotten really fired up about the Lord at that time in my life, and I was sitting on the front row.

C. I had three dollars in my wallet, too, but I wasn't about to give in response to an offering like that.

D. So, I sat in the front row with my arms folded across my chest, looking the pastor in the eye and thinking, *I dare you to point me out and make an issue of it. Give me an opportunity, and I'll stand up in front of this crowd and rebuke you!*

E. He never did look at me, but he continued to pressure people to hold up their three dollars.

XIV. Some people might think I had a bad attitude, but I didn't.

A. I defied him because I think that kind of manipulation is wrong.

B. If the body of Christ would quit giving to ministers who use manipulation, then those ministers would be out of business: they wouldn't be on television, and they wouldn't be in a position to continue manipulating people.

C. It isn't going to change unless people learn to give with the right motivation.

D. *God loves a cheerful giver!*

E. I encourage you to give and to tithe, but don't do it out of fear or guilt.

F. Do it because you love God, and you want to show your appreciation for all He has done for you.

G. When you purify your motives for tithing and start doing it as you desire in your heart, then you'll begin to see the hundredfold return on your giving—and you'll probably find yourself wanting to give a lot more than 10 percent.

TEACHER'S GUIDE

1. I was taught to believe that the tithe is mandatory. We were told that we owed God a tenth of our income, and if we didn't pay up, we'd be cursed. Not tithing, we were told, is the same as stealing from God. Fortunately, none of that is true—God loves us independent of our works, which includes whether or not we tithe.

    1a. What is a tithe?
        A. An offering prescribed by the Law
        B. A mandatory payment of money to your church
        C. A tenth part
        D. All of the above
        E. None of the above
    1b. True or false: Not tithing is stealing from God.
        False

2. New Testament giving isn't a debt or an obligation. Scripture says,

> *But this I say, He which soweth sparingly shall reap also sparingly; and he which soweth bountifully shall reap also bountifully. Every man according as he purposeth in his heart, so let him give; not grudgingly, or of necessity: for God loveth a cheerful giver.*
>
> 2 CORINTHIANS 9:6-7

I don't know how anyone can read these verses and still think you are obligated to tithe. If the reason you pay a tithe is because you don't want to be under a curse, then you are paying out of necessity. Under the New Covenant, you should be giving from a cheerful heart. You should be giving because you want to, not to pay God hush money. The Apostle Paul ended his teaching on giving by saying,

> *Thanks be unto God for his unspeakable gift.*
>
> 2 CORINTHIANS 9:15

This summarizes why you should give back to the Lord under the New Covenant: He has already given to you beyond measure. God has provided everything for you, and your giving is actually an expression of appreciation for all He has done for you. It goes back to the scripture that says nothing you do is of any benefit unless it is motivated by love (1 Cor. 13:3).

    2a. Read 2 Corinthians 9:6-7. How does this passage say you should give?
        As you purpose in your heart, not grudgingly or of necessity
    2b. Read 2 Corinthians 9:15. Why should you give back to the Lord under the New Covenant?
        Because He has already given to you beyond measure

3. The very first time the tithe was mentioned in Scripture is when Abraham gave tithes to Melchizedek, the king of Salem. It was the same incident where Abraham refused to keep the king of Sodom's money because he didn't want anyone trying to say they made him rich. This incident happened more than 400 years before Moses gave the Law to Israel. We have been redeemed from the curse of the Law and we aren't under the bondage of legalism to tithe, but we should also recognize that tithing was a biblical principle before the Law came along. Abraham wasn't living under the Law, yet he tithed. I believe that we are supposed to tithe too. Actually, I think the tithe is a starting place. Everything we have under the New Covenant is far superior to the Old Covenant, so I think we should be doing more than what was required under the Law.

    3a. How do you know that the tithe was instituted before the Law?
        Because Abraham gave a tithe to Melchizedek 400 years before the Law was given
    3b. True or false: Tithing is a starting place.
        True

4. Let's look at the classic passage from Malachi that is used to teach on the tithe:

> *Will a man rob God? Yet ye have robbed me. But ye say, Wherein have*
> *we robbed thee? In tithes and offerings. Ye are cursed with a curse: for ye*
> *have robbed me, even this whole nation. Bring ye all the tithes into the*
> *storehouse, that there may be meat in mine house, and prove me now*
> *herewith, saith the LORD of hosts, if I will not open you the windows of*
> *heaven, and pour you out a blessing, that there shall not be room enough*
> *to receive it. And I will rebuke the devourer for your sakes, and he shall*
> *not destroy the fruits of your ground; neither shall your vine cast her fruit*
> *before the time in the field, saith the LORD of hosts.*
>
> MALACHI 3:8-11

Nearly everyone who teaches on the tithe cites this passage. Usually, this passage is used like a club to beat people into submission. But there is a huge difference between the punishment that came for disobeying the Law under the Old Covenant and the grace that we live under in the New Testament. We don't tithe in an attempt to keep the Law. In fact, it would be a bad idea to even try.

> *For as many as are of the works of the law are under the curse: for it is*
> *written, Cursed is every one that continueth not in all things which are*
> *written in the book of the law to do them.*
>
> GALATIANS 3:10

We are cursed if we don't keep all of the Law, which includes all the commandments and sacrifices. We can't just keep some of it, or do the best we can and God will make up the difference. This is why Jesus came—because we are absolutely incapable of keeping the Law. The people who are trying to say we are cursed if we don't tithe are missing this point. We either trust the grace of God, or we reject Jesus' sacrifice and put our trust in our own works and forfeit God's grace. We have to be 100 percent perfect—never making a single mistake in thought, word, or deed for our entire lives—or we have to humble ourselves and receive the gift of God's grace. Scripture says,

> *But that no man is justified by the law in the sight of God, it is evident: for,*
> *The just shall live by faith. And the law is not of faith: but, The man that*
> *doeth them shall live in them. Christ hath redeemed us from the curse of*
> *the law, being made a curse for us: for it is written, Cursed is every one that*
> *hangeth on a tree: That the blessing of Abraham might come on the Gentiles*
> *through Jesus Christ; that we might receive the promise of the Spirit*
> *through faith.*
>
> GALATIANS 3:11-14

This passage couldn't be any clearer. The verse in Malachi says we **"are cursed with a curse"** if we don't tithe—this is exactly what we have been redeemed from. The whole attitude that God is going to punish us for not paying a tithe is completely unscriptural. The church I went to as a child used to say that if people didn't pay their tithes, God would take it from them in doctors' bills. Under the New Covenant, God doesn't relate to us that way. Trying to pay off God like He's some kind of mobster is the wrong motivation. We're not going to benefit from that kind of giving.

4a. Read Galatians 3:10. Why is it a bad idea to tithe in order to keep the Law?
Because if you tithe according to the Law, you are obligated to keep all of the Law as well, which includes all the commandments and sacrifices

4b. According to Galatians 3:11-14, who can be justified by the Law?
No one

4c. If you try to live by the Law and fail, what are you?
Cursed

5. It's also worth mentioning that the passage in Malachi 3 says the curse comes for robbing God in tithes *and* offerings. The people who use this verse to teach about tithing from a Law perspective conveniently overlook that you also have to give offerings to keep the Law. I've never personally sat down and figured it out, but I've heard other ministers say that there were so many offerings that all together, the mandatory giving totaled more like 33 percent. So, if you are trying to live by the Law, you are cursed unless you are giving at least 33 percent. It's hypocritical to say you are cursed for not paying tithes and just leave out the offerings.

    5a. According to Malachi 3, the curse comes from robbing God in tithes *and* _____ .
        Offerings

6. You can see the natural reasons tithing is beneficial. God gives you seed, and you have a choice about what to do with that seed. You can eat all of the seed that God gives you, or you can plant some of it and reap a crop. Planting seeds ensures a future crop, and tithing moves money into your future—in addition to the eternal benefit. Money is like seed, and when you consume every dollar that comes your way, you aren't investing in your future. God loves you if you eat all of your seed, but don't be surprised when the money runs out and you're crying out to Him about not meeting your needs. It's not His fault you ate all of your seed. You need to be disciplined enough to take a portion of what God has given you and sow it into your future.

    6a. Tithing moves money into your future but also has what?
        An eternal benefit
    6b. What is money like?
        Seed
    6c. Why shouldn't you consume all of your money?
        Because you aren't investing in your future if you do
    6d. How does God view you even if you eat all of your seed?
        He loves you

7. God the Father put all of His wrath on Jesus, so He isn't mad at us for not tithing. He's not even in a bad mood. But just because the punishment for not tithing has been taken away, that doesn't mean we should stop giving. It's similar to how parents teach children to do the right thing by using punishment, or the threat of it, to keep them in line. Old Testament believers didn't have the capacity to understand why they should or shouldn't do certain things, because the natural mind can't understand the things of God (1 Cor. 2:14). The people under the Law were spiritually dead, as all people are until they are born again by believing in Jesus. God couldn't explain to them the spiritual benefits of godly behavior, so, in a sense, He treated them like children and threatened punishment to keep them from hurting themselves. Even a lost man could understand that it was in his best interests to tithe when the alternative was to be cursed. Now that we are born again and God's Spirit lives in us, He has removed the curse. Now we do what is right out of good hearts and because we understand spiritual things. I give tithes and offerings because it's a way of showing my faith and using the finances God gave me to help build His kingdom. I believe in tithing just like I still look both ways before crossing the street; I just give with a different motivation than they did under the Old Covenant.

7a. Under the Old Covenant, the penalty for not tithing is similar to what?
   To how parents teach children to do the right thing by using punishment, or the threat of it, to keep them in line
7b. Why did God treat people in the Old Covenant like children, in a sense, and threaten punishment to keep them from hurting themselves?
   A. Because the people didn't know any better
   B. Because that was better than just destroying them all
   C. Because He found that they responded better to that kind of treatment
   D. Because He couldn't explain to them the spiritual benefits of godly behavior
   E. Because it was either that or let them bite and devour each other until they were consumed
7c. This could even be understood by whom?
   A lost man
7d. Why don't New Testament born-again believers need threats and punishments to live by the Law?
   Because they do what is right out of good hearts and because they understand spiritual things

8. A long time ago, a man heard me preach on how giving out of a sense of obligation profits nothing, and he decided to change how he was giving. He was tithing because he felt obligated to give God 10 percent of his income and still felt like he was always behind financially. So, after hearing me teach, he and his wife decided they were going to start giving as they purposed in their hearts. He stopped calculating his tithe exactly, and they just started giving whatever they wanted. About six months later, he realized that they had more money in the bank than they'd ever had before. His first thought was, *I bet I've decreased my giving*. What he discovered surprised him: He had moved his giving up to 24 percent of his income. He was giving more than twice as much as he ever had, yet he was more prosperous than ever—because God was prospering him supernaturally.

9. When you give grudgingly or of necessity, you get zero benefit from that kind of giving. It isn't going to come back to you or influence your future. Scripture says **"Give, and it shall be given unto you; good measure, pressed down, and shaken together, and running over, shall men give into your bosom. For with the same measure that ye mete withal it shall be measured to you again"** (Luke 6:38), but if that was all there was to prosperity, then nearly every Christian would be prosperous. If all people had to do was give and—*boom*—it came back to them a hundredfold, then every church would be packed full of millionaires. So, why hasn't every believer seen that kind of return? Because the motive behind the gift is more important than the gift itself. You have to plant your financial seed with a cheerful heart, motivated by love, because your gift is ruined when you give with the wrong motive. Let's say you have a hundred seeds. It would be better to plant one seed that produces fruit than to plant ten seeds that don't produce anything. The same is true with your giving: It would be better to give a little with the right motivation than to give 10 percent without any benefit. It would also build your faith to see a return come from giving with the right motive.

    9a. What do you get from giving grudgingly or of necessity?
       Zero benefit
    9b. It would be better to give a _____ with the right motivation than to give 10 percent without any benefit.
       Little

10. Read what the Lord said in Malachi 3:10 again:

> *Bring ye all the tithes into the storehouse, that there may be meat in mine house, and prove me now herewith, saith the LORD of hosts, if I will not open you the windows of heaven, and pour you out a blessing, that there shall not be room enough to receive it.*

As far as I know, this is the only instance in Scripture where the Lord says "prove Me." Basically, He's saying, "Try it, and see if it doesn't work!" I think He said it this way because He knows it is scary for people to take a portion of what they need to survive and give it away. When you are dependent upon money to pay bills and buy food, it's hard to move your trust over to a God you can't see. God knows that, so He said, "Try Me."

    10a. Read Malachi 3:10. What will happen when you prove (try) Him?
       He will open the windows of heaven to you and pour out a blessing on you that you won't have room to receive

11. When you first start giving, it might be better for you to give 2 or 5 percent if that is what you can trust God with and do it with joy and peace. If that is what you can give cheerfully, then start there. You should start where you are comfortable—or where you "purpose in your heart." I'm not encouraging people who are giving 10 percent to drop down in their giving. If you need to drop back until your faith can build up and you can give 10 percent with a good heart, then do it. But eventually you want to get to where you are thinking, *God, this is Your money. What do You want me to do with it?*

   11a.   Should you give a minimum of 10 percent of your income whether you want to or not?
       <u>No, you should start where you are comfortable—or where you "purpose in your heart"</u>
   11b.   Eventually you want to think what?
       <u>God, this is Your money. What do You want me to do with it?</u>

12. Giving out of fear is the same thing as giving **"grudgingly,"** and giving out of manipulation and condemnation is the same as giving **"of necessity."** Unfortunately, you sometimes hear ministers at church or on television manipulating people into giving **"of necessity."** I actually heard someone on a television fundraiser say that if anyone gave one thousand dollars within the next ten minutes, then God was going to open up the heavens and pour out all kinds of blessings. When the ten minutes were up, the television minister said, "I believe the Lord is extending the window another seven minutes." I'm telling you, it would be funny if it wasn't so pathetic how believers are regularly manipulated into giving. The sad part is that ministers only do that kind of stuff because it works. "You've got to get in on this opportunity to give," they say, "because after five minutes, God is going to cut off His blessings." But the blessings of God don't come with an expiration date. The only gift that is acceptable to God is that which you purpose in your own heart and give cheerfully—not grudgingly or of necessity. You aren't going to buy prosperity from God or force Him to bless you. All of that stuff is manipulation and condemnation, and giving with those motivations profits you nothing.

   12a.   True or false: With your giving, you can buy prosperity from God.
       <u>False</u>

13. When I was eighteen years old, I went to hear a man speak at a Baptist church in Texas. He said, "If you were going to a movie, you'd pay three dollars to get in. I don't want some people giving twenty or fifty dollars in this offering; I just want every person in here to get three dollars and hold it up so I can see. If you don't have three dollars, then borrow it from your neighbor." I had just gotten really fired up about the Lord at that time in my life, and I was sitting on the front row. I had three dollars in my wallet, too, but I wasn't about to give in response to an offering like that. So, I sat in the front row with my arms folded across my chest, looking the pastor in the eye and thinking, *I dare you to point me out and make an issue of it. Give me an opportunity, and I'll stand up in front of this crowd and rebuke you!* He never did look at me, but he continued to pressure people to hold up their three dollars.

14. Some people might think I had a bad attitude, but I didn't. I defied him because I think that kind of manipulation is wrong. If the body of Christ would quit giving to ministers who use manipulation, then those ministers would be out of business: they wouldn't be on television, and they wouldn't be in a position to continue manipulating people. It isn't going to change unless people learn to give with the right motivation. *God loves a cheerful giver!* I encourage you to give and to tithe, but don't do it out of fear or guilt. Do it because you love God, and you want to show your appreciation for all He has done for you. When you purify your motives for tithing and start doing it as you desire in your heart, then you'll begin to see the hundredfold return on your giving—and you'll probably find yourself wanting to give a lot more than 10 percent.

14a. What would happen if the body of Christ quit giving to ministers who use manipulation?
They would be out of business: they wouldn't be on television, and they wouldn't be in a position to continue manipulating people

14b. If you love God and want to show your appreciation for all He has done for you, what should you do?
A. Make a vow to Him
B. Give and tithe
C. Honor Him with your lips
D. All of the above
E. None of the above

14c. You'll begin to see the hundredfold return on your giving—and you'll probably find yourself wanting to give a lot more than 10 percent—when you what?
Purify your motives for tithing and start doing it as you desire in your heart

DISCIPLESHIP
── QUESTIONS ──

1. What is a tithe?
   A. An offering prescribed by the Law
   B. A mandatory payment of money to your church
   C. A tenth part
   D. All of the above
   E. None of the above

2. True or false: Not tithing is stealing from God.

3. Read 2 Corinthians 9:6-7. How does this passage say you should give?

4. Read 2 Corinthians 9:15. Why should you give back to the Lord under the New Covenant?

5. How do you know that the tithe was instituted before the Law?

6. True or false: Tithing is a starting place.

7. Read Galatians 3:10. Why is it a bad idea to tithe in order to keep the Law?

8. According to Galatians 3:11-14, who can be justified by the Law?

9. If you try to live by the Law and fail, what are you?

_____

_____

_____

10. According to Malachi 3, the curse comes from robbing God in tithes *and*

_____ .

11. Tithing moves money into your future but also has what?

_____

_____

_____

12. What is money like?

_____

_____

_____

13. Why shouldn't you consume all of your money?

_____

_____

_____

14. How does God view you even if you eat all of your seed?

_____

_____

_____

15. Under the Old Covenant, the penalty for not tithing is similar to what?

_____

_____

_____

16. Why did God treat people in the Old Covenant like children, in a sense, and threaten punishment to keep them from hurting themselves?
    A. Because the people didn't know any better
    B. Because that was better than just destroying them all
    C. Because He found that they responded better to that kind of treatment
    D. Because He couldn't explain to them the spiritual benefits of godly behavior
    E. Because it was either that or let them bite and devour each other until they were consumed

17. This could even be understood by whom?

_____
_____
_____

18. Why don't New Testament born-again believers need threats and punishments to live by the Law?

_____
_____
_____

19. What do you get from giving grudgingly or of necessity?

_____
_____
_____

20. It would be better to give a _____ with the right motivation than to give 10 percent without any benefit.

21. Read Malachi 3:10. What will happen when you prove (try) Him?

_____
_____
_____

22. Should you give a minimum of 10 percent of your income whether you want to or not?

_____
_____
_____

23. Eventually you want to think what?

_____
_____
_____

24. True or false: With your giving, you can buy prosperity from God.

25. What would happen if the body of Christ quit giving to ministers who use manipulation?

_____
_____
_____

26. If you love God and want to show your appreciation for all He has done for you, what should you do?
    A. Make a vow to Him
    B. Give and tithe
    C. Honor Him with your lips
    D. All of the above
    E. None of the above

27. You'll begin to see the hundredfold return on your giving—and you'll probably find yourself wanting to give a lot more than 10 percent—when you what?

    _____

    _____

    _____

ANSWER
—KEY—

1. C. A tenth part

2. False

3. As you purpose in your heart, not grudgingly or of necessity

4. Because He has already given to you beyond measure

5. Because Abraham gave a tithe to Melchizedek 400 years before the Law was given

6. True

7. Because if you tithe according to the Law, you are obligated to keep all of the Law as well, which includes all the commandments and sacrifices

8. No one

9. Cursed

10. Offerings

11. An eternal benefit

12. Seed

13. Because you aren't investing in your future if you do

14. He loves you

15. To how parents teach children to do the right thing by using punishment, or the threat of it, to keep them in line

16. D. Because He couldn't explain to them the spiritual benefits of godly behavior

17. A lost man

18. Because they do what is right out of good hearts and because they understand spiritual things

19. Zero benefit

20. Little

21. He will open the windows of heaven to you and pour out a blessing on you that you won't have room to receive

22. No, you should start where you are comfortable—or where you "purpose in your heart"

23. *God, this is Your money. What do You want me to do with it?*

24. False

25. They would be out of business: they wouldn't be on television, and they wouldn't be in a position to continue manipulating people

26. B. Give and tithe

27. Purify your motives for tithing and start doing it as you desire in your heart

——SCRIPTURES——

2 CORINTHIANS 9:6-7

But this I say, He which soweth sparingly shall reap also sparingly; and he which soweth bountifully shall reap also bountifully. [7] Every man according as he purposeth in his heart, so let him give; not grudgingly, or of necessity: for God loveth a cheerful giver.

2 CORINTHIANS 9:15

Thanks be unto God for his unspeakable gift.

1 CORINTHIANS 13:3

And though I bestow all my goods to feed the poor, and though I give my body to be burned, and have not charity, it profiteth me nothing.

MALACHI 3:8-11

Will a man rob God? Yet ye have robbed me. But ye say, Wherein have we robbed thee? In tithes and offerings. [9] Ye are cursed with a curse: for ye have robbed me, even this whole nation. [10] Bring ye all the tithes into the storehouse, that there may be meat in mine house, and prove me now herewith, saith the Lord of hosts, if I will not open you the windows of heaven, and pour you out a blessing, that there shall not be room enough to receive it. [11] And I will rebuke the devourer for your sakes, and he shall not destroy the fruits of your ground; neither shall your vine cast her fruit before the time in the field, saith the Lord of hosts.

GALATIANS 3:10-14

For as many as are of the works of the law are under the curse: for it is written, Cursed is every one that continueth not in all things which are written in the book of the law to do them. [11] But that no man is justified by the law in the sight of God, it is evident: for, The just shall live by faith. [12] And the law is not of faith: but, The man that doeth them shall live in them. [13] Christ hath redeemed us from the curse of the law, being made a curse for us: for it is written, Cursed is every one that hangeth on a tree: [14] That the blessing of Abraham might come on the Gentiles through Jesus Christ; that we might receive the promise of the Spirit through faith.

1 CORINTHIANS 2:14

But the natural man receiveth not the things of the Spirit of God: for they are foolishness unto him: neither can he know them, because they are spiritually discerned.

LUKE 6:38

Give, and it shall be given unto you; good measure, pressed down, and shaken together, and running over, shall men give into your bosom. For with the same measure that ye mete withal it shall be measured to you again.

2 CORINTHIANS 9:11

Being enriched in every thing to all bountifulness, which causeth through us thanksgiving to God.

GIVE WHERE YOU'RE FED

A lot of people are confused about where they should give their tithes and offerings, or how the money they give should be used. Scripture says, **"Bring ye all the tithes into the storehouse"** (Mal. 3:10). In the Old Testament, the tithe was given toward the work of God. It was either given to a priest who offered the sacrifices, or it was brought directly to the temple (for those who lived in Jerusalem). There were other offerings the people had to pay for, but the tithe went directly to the ministers. That was how God supported the ministers who were doing His work.

Most pastors teach that the storehouse is your local church and that parachurch and other social-welfare ministries are meant to be supported by offerings above the tithe. In a perfect world, I'd have to agree with that, but this isn't a perfect world. Technically, a storehouse is where you put your food. In Old Testament times, it was where they would hang meat and store grain, and when they got hungry, they would go there to get something to eat. You could say that a storehouse is where you get fed—so you should be giving your tithe where you get fed, and that may not be your local church.

However, you should recognize that a good church does more than just teach the Word. It fosters community and is an important part of spiritual growth. You need the maturity that comes through fellowshipping with other believers. A good local church helps you raise your children and gives them a place to meet other Christian kids. It offers one-on-one counseling and marriage counseling. Your local pastor helps you deal with grief and get through hard times.

A good local church does a lot of things that a television minister can't do for you. You can't call me in the middle of the night when tragedy strikes. You can't meet at my house and fellowship with other believers, and I can't bring you food when a loved one dies. So, if you are in a good local church that is preaching the Word, helping widows and orphans, and doing what a godly church is supposed to do, then you should be tithing at your church—no question about it.

Unfortunately, I don't believe most churches are teaching about the grace of God and preaching the true Gospel. The most common question I get is from people who are looking for a church that is teaching about the love of God and the finished work of Jesus. From what I can tell, I would say that the majority of believers are not in churches that are truly preaching the Word of God. Many people are going to churches they know aren't good, but they go there out of a sense of obligation or because there are no other options. Maybe their whole family goes there, or it's the one they've always gone to and don't want to change where they go.

In fact, many people are going to churches that preach things completely contrary to the Gospel message. They leave church feeling condemned and beat up—the exact opposite of what a church is supposed to do. It would be wrong for me to tell you to put your tithes into the local church and not qualify that by saying a *good* local church—one that is meeting the needs of its members.

It matters where you plant your seed. Some people think that God sees their hearts when they give, and they reap a benefit from their giving regardless of what the church does with their money—but that's not true. You'd be a very poor farmer with that kind of attitude. You can't expect the same results from casting your seed on pavement that you would get from planting it in fertile soil. In addition, every time you give to a church or minister, you are casting a vote in support of how they conduct themselves. Every time you give money to a church, you are helping support what they do—whether it's good or bad—so it absolutely matters where you give your money.

I'm not saying the church has to be perfect—no church is. Maybe your church isn't hitting on all cylinders, but they are preaching the Truth and being a light to the community. In that case, I would recommend giving your tithe there because you need what a local church offers. But if you feel worse after you go to church than you did when you went in or the church is supporting causes that are contrary to the Word or not doing anything in the community, then you shouldn't be subsidizing that with your giving.

WHERE YOU GIVE YOUR MONEY IS IMPORTANT.

Scripture says to bring the tithes into the storehouse, so you should be giving where you get fed. It's wrong to put your money into something that you don't agree with and then go get fed by ministries you don't support financially. That's like eating at McDonald's and going across the street to Wendy's to pay for your meal. No, you pay your bill where you ate—and you should give your tithe where you get fed. If you aren't being fed at your church, then you shouldn't be tithing there.

I travel a lot. It's not uncommon for me to be out of town three Sundays every month. So, I'm not at my local church every weekend. I give to the local church when I'm there, but I don't give an exact tithe of my income, because I may only be there six or seven times in an entire year. I don't get fed by my church much and my kids are grown, so we spread our giving around. I give God well more than 10 percent of my income, but I split my tithing and giving among my church and the other ministries that feed me.

You also need to keep in mind that giving where you are fed can't be the only criteria for your giving. If that was the only reason for giving, then missionaries who work in faraway countries wouldn't have any income, and no one would be helping widows and orphans. The people that missionaries help are often impoverished and unable to support them. Missionaries need financial partners who will help them spread the Gospel but who don't directly benefit from their ministries. So, giving where you are fed isn't the only guideline for tithing, but I believe it should be the primary one.

Your tithe, or at least a portion of it, should be going to the ministry that is feeding you. Widows and orphans may not minister to you, but it is a godly thing to give and support them. That falls under what is called benevolence giving. There is also giving that goes toward missionary work. So, not all of your giving should go to where you are being fed, but the bulk of it should.

A good local church will feed us in ways that no other ministry can. The body of Christ is dependent upon the local church. If we didn't have local churches to meet our needs and we were solely dependent upon television preachers (of which I'm one), then the body of Christ would be in a crisis situation. The local church is the backbone of the body, and it's best for us to be in good local churches where we can give our tithes—but we shouldn't put our tithes into dead churches.

In the first place, if you are in a dead church, then get out! Go find yourself a church that is preaching the Gospel, and then give your tithe to that church, and use offerings to support other parts of the body of Christ. Maybe you live in a rural area with limited options or your spouse will only go to one certain church or something else keeps you tied to a church that isn't preaching the Gospel. If, for some reason, you can't find a good local church or get out of the dead one you're in, then, at a minimum, you shouldn't give all of your money there. The best option is to get out of the dead church, but if you can't—or won't—do that, then you should at least split your tithe.

This principle of giving where you are fed is really simple, and it would solve a lot of problems if believers followed it. The preachers who are lying and manipulating people in order to get their money are not truly feeding the body of Christ. They would go out of business if people would just stop giving them money. They'd have to come up with some other con and move on with their lives. Then only the people who are really feeding Christians would be getting all of the resources, and the believers would have an abundance of finances. The good churches wouldn't have to hold car washes and bake sales to raise money.

YOUR RETURN IS GOING TO DEPEND TO A DEGREE ON HOW FRUITFUL THE GROUND IS THAT YOU ARE SOWING INTO.

Our television show has the potential of reaching three billion people on a daily basis. I don't know what percentage of that potential actually watches, but let's just say it's 1 percent, which is thirty million people. If thirty million people were being encouraged and built up in the Word by our ministry and they started sending us money because we are feeding them, I'm not sure we'd know what to do with it all. Yet only a very small percentage of our viewers gives to the ministry. I'm sure there are lots of people who are getting fed by us, but they are giving their money elsewhere because they don't know this simple principle of giving where they are fed.

Giving where you are fed makes a difference for you too. The return on your giving is going to depend to a degree on how fruitful the ground is that you are sowing into, just like there is a difference between planting in dirt and concrete. If you give to a church or ministry that isn't really accomplishing the Lord's work, then you are going to get marginal returns. When you plant your seed in a place that is fruitful and ministering the Word of God, then you are going to receive a better return. Don't give where you are begged or pressured, or where you've always given—give where you are fed. Bring the tithes into the storehouse! Wherever you get your food from is where you should be giving. It's that simple.

Quit giving where you are coerced, intimidated, and condemned. I actually had a woman come to me one time with a personalized letter that said, *Dear Stella*—or whatever her name was—*God woke me up at three o'clock this morning and gave me your name and told me to tell you that if you send me a thousand dollars, then all of the people you have been praying for will get saved.* The letter went on to promise healing, prosperity, and deliverance if she would just send in some money.

She was a poor woman, and she told me that she could scrape together the thousand dollars, but she wasn't really sure she should give it. On the other hand, she felt compelled to because the letter was personalized, and the minister claimed God had woken him at three in the morning with a special message for her. She said, "What should I do?" I just took the letter and tore it up. I had to explain that the exact same computer-generated letter was probably sent to thousands of people. But the reason crooks send those kinds of letters is because Christians actually send money in response.

I hate to say it, but I believe the majority of giving in the body of Christ is in response to begging or some sort of emotional coercion. Some preachers are raising a lot of money by manipulating people and doing all kinds of ungodly things, and it bothers me that Christians respond to that. The body of Christ is empowering those preachers and perpetuating all of that manipulation by giving money to support it. It's possible that some good could come out of that kind of giving because God can use anything, but those practices are wrong. If we would learn the biblical guidelines for when and why to give, then we would starve out the charlatans. The people who are truly preaching the Word of God would have such an abundance that they would never have to mention money again.

Giving out of desperation because somebody said that God would supply your needs is an ungodly principle. In a sense, it's like trying to buy a miracle. As a matter of fact, the book of Acts tells a story about a man named Simon who tried to do that very thing. Simon had been a magician in Samaria, but he was born again when he heard Philip preach the Gospel. Later, Peter and John went down to Samaria and prayed for people to receive the Holy Spirit. Simon saw that people were receiving the gift of speaking in tongues when Peter and John laid hands on them. Simon also wanted to be able lay hands on people and have them receive the Holy Spirit, so he offered Peter money to give him the same gift. On the surface, that seems like a good desire, but Peter responded differently:

*Thy money perish with thee, because thou hast thought that the gift of
God may be purchased with money. Thou hast neither part nor lot in this
matter: for thy heart is not right in the sight of God… For I perceive that
thou art in the gall of bitterness, and in the bond of iniquity.*

ACTS 8:20-21 AND 23

I'm not sure whether being **"in the gall of bitterness, and in the bond of iniquity"** means
that Simon was never really born again or whether his heart was just wrong, but it's not good
either way. Simon thought he could buy God's anointing by giving Peter money, and Peter
rebuked him. This shows that your heart is not right if you are trying to buy God's blessings.
At the same time, it's possible to be in the process of believing God for a miracle, and it may
be that letting go of some of your money could be a step of faith for you. See, it isn't giving
money that makes the miracle happen—it's stepping out in faith.

A lot of people only give when they're begged—partly because that's what they've been
taught. When Jamie and I first moved to Colorado Springs, a man gave our ministry a
building and then came to work for us for about six months. Back then, we used to send out
teachings on cassette tape. He noticed that for a couple of weeks at a time, we couldn't fill
orders for tapes. It was because we'd run out of money and had to wait a week or two until
we had enough to get in another shipment of blank tapes. Then we would duplicate more
teachings and start filling orders again.

When he saw what was going on, he asked me why I wasn't telling people how desperate
the ministry was for additional finances. He told me he had given away twenty-five thousand
dollars the previous year, and he always asked God where to send the money before he gave.
He said I was the first person who came to mind every time he prayed, because our ministry
had helped him transform his life, but he didn't give to us, because I never asked. Do you
know who he gave to? He gave to a television minister who was always begging for money and
telling people he was going to go off the air if they didn't give!

I was invited to be a guest on that same minister's network much later, and the head of his
ministry showed me a room filled with hundreds of thousands of letters stuffed and sealed in
envelopes. All they had to do was slap a stamp and an address on the envelopes and mail them
out. The letters talked about a pending financial crisis if people didn't give. They sent out those
letters at six-month intervals and had printed them out for two years in advance. *They didn't
even have a crisis yet!* It was all lies and manipulation. They begged and people gave.

We're not supposed to give where we are begged—we're supposed to give as we purpose in
our own hearts. Not just that, but we're supposed to give where we are fed. The people who are
using manipulation are not truly in tune with God. I'm not saying they aren't born again, but
I'm saying they are carnal. Those people aren't really feeding the body of Christ. If we'd stop
giving to them, they would go away.

I had a publicity group come to me one time and guarantee that they could raise a million dollars by sending out letters for us. It was back when our income was about eighty thousand dollars a month, and we needed the extra income, so I told them I would fly them out and meet with them. They started by telling me about the color ink that people respond to, the font we should use, and how to underline certain statements. They had the whole business down to a science. They also told me how they had raised another client twenty million dollars using the same techniques just a couple of months before.

I said, "Well, we could sure use twenty million dollars. But what are you going to say? What are you going to do?"

They said, "Just leave that up to us."

"No," I said, "I need to know what you are going to say."

So, they started telling me how they would put in a picture of children with distended bellies and flies crawling all over them. Then they'd say we help support orphanages and things like that.

I said, "But I don't support any orphanages."

"Neither does the guy we raised the twenty million dollars for," they said.

I told them I wasn't interested in using dishonest practices. They argued that once I had the money, I could use it any way I wanted, but I wasn't going to compromise. My integrity is more important to me than getting millions of dollars, so I sent them away. But the reason those people are in business is because what they do works.

It's okay to give when you are touched emotionally sometimes, but don't let that be the driving motivation behind your giving. Give from your first fruits, and give where you are fed. Give to the people who have really affected your life. If the body of Christ would start doing that, then the people who are truly ministering the Word of God would have a super abundance, and the crooks would have to repent or get out of ministry. Proper giving would also increase the harvest you receive on your giving—because just like a farmer reaps a bigger harvest by planting in fertile soil, your giving achieves better returns when you plant it in a ministry that is doing kingdom work.

— OUTLINE —

I.   A lot of people are confused about where they should give their tithes and offerings, or how the money they give should be used.

   A. Scripture says, **"Bring ye all the tithes into the storehouse"** (Mal. 3:10).

   B. In the Old Testament, the tithe went directly to the ministers—that was how God supported the ministers who were doing His work.

   C. Most pastors teach that the storehouse is your local church and that parachurch and other social-welfare ministries are meant to be supported by offerings above the tithe.

   D. In a perfect world, I'd have to agree with that, but this isn't a perfect world.

   E. Technically, a storehouse is where you put your food.

   F. You could say that a storehouse is where you get fed—so you should be giving your tithe where you get fed, and that may not be your local church.

II. You should recognize that a good church does more than just teach the Word.

   A. It fosters community and is an important part of spiritual growth.

   B. You need the maturity that comes through fellowshipping with other believers.

   C. A good local church helps you raise your children and gives them a place to meet other Christian kids.

   D. It offers one-on-one counseling and marriage counseling.

   E. Your local pastor helps you deal with grief and get through hard times.

   F. So, if you are in a good local church that is preaching the Word, helping widows and orphans, and doing what a godly church is supposed to do, then you should be tithing at your church—no question about it.

III. Unfortunately, I don't believe most churches are teaching about the grace of God and preaching the true Gospel.

   A. The most common question I get is from people who are looking for a church that is teaching about the love of God and the finished work of Jesus.

   B. Many people are going to churches they know aren't good, but they go there out of a sense of obligation or because there are no other options—maybe their whole family goes there, or it's the one they've always gone to, and they don't want to change where they go.

C. In fact, many people are going to churches that preach things completely contrary to the Gospel message.

D. They leave church feeling condemned and beat up—the exact opposite of what a church is supposed to do.

E. It would be wrong for me to tell you to put your tithes into the local church and not qualify that by saying a *good* local church—one that is meeting the needs of its members.

IV. It matters where you plant your seed.

A. Some people think that God sees their hearts when they give, and they reap a benefit from their giving regardless of what the church does with their money—but that's not true.

B. You'd be a very poor farmer with that kind of attitude.

C. You can't expect the same results from casting your seed on pavement that you would get from planting it in fertile soil.

D. In addition, every time you give to a church or minister, you are casting a vote in support of how they conduct themselves.

E. Every time you give money to a church, you are helping support what they do—whether it's good or bad—so it absolutely matters where you give your money.

F. I'm not saying the church has to be perfect—no church is.

G. Maybe your church isn't hitting on all cylinders, but they are preaching the Truth and being a light to the community.

H. In that case, I would recommend giving your tithe there because you need what a local church offers.

I. It's wrong to put your money into something that you don't agree with and then go get fed by ministries you don't support financially.

J. That's like eating at McDonald's and going across the street to Wendy's to pay for your meal.

K. If you aren't being fed at your church, then you shouldn't be tithing there.

V. Giving where you are fed isn't the only guideline for tithing, but I believe it should be the primary one.

A. Widows and orphans may not minister to you, but it is a godly thing to give and support them.

B. That falls under what is called benevolence giving.

C. There is also giving that goes toward missionary work.

D. So, not all of your giving should go to where you are being fed, but the bulk of it should.

VI. The local church is the backbone of the body, and it's best for you to be in a good local church where you can give your tithes—but you shouldn't put your tithes into a dead church.

    A. In the first place, if you are in a dead church, then get out!

    B. Go find yourself a church that is preaching the Gospel, and then give your tithe to that church, and use offerings to support other parts of the body of Christ.

    C. If, for some reason, you can't find a good local church or get out of the dead one you're in, then, at a minimum, you shouldn't give all of your money there.

VII. This principle of giving where you are fed is really simple, and it would solve a lot of problems if believers followed it.

    A. The preachers who are lying and manipulating people in order to get their money are not truly feeding the body of Christ.

    B. They would go out of business if people would just stop giving them money.

    C. Then only the people who are really feeding Christians would be getting all of the resources, and the believers would have an abundance of finances.

    D. The good churches wouldn't have to hold car washes and bake sales to raise money.

VIII. Giving where you are fed makes a difference for you too.

    A. The return on your giving is going to depend to a degree on how fruitful the ground is that you are sowing into.

    B. If you give to a church or ministry that isn't really accomplishing the Lord's work, then you are going to get marginal returns.

    C. When you plant your seed in a place that is fruitful and ministering the Word of God, then you are going to receive a better return.

IX. I actually had a woman come to me one time with a personalized letter that said, *Dear Stella*—or whatever her name was—*God woke me up at three o'clock this morning and gave me your name and told me to tell you that if you send me a thousand dollars, then all of the people you have been praying for will get saved.*

    A. The letter went on to promise healing, prosperity, and deliverance if she would just send in some money.

    B. She was a poor woman, and she told me that she could scrape together the thousand dollars, but she wasn't really sure she should give it.

    C. On the other hand, she felt compelled to because the letter was personalized, and the minister claimed God had woken him at three in the morning with a special message for her.

D. She said "What should I do?" and I took the letter, tore it up, and explained that the exact same computer-generated letter was probably sent to thousands of people.

E. The reason crooks send those kinds of letters is because Christians actually send money in response.

F. I hate to say it, but I believe the majority of giving in the body of Christ is in response to begging or some sort of emotional coercion.

G. It's possible that some good could come out of that kind of giving because God can use anything, but those practices are wrong—giving out of desperation because somebody said that God would supply your needs is an ungodly principle.

H. In a sense, it's like trying to buy a miracle.

X. The book of Acts tells a story about a man named Simon who tried to do that very thing.

A. Simon had been a magician in Samaria, but he was born again when he heard Philip preach the Gospel.

B. Later, Peter and John went down to Samaria and prayed for people to receive the Holy Spirit.

C. Simon saw that people were receiving the gift of speaking in tongues when Peter and John laid hands on them.

D. Simon also wanted to be able lay hands on people and have them receive the Holy Spirit, so he offered Peter money to give him the same gift.

E. On the surface, that seems like a good desire, but Peter responded differently:

Thy money perish with thee, because thou hast thought that the gift of God may be purchased with money. Thou hast neither part nor lot in this matter: for thy heart is not right in the sight of God... For I perceive that thou art in the gall of bitterness, and in the bond of iniquity.
ACTS 8:20-21 AND 23

i. I'm not sure whether being **"in the gall of bitterness, and in the bond of iniquity"** means that Simon was never really born again or whether his heart was just wrong, but it's not good either way.

F. This shows that your heart is not right if you are trying to buy God's blessings.

G. At the same time, it's possible to be in the process of believing God for a miracle, and it may be that letting go of some of your money could be a step of faith for you.

H. See, it isn't giving money that makes the miracle happen—it's stepping out in faith.

XI. When Jamie and I first moved to Colorado Springs, a man gave our ministry a building and then came to work for us for about six months.

A. Back then, we used to send out teachings on cassette tape.

B. He noticed that for a couple of weeks at a time, we couldn't fill orders for tapes.

C. It was because we'd run out of money and had to wait a week or two until we had enough to get in another shipment of blank tapes.

D. When he saw what was going on, he asked me why I wasn't telling people how desperate the ministry was for additional finances.

E. He told me he had given away twenty-five thousand dollars the previous year, and he always asked God where to send the money before he gave.

F. He said I was the first person who came to mind every time he prayed, because our ministry had helped him transform his life, but he didn't give to us, because I never asked.

G. Instead he gave to a television minister who was always begging for money and telling people he was going to go off the air if they didn't give!

XII. I was invited to be a guest on that same minister's network much later, and the head of his ministry showed me a room filled with hundreds of thousands of letters stuffed and sealed in envelopes.

A. The letters talked about a pending financial crisis if people didn't give.

B. They sent out those letters at six-month intervals and had printed them out for two years in advance.

C. *They didn't even have a crisis yet*—it was all lies and manipulation!

D. The people who are using manipulation are not truly in tune with God.

E. I'm not saying they aren't born again, but I'm saying they are carnal.

XIII. I had a publicity group come to me one time and guarantee that they could raise one million dollars by sending out letters for us.

A. They started by telling me about the color ink that people respond to, the font we should use, and how to underline certain statements.

B. They had the whole business down to a science.

C. They also told me how they had raised another client twenty million dollars using the same techniques just a couple of months before.

D. I said, "Well, we could sure use twenty million dollars. But what are you going to say? What are you going to do?" They said, "Just leave that up to us." "No," I said, "I need to know what you are going to say."

E. So, they started telling me how they would put in a picture of children with distended bellies and flies crawling all over them, and they'd say we help support orphanages and things like that.

F. I said "But I don't support any orphanages," but they said, "Neither does the guy we raised the twenty million dollars for."

G. I told them I wasn't interested in using dishonest practices.

H. They argued that once I had the money, I could use it any way I wanted, but I wasn't going to compromise—my integrity is more important to me than getting millions of dollars.

XIV. It's okay to give when you are touched emotionally sometimes, but don't let that be the driving motivation behind your giving.

A. Give from your first fruits, and give where you are fed.

B. Give to the people who have really affected your life.

C. If the body of Christ would start doing that, then the people who are truly ministering the Word of God would have a super abundance, and the crooks would have to repent or get out of ministry.

D. Proper giving would also increase the harvest you receive on your giving—because just like a farmer reaps a bigger harvest by planting in fertile soil, your giving achieves better returns when you plant it in a ministry that is doing kingdom work.

TEACHER'S
—— GUIDE ——

1. A lot of people are confused about where they should give their tithes and offerings, or how the money they give should be used. Scripture says, **"Bring ye all the tithes into the storehouse"** (Mal. 3:10). In the Old Testament, the tithe went directly to the ministers—that was how God supported the ministers who were doing His work. Most pastors teach that the storehouse is your local church and that parachurch and other social-welfare ministries are meant to be supported by offerings above the tithe. In a perfect world, I'd have to agree with that, but this isn't a perfect world. Technically, a storehouse is where you put your food. You could say that a storehouse is where you get fed—so you should be giving your tithe where you get fed, and that may not be your local church.

    1a. Read Malachi 3:10. Where should the tithes be brought?
        Into the storehouse
    1b. A storehouse is where you get what?
        A. Sleep
        B. Money
        C. Fed
        D. All of the above
        E. None of the above

2. You should recognize that a good church does more than just teach the Word. It fosters community and is an important part of spiritual growth. You need the maturity that comes through fellowshipping with other believers. A good local church helps you raise your children and gives them a place to meet other Christian kids. It offers one-on-one counseling and marriage counseling. Your local pastor helps you deal with grief and get through hard times. So, if you are in a good local church that is preaching the Word, helping widows and orphans, and doing what a godly church is supposed to do, then you should be tithing at your church—no question about it.

    2a. If you are in a good local church that is preaching the Word, helping widows and orphans, and doing what a godly church is supposed to do, what should you do?
        Tithe there

3. Unfortunately, I don't believe most churches are teaching about the grace of God and preaching the true Gospel. The most common question I get is from people who are looking for a church that is teaching about the love of God and the finished work of Jesus. Many people are going to churches they know aren't good, but they go there out of a sense of obligation or because there are no other options—maybe their whole family goes there, or it's the one they've always gone to, and they don't want to change where they go. In fact, many people are going to churches that preach things completely contrary to the Gospel message. They leave church feeling condemned and beat up—the exact opposite of what a church is supposed to do. It would be wrong for me to tell you to put your tithes into the local church and not qualify that by saying a *good* local church—one that is meeting the needs of its members.

4. It matters where you plant your seed. Some people think that God sees their hearts when they give, and they reap a benefit from their giving regardless of what the church does with their money—but that's not true. You'd be a very poor farmer with that kind of attitude. You can't expect the same results from casting your seed on pavement that you would get from planting it in fertile soil. In addition, every time you give to a church or minister, you are casting a vote in support of how they conduct themselves. Every time you give money to a church, you are helping support what they do—whether it's good or bad—so it absolutely matters where you give your money. I'm not saying the church has to be perfect—no church is. Maybe your church isn't hitting on all cylinders, but they are preaching the Truth and being a light to the community. In that case, I would recommend giving your tithe there because you need what a local church offers. It's wrong to put your money into something that you don't agree with and then go get fed by ministries you don't support financially. That's like eating at McDonald's and going across the street to Wendy's to pay for your meal. If you aren't being fed at your church, then you shouldn't be tithing there.

    4a. Why does it matter where you plant (give) your seed (money)?
       Because you can't expect the same results from casting your seed on pavement that you would get from planting it in fertile soil, and every time you give money to a church, you are helping support what they do—whether it's good or bad)

    4b. To put your money into something that you don't agree with and then go get fed by ministries you don't support financially is _____ .
       Wrong

    4c. True or false: Even if you aren't being fed at your church, you should still tithe there.
       False

5. Giving where you are fed isn't the only guideline for tithing, but I believe it should be the primary one. Widows and orphans may not minister to you, but it is a godly thing to give and support them. That falls under what is called benevolence giving. There is also giving that goes toward missionary work. So, not all of your giving should go to where you are being fed, but the bulk of it should.

    5a. Why shouldn't all of your money go to where you are fed?
       Because you should also do benevolence giving, which is supporting widows and orphans, and you should give toward missionary work

6. The local church is the backbone of the body, and it's best for you to be in a good local church where you can give your tithes—but you shouldn't put your tithes into a dead church. In the first place, if you are in a dead church, then get out! Go find yourself a church that is preaching the Gospel, and then give your tithe to that church, and use offerings to support other parts of the body of Christ. If, for some reason, you can't find a good local church or get out of the dead one you're in, then, at a minimum, you shouldn't give all of your money there.

    6a. What should you do if you're in a dead church?
       Get out!

7. This principle of giving where you are fed is really simple, and it would solve a lot of problems if believers followed it. The preachers who are lying and manipulating people in order to get their money are not truly feeding the body of Christ. They would go out of business if people would just stop giving them money. Then only the people who are really feeding Christians would be getting all of the resources, and the believers would have an abundance of finances. The good churches wouldn't have to hold car washes and bake sales to raise money.

    7a. What would believers have if they gave where they are fed?
    <u>An abundance of finances</u>

8. Giving where you are fed makes a difference for you too. The return on your giving is going to depend to a degree on how fruitful the ground is that you are sowing into. If you give to a church or ministry that isn't really accomplishing the Lord's work, then you are going to get marginal returns. When you plant your seed in a place that is fruitful and ministering the Word of God, then you are going to receive a better return.

    8a. When you plant your seed in a place that is fruitful and ministering the Word of God, then you are going to receive what kind of return?
    A. A marginal one
    B. A quick one
    C. An equal one
    D. A surprising one
    <u>E. A better one</u>

9. I actually had a woman come to me one time with a personalized letter that said, *Dear Stella*—or whatever her name was—*God woke me up at three o'clock this morning and gave me your name and told me to tell you that if you send me a thousand dollars, then all of the people you have been praying for will get saved*. The letter went on to promise healing, prosperity, and deliverance if she would just send in some money. She was a poor woman, and she told me that she could scrape together the thousand dollars, but she wasn't really sure she should give it. On the other hand, she felt compelled to because the letter was personalized, and the minister claimed God had woken him at three in the morning with a special message for her. She said "What should I do?" and I took the letter, tore it up, and explained that the exact same computer-generated letter was probably sent to thousands of people. The reason crooks send those kinds of letters is because Christians actually send money in response. I hate to say it, but I believe the majority of giving in the body of Christ is in response to begging or some sort of emotional coercion. It's possible that some good could come out of that kind of giving because God can use anything, but those practices are wrong—giving out of desperation because somebody said that God would supply your needs is an ungodly principle. In a sense, it's like trying to buy a miracle.

    9a. Why is giving out of desperation because somebody said that God would supply your needs an ungodly principle?
    <u>Because it's like trying to buy a miracle</u>

10. The book of Acts tells a story about a man named Simon who tried to do that very thing. Simon had been a magician in Samaria, but he was born again when he heard Philip preach the Gospel. Later, Peter and John went down to Samaria and prayed for people to receive the Holy Spirit. Simon saw that people were receiving the gift of speaking in tongues when Peter and John laid hands on them. Simon also wanted to be able lay hands on people and have them receive the Holy Spirit, so he offered Peter money to give him the same gift. On the surface, that seems like a good desire, but Peter responded differently:

> *Thy money perish with thee, because thou hast thought that the gift of God may be purchased with money. Thou hast neither part nor lot in this matter: for thy heart is not right in the sight of God... For I perceive that thou art in the gall of bitterness, and in the bond of iniquity.*
>
> ACTS 8:20-21 AND 23

I'm not sure whether being **"in the gall of bitterness, and in the bond of iniquity"** means that Simon was never really born again or whether his heart was just wrong, but it's not good either way. This shows that your heart is not right if you are trying to buy God's blessings. At the same time, it's possible to be in the process of believing God for a miracle, and it may be that letting go of some of your money could be a step of faith for you. See, it isn't giving money that makes the miracle happen—it's stepping out in faith.

    10a. Read Acts 8:20-21 and 23. What happened when Simon the magician tried to buy the gift of giving the Spirit to those he laid hands on?
        A. Peter rebuked him
        B. Peter corrected him
        C. Peter took the money but denied him the gift
        D. All of the above
        E. None of the above
    10b. If you're in the process of believing God for a miracle, how could giving money be the right thing?
        If it's a step of faith for you

11. When Jamie and I first moved to Colorado Springs, a man gave our ministry a building and then came to work for us for about six months. Back then, we used to send out teachings on cassette tape. He noticed that for a couple of weeks at a time, we couldn't fill orders for tapes. It was because we'd run out of money and had to wait a week or two until we had enough to get in another shipment of blank tapes. When he saw what was going on, he asked me why I wasn't telling people how desperate the ministry was for additional finances. He told me he had given away twenty-five thousand dollars the previous year, and he always asked God where to send the money before he gave. He said I was the first person who came to mind every time he prayed, because our ministry had helped him transform his life, but he didn't give to us, because I never asked. Instead he gave to a television minister who was always begging for money and telling people he was going to go off the air if they didn't give!

12. I was invited to be a guest on that same minister's network much later, and the head of his ministry showed me a room filled with hundreds of thousands of letters stuffed and sealed in envelopes. The letters talked about a pending financial crisis if people didn't give. They sent out those letters at six-month intervals and had printed them out for two years in advance. *They didn't even have a crisis yet*—it was all lies and manipulation! The people who are using manipulation are not truly in tune with God. I'm not saying they aren't born again, but I'm saying they are carnal.

    12a. Ministers who use manipulation to get money are _____.
        Not truly in tune with God and carnal

13. I had a publicity group come to me one time and guarantee that they could raise one million dollars by sending out letters for us. They started by telling me about the color ink that people respond to, the font we should use, and how to underline certain statements. They had the whole business down to a science. They also told me how they had raised another client twenty million dollars using the same techniques just a couple of months before. I said, "Well, we could sure use twenty million dollars. But what are you going to say? What are you going to do?" They said, "Just leave that up to us." "No," I said, "I need to know what you are going to say." So, they started telling me how they would put in a picture of children with distended bellies and flies crawling all over them, and they'd say we help support orphanages and things like that. I said "But I don't support any orphanages," but they said, "Neither does the guy we raised the twenty million dollars for." I told them I wasn't interested in using dishonest practices. They argued that once I had the money, I could use it any way I wanted, but I wasn't going to compromise—my integrity is more important to me than getting millions of dollars.

14. It's okay to give when you are touched emotionally sometimes, but don't let that be the driving motivation behind your giving. Give from your first fruits, and give where you are fed. Give to the people who have really affected your life. If the body of Christ would start doing that, then the people who are truly ministering the Word of God would have a super abundance, and the crooks would have to repent or get out of ministry. Proper giving would also increase the harvest you receive on your giving—because just like a farmer reaps a bigger harvest by planting in fertile soil, your giving achieves better returns when you plant it in a ministry that is doing kingdom work.

    14a. Is it ever okay to give when you are touched emotionally?
        Yes
    14b. You should give where you are fed, but you should give from your what?
        A. Abundance
        B. First fruits
        C. Own wallet
        D. Leftovers
        E. Taxes

DISCIPLESHIP
——— QUESTIONS ———

1. Read Malachi 3:10. Where should the tithes be brought?

   _____
   _____
   _____

2. A storehouse is where you get what?
   A. Sleep
   B. Money
   C. Fed
   D. All of the above
   E. None of the above

3. If you are in a good local church that is preaching the Word, helping widows and orphans, and doing what a godly church is supposed to do, what should you do?

   _____
   _____
   _____

4. Why does it matter where you plant (give) your seed (money)?

   _____
   _____
   _____

5. To put your money into something that you don't agree with and then go get fed by ministries you don't support financially is _____ .

6. True or false: Even if you aren't being fed at your church, you should still tithe there.

7. Why shouldn't all of your money go to where you are fed?

   _____
   _____
   _____

8. What should you do if you're in a dead church?

   _____
   _____
   _____

9. What would believers have if they gave where they are fed?

    _____
    _____
    _____

10. When you plant your seed in a place that is fruitful and ministering the Word of God, then you are going to receive what kind of return?
    A. A marginal one
    B. A quick one
    C. An equal one
    D. A surprising one
    E. A better one

11. Why is giving out of desperation because somebody said that God would supply your needs an ungodly principle?

    _____
    _____
    _____

12. Read Acts 8:20-21 and 23. What happened when Simon the magician tried to buy the gift of giving the Spirit to those he laid hands on?
    A. Peter rebuked him
    B. Peter corrected him
    C. Peter took the money but denied him the gift
    D. All of the above
    E. None of the above

13. If you're in the process of believing God for a miracle, how could giving money be the right thing?

    _____
    _____
    _____

14. Ministers who use manipulation to get money are _____.

15. Is it ever okay to give when you are touched emotionally?

    _____
    _____
    _____

16. You should give where you are fed, but you should give from your what?
    A. Abundance
    B. First fruits
    C. Own wallet
    D. Leftovers
    E. Taxes

ANSWER
—KEY—

1. Into the storehouse

2. C. Fed

3. Tithe there

4. Because you can't expect the same results from casting your seed on pavement that you would get from planting it in fertile soil, and every time you give money to a church, you are helping support what they do—whether it's good or bad

5. Wrong

6. False

7. Because you should also do benevolence giving, which is supporting widows and orphans, and you should give toward missionary work

8. Get out!

9. An abundance of finances

10. E. A better one

11. Because it's like trying to buy a miracle

12. A. Peter rebuked him

13. If it's a step of faith for you

14. Not truly in tune with God and carnal

15. Yes

16. B. First fruits

——SCRIPTURES——

MALACHI 3:10

Bring ye all the tithes into the storehouse, that there may be meat in mine house, and prove me now herewith, saith the LORD of hosts, if I will not open you the windows of heaven, and pour you out a blessing, that there shall not be room enough to receive it.

ACTS 8:20-21

But Peter said unto him, Thy money perish with thee, because thou hast thought that the gift of God may be purchased with money. [21] Thou hast neither part nor lot in this matter: for thy heart is not right in the sight of God.

ACTS 8:23

For I perceive that thou art in the gall of bitterness, and in the bond of iniquity.

PARTNERSHIP

One of the best known scriptures about prosperity is the Apostle Paul's statement to the Philippians that his **"God shall supply all your need"** (Phil. 4:19). Often, you hear that verse taught like it applies to every person on the face of the planet. It's true that God wants to supply all of your needs, and there are plenty of scriptures that talk about that—like how God provides for the birds of the air and the lilies of the field—but Paul wrote that particular verse about people who had partnered with him in spreading the Gospel. He was talking about the special blessing on partnership. Earlier in his letter, Paul said,

> *I thank my God upon every remembrance of you, Always in every prayer of*
> *mine for you all making request with joy, For your fellowship in the gospel*
> *from the first day until now.*
>   PHILIPPIANS 1:3-5

The word translated **"fellowship"** in verse 5 is the Greek word *koinonia*, and it literally means "partnership" (*Strong's Concordance*). Paul was thanking the Philippians for their partnership in the Gospel. They were people who gave to Paul in a greater way than any other church had. Paul made specific mention of how eager they were to care for him and provide for his needs. He said,

> *But I rejoiced in the Lord greatly, that now at the last your care of me hath*
> *flourished again; wherein ye were also careful, but ye lacked opportunity.*
>   PHILIPPIANS 4:10

The Philippians were regular supporters of Paul as he traveled from place to place preaching the Good News. They were helping him take the Gospel to other places around the world. When he said they were careful but lacked opportunity, he was saying they didn't always know where to send their money. Paul had been arrested in Jerusalem, locked in prison, and shipwrecked on his way to trial in Rome. Basically, his location was constantly changing for about three years. They didn't have the communications to know exactly where Paul was, so they **"lacked opportunity"** to give. But the moment they heard Paul was in Rome, they sent clothes, finances, and things for him to study. They were eager to help him, but Paul wasn't rejoicing over them just because they took care of him:

> *Not that I speak in respect of want: for I have learned, in whatsoever state*
> *I am, therewith to be content. I know both how to be abased, and I know*
> *how to abound: every where and in all things I am instructed both to be*
> *full and to be hungry, both to abound and to suffer need. I can do all things*
> *through Christ which strengtheneth me.*
>   PHILIPPIANS 4:11-13

Paul said he had learned how to live in need and in abundance. He was rejoicing because he saw their hearts to give, and he knew that by supporting him, they were actually giving to God. He saw that their giving would cause God to pour out a blessing on them and result in a hundredfold return. He went on to say,

Notwithstanding ye have well done, that ye did communicate with my
affliction. Now ye Philippians know also, that in the beginning of the gospel,
when I departed from Macedonia, no church communicated with me as
concerning giving and receiving, but ye only.

PHILIPPIANS 4:14-15

When Paul said **"communicated,"** he was talking about how they gave financially. The amazing thing here is that Paul says no other churches were giving him money to help preach the Gospel—only the Philippians! Paul and his companions were in constant jeopardy, and they endured great persecution and suffering to preach the Good News, but none of the other churches Paul started were supporting him in his work. I think that's tragic.

It seems people gave to Paul only while he was in their town preaching. They fed him and gave him a place to stay, but as soon as he left town, he was on his own again. So, every time he went to a new place, he had to start all over financially. I don't think Paul should have had to scrape by like that. People should have been so thankful for what God was doing through him that they took care of him no matter where he was, but only the Philippians blessed Paul after he went away. You can see why Paul was thankful every time he thought about the Philippians and how they helped establish churches in other areas.

For even in Thessalonica ye sent once and again unto my necessity. Not
because I desire a gift: but I desire fruit that may abound to your account.

PHILIPPIANS 4:16-17

"Once and again" just means they sent money to Paul more than once. It's a good thing, too, because Paul's ministry wasn't well received in Thessalonica. He was basically run out of town. So, if it wasn't for the financial support of the Philippians, he might not have been able to continue his ministry there. Their giving wasn't just benefiting Paul personally; it was helping to establish God's kingdom abroad, and Paul was rejoicing because he knew that God gives prosperity to help establish His covenant. Paul understood that their giving would result in a supernatural return—because God gives seed to sowers. Paul talked about how their giving caused him to abound, and then he said,

But my God shall supply all your need according to his riches in glory by
Christ Jesus.

PHILIPPIANS 4:19

There is no doubt that God delights in the prosperity of His servants, or that He sends sun and rain on the just and the unjust alike.[1] God desires to bless both believers and unbelievers, but this particular verse is talking about people who had partnered with Paul in sharing the Gospel

---

[1] See, for example, Ps. 35:27, Matt. 5:45, and 3 John 2

and were helping to establish God's covenant upon the earth. They weren't just giving to Paul because they were receiving from him. They were giving when Paul was blessing people beyond their own city, and they weren't receiving anything in return. In modern terms, you could say they weren't just giving to get books and videos—they were giving toward missionary work.

Philippians 4:19 is talking about the special blessing on those who become partners in spreading the Gospel, which means that if you really want to be blessed, then partner with a ministry that has a big vision and is doing a great job of spreading the Gospel. The way God gets money to a ministry is by giving it to the believers who support it. In order for the money to get to the ministry, it has to pass through the hands of partners first—and as the money passes *through*, there will be plenty left over for *you*. So, one of the best ways to prosper is to find a ministry that is powerfully anointed by God and become a partner with it.

I couldn't provide one week's worth of the income it takes to run our ministry; it takes the support of our partners to supply our financial needs and enable us to do what God has called us to do. I know that our partners have to prosper before our ministry can prosper, so I pray that God blesses our partners and causes them to abound, because my ability to accomplish God's will is directly dependent upon other people joining with me and becoming partners. All of the money God needs to get to our ministry has to come through our partners first. The same is true for every other ministry out there.

This is why God causes a supernatural flow of finances to go your way when you identify yourself as a giver. God has made provision for every believer, but there is a special anointing on people who give to help spread the Gospel. When you say "I want to help this church change my city, and I want to help this person go around the world and spread the Gospel," then God is going to prosper you. God gives money to people who will use it to advance the kingdom (Deut. 8:18), and He gives more than enough, so there is always plenty left over for the giver.

Aside from causing a flow of finances to pass through partners' hands, there is an additional benefit to partnering with a ministry. Scripture says,

> *A man's gift maketh room for him, and bringeth him before great men.*
> PROVERBS 18:16

I used to think that **"gift"** in this verse meant a God-given ability or anointing. I thought that if I would use my gift of teaching properly, for instance, it would open up doors and bring me before great people. But the Hebrew word used for **"gift"** here is *mattan*, and it literally means "a present" (*Strong's Concordance*). It's clear from its other uses in Scripture that it means some kind of monetary gift.[2] It's not talking about the anointing on one's life. This verse is simply saying that even in the natural realm, a gift opens doors.

---

[2]For example, Prov. 15:27 and 19:6

In a negative sense, you could understand this kind of gift to be a bribe, but there is also a positive side to this, because a gift doesn't have to be used in a negative way. You can turn away wrath with a gift or gain favor with people. Gifts also have an effect in the spiritual realm. When you give, it opens doors for you. It can create opportunities and bring you before powerful people. This is different from a bribe, and Scripture gives an example of a gift being used in this positive sense.

In the Old Testament, it says that when the Queen of Sheba heard how wise and prosperous King Solomon was, she traveled to Jerusalem to witness it for herself. It says she went up with **"a very great train"** of camels bearing spices, precious stones, and **"very much gold"** (1 Kin. 10:2). The Queen of Sheba was astounded by what she saw in King Solomon's court, and she said,

> *It was a true report that I heard in mine own land of thy acts and of thy wisdom. Howbeit I believed not the words, until I came, and mine eyes had seen it: and, behold, the half was not told me: thy wisdom and prosperity exceedeth the fame which I heard.*
>
> 1 KINGS 10:6-7

Solomon was the wisest and wealthiest man on the face of the earth. The Bible says that people came from all over the world to inquire of him and search out his wisdom. Think about that. Today, if you tried to meet with the president of the United States or the prime minister of Israel, do you think you would be able to walk right into his office and sit down? No way. There are protocols and you have to get in line. I believe Solomon had more fame and notoriety than the leader of any country today. So, the Queen of Sheba brought gifts to get Solomon's attention and gain access to him.

> *And she gave the king an hundred and twenty talents of gold, and of spices very great store, and precious stones: there came no more such abundance of spices as these which the queen of Sheba gave to king Solomon.*
>
> 1 KINGS 10:10

A talent is equal to about 75.5 pounds, so that means the queen gave Solomon 9,000 pounds, or 145,000 ounces, of gold. At today's price of $1,730 per ounce, that gold would be worth more than $250,000,000, and there's no telling how much her other gifts were worth. I can guarantee that a gift that size is going to make room for you. I don't know how long the line was of people waiting to see King Solomon, but the queen's gift moved her right to the front. Not only did she get to spend a little time with him; she ate with him and saw all the different aspects of his kingdom. The implication is that she was able to spend a number of days with Solomon. I don't know the exact details, but the queen's gift opened up a door. It made room for her and brought her before the greatest man of her day—that's the positive power of a gift.

In a spiritual sense, when you give by partnering with a ministry, it makes room for you. It's like you start drawing on the anointing that is on the ministry. You end up partaking of the fruits of that ministry. When you partner with someone who is preaching the Good News, then you receive the benefit of prospering from their blessing.

Here's something else to consider: I bet the Queen of Sheba could have used that $250,000,000 for needs within her own kingdom. Can you imagine the length of the camel train she would have needed to carry all of those goods, plus the soldiers to guard it? They must have traveled to Jerusalem with hundreds of camels and an entourage the size of a small army. It couldn't have been inconspicuous, and the people in her kingdom probably wondered where she was going with all of that wealth. I bet it raised some eyebrows when people heard that she was planning to give all of that money to a king who was already the richest man on earth.

I'm sure some people were thinking, *Why give so much money to King Solomon? Think of how many poor people she could help with that money.* She could have changed entire nations with that money. She could have built buildings and helped farmers in every town she passed through. But the Queen of Sheba decided she was going to use that money to go find out how King Solomon had become so successful in running his kingdom. Then she could apply that knowledge to improving her own land. She passed up all of the beggars and cities that could have used her resources, and took these resources to the wealthiest man alive. She did it because she wanted to partake of the success Solomon was experiencing. And it worked. The Scripture says,

> *And king Solomon gave unto the queen of Sheba all her desire, whatsoever she asked, beside that which Solomon gave her of his royal bounty. So she turned and went to her own country, she and her servants.*
>
> 1 KINGS 10:13

It would be interesting to know how much of his royal bounty Solomon gave to the Queen of Sheba. The next verses tell us that Solomon received 666 talents of gold annually plus the profits he made from businesses and the kings of other countries who paid him taxes—which means the queen's gift was only a fraction of King Solomon's yearly earnings. Solomon was so rich, he didn't even keep track of silver. It was thrown into the streets and treated like rock. He was unbelievably wealthy. So, when it says that Solomon gave to her of his bounty, I think the Queen of Sheba received more from Solomon than she gave. I think she left Jerusalem with more money than she had when she came.

As the queen traveled toward Jerusalem, I'm sure many beggars and kings wondered what she thought she was going to accomplish by giving such a huge gift to a man who was already filthy rich. But she wasn't giving the money to help Solomon; she gave that gift to help herself. She used it to gain entry and to partake of Solomon's wisdom, favor, and anointing—and she ended up leaving Jerusalem with all of the bounty Solomon gave her. So, on her return journey, she still had tremendous wealth to use to aid beggars and farmers, but she also had wisdom and anointing she could use to build her entire nation. Benevolent giving would have been a short-term solution, but using wisdom and anointing to lift the kingdom out of need was a long-term solution.

It isn't wrong to give to people in need. As a matter of fact, Scripture says that if you see your brother in need and don't help, then the love of God doesn't dwell in you (1 John 3:17). So, you are definitely supposed to give when you see people in need, but that isn't the only reason to give. Sometimes, like the Queen of Sheba did, you should give because you need what a church or minister can give to you. I tell my Bible college students to "sow where you want to go." In other words, if you feel called into missionary work, then find people who are doing good work in that field and support them. By partnering with them, you begin to draw on the anointing and experience they have. It will come to you and help you fulfill your own calling.

It's kind of like finding someone who has reached a destination you want to travel to, and latching on to them to help you get there. You find someone who has gone further than you have gone, and you sow into their life to help get yourself to the same place. That's what the Queen of Sheba did. She found a man who had more favor, more wisdom, and greater wealth, and she used a gift to gain access to him in order to glean more wisdom, wealth, and favor for herself.

It's important to recognize that when you partner with a ministry and give deliberately, you can partake of the blessing that is on that ministry—not giving just to get, but giving to help bring you where you want to go. When you do that, it starts a supernatural flow of God's finances toward you so that you are able to both meet your own needs and also abound unto every good work.

God won't let you outgive Him. God always blesses you back when you show faith in Him by giving of your substance. You will never be more faithful to God than He is to you. I'm not saying that partnering with a ministry is about giving just to get. That's why I spent so much time in earlier lessons talking about your heart motives being more important than your gift. But when your heart is right, partnering with a ministry to help it get the Gospel out is going to open doors for you and cause you to prosper.

Giving is a powerful part of tapping into God's prosperity. Several different things help determine the harvest you get from your giving—like the attitude you give with, where you give, and trusting God as your source—so there isn't a formula. But you can't really prosper in God's economy until you start sowing into His kingdom. I recommend you do it regularly by tithing and giving from the first fruits of your income. That way, you won't spend your money before you can give, and end up missing out on God's supernatural supply. As you become a deliberate, on-purpose giver—and you do it motivated by love—it will start a flow of God's blessings into your life that will cause you to prosper like never before.

— OUTLINE —

I. Early in his letter to the Philippians, Paul said,

> *I thank my God upon every remembrance of you, Always in every prayer of mine for you all making request with joy, For your fellowship in the gospel from the first day until now.*
> PHILIPPIANS 1:3-5

   A. The word translated **"fellowship"** in verse 5 is the Greek word *koinonia*, and it literally means **"partnership"** (*Strong's Concordance*).

   B. Paul was thanking the Philippians for their partnership in the Gospel.

   C. They were people who gave to Paul in a greater way than any other church had.

   D. Paul made specific mention of how eager they were to care for him and provide for his needs.

   E. They were helping him take the Gospel to other places around the world.

   F. When he said they were careful but lacked opportunity (Phil. 4:10), he was saying they didn't always know where to send their money, but the moment they heard Paul was in Rome, they sent clothes, finances, and things for him to study.

   G. But Paul wasn't rejoicing over them just because they took care of him (Phil. 4:11-13); he was rejoicing because he saw their hearts to give, and he knew that by supporting him, they were actually giving to God.

   H. He saw that their giving would cause God to pour out a blessing on them and result in a hundredfold return.

II. The amazing thing here is that Paul said no other churches were giving him money to help preach the Gospel (Phil. 4:15).

   A. It seems people gave to Paul only while he was in their town preaching: they fed him and gave him a place to stay, but as soon as he left town, he was on his own again.

   B. So, every time he went to a new place, he had to start all over financially.

   C. I don't think Paul should have had to scrape by like that.

   D. People should have been so thankful for what God was doing through him that they took care of him no matter where he was.

III. You can see why Paul was thankful every time he thought about the Philippians and how they helped establish churches in other areas.

For even in Thessalonica ye sent once and again unto my necessity. Not because I desire a gift: but I desire fruit that may abound to your account.
PHILIPPIANS 4:16-17

A. **"Once and again"** just means they sent money to Paul more than once.

B. Their giving wasn't just benefiting Paul personally; it was helping to establish God's kingdom abroad, and Paul understood that their giving would result in a supernatural return—because God gives seed to sowers.

C. Paul talked about how their giving caused him to abound, and then he said,

But my God shall supply all your need according to his riches in glory by Christ Jesus.
PHILIPPIANS 4:19

D. God desires to bless both believers and unbelievers, but this particular verse is talking about people who had partnered with Paul in sharing the Gospel and were helping to establish God's covenant upon the earth.

E. They weren't just giving to Paul because they were receiving from him; they were giving when Paul was blessing people beyond their own city, and they weren't receiving anything in return.

F. In modern terms, you could say they weren't just giving to get books and videos—they were giving toward missionary work.

IV. Philippians 4:19 is talking about the special blessing on those who become partners in spreading the Gospel, which means that if you really want to be blessed, then partner with a ministry that has a big vision and is doing a great job of spreading the Gospel.

A. The way God gets money to a ministry is by giving it to the believers who support it.

B. So, one of the best ways to prosper is to find a ministry that is powerfully anointed by God and become a partner with it.

C. I pray that God blesses our partners and causes them to abound, because my ability to accomplish God's will is directly dependent upon other people joining with me and becoming partners.

D. God has made provision for every believer, but there is a special anointing on people who give to help spread the Gospel.

E. When you say "I want to help this church change my city, and I want to help this person go around the world and spread the Gospel," then God is going to prosper you.

F. God gives money to people who will use it to advance the kingdom (Deut. 8:18), and He gives more than enough, so there is always plenty left over for the giver.

V. Aside from causing a flow of finances to pass through partners' hands, there is an additional benefit to partnering with a ministry:

A man's gift maketh room for him, and bringeth him before great men.
PROVERBS 18:16

A. I used to think this meant **"gift"** in the sense of God-given ability or anointing.

B. I thought that if I would use my gift of teaching properly, for instance, it would open up doors and bring me before great people.

C. But the Hebrew word used for gift here is *mattan*, and it literally means "a present" (*Strong's Concordance*).

D. It's clear from its other uses in Scripture that it means some kind of monetary gift.[1]

E. This verse is simply saying that even in the natural realm, a gift opens doors.

F. In a negative sense, you could understand this kind of gift to be a bribe, but there is also a positive side to this.

G. You can turn away wrath with a gift or gain favor with people.

H. Gifts also have an effect in the spiritual realm.

I. It can create opportunities and bring you before powerful people.

J. This is different from a bribe, and Scripture gives us an example of a gift being used in this positive sense.

VI. In the Old Testament, it says that when the Queen of Sheba heard how wise and prosperous King Solomon was, she traveled to Jerusalem to witness it for herself.

A. It says she went up with **"a very great train"** of camels bearing spices, precious stones, and **"very much gold"** (1 Kin. 10:2).

B. The Queen of Sheba was astounded by what she saw in King Solomon's court, and she said,

It was a true report that I heard in mine own land of thy acts and of thy wisdom. Howbeit I believed not the words, until I came, and mine eyes had seen it: and, behold, the half was not told me: thy wisdom and prosperity exceedeth the fame which I heard.
1 KINGS 10:6-7

C. Solomon was the wisest and wealthiest man on the face of the earth.

D. The Bible says that people came from all over the world to inquire of him and search out his wisdom.

E. I believe Solomon had more fame and notoriety than the leader of any country today.

---

[1]For example, Prov. 15:27 and 19:6

F. So, the Queen of Sheba brought gifts to get Solomon's attention and gain access to him.

And she gave the king an hundred and twenty talents of gold, and of spices very great store, and precious stones: there came no more such abundance of spices as these which the queen of Sheba gave to king Solomon.

1 KINGS 10:10

G. A talent is equal to about 75.5 pounds, so that means the queen gave Solomon 9,000 pounds, or 145,000 ounces, of gold.

H. At today's price of $1,730 per ounce, that gold would be worth more than $250,000,000, and there's no telling how much her other gifts were worth.

I. I don't know how long the line was of people waiting to see King Solomon, but the queen's gift moved her right to the front.

J. Not only did she get to spend a little time with him; she ate with him and saw all the different aspects of his kingdom.

K. In a spiritual sense, when you give by partnering with a ministry, it's like you start drawing on the anointing that is on the ministry.

L. You end up partaking of the fruits of that ministry.

M. You receive the benefit of prospering from their blessing.

VII. Here's something else to consider: I bet the Queen of Sheba could have used that 250 million dollars for needs within her own kingdom.

A. I bet it raised some eyebrows when people heard that she was planning to give all of that money to a king who was already the richest man on earth.

B. She could have changed entire nations with that money.

C. She could have built buildings and helped farmers in every town she passed through.

D. But the Queen of Sheba decided she was going to use that money to go find out how King Solomon had become so successful in running his kingdom.

E. Then she could apply that knowledge to improving her own land.

F. She did it because she wanted to partake of the success Solomon was experiencing—and it worked.

And king Solomon gave unto the queen of Sheba all her desire, whatsoever she asked, beside that which Solomon gave her of his royal bounty. So she turned and went to her own country, she and her servants.

1 KINGS 10:13

G. The queen's gift was only a fraction of King Solomon's yearly earnings, so when it says that Solomon gave to her of his bounty, I think the Queen of Sheba received more from Solomon than she gave.

H. On her return journey, she still had tremendous wealth to use to aid beggars and farmers, but she also had wisdom and anointing she could use to build her entire nation.

I. Benevolent giving would have been a short-term solution, but using wisdom and anointing to lift the kingdom out of need was a long-term solution.

VIII. Sometimes, like the Queen of Sheba did, you should give because you need what a church or minister can give to you.

A. I tell my Bible college students to "sow where you want to go."

B. In other words, if you feel called into missionary work, then find people who are doing good work in that field and support them.

C. By partnering with them, you begin to draw on the anointing and experience they have.

D. It will come to you and help you fulfill your own calling.

E. You find someone who has gone further than you have gone, and you sow into their life to help get yourself to the same place.

F. The Queen of Sheba found a man who had more favor, more wisdom, and greater wealth, and she used a large gift to gain access to him in order to glean more wisdom, wealth, and favor for herself.

G. When you do that, it starts a supernatural flow of God's finances toward you so that you are able to both meet your own needs and also abound unto every good work.

IX. God always blesses you back when you show faith in Him by giving of your substance.

A. You will never be more faithful to God than He is to you.

B. I'm not saying that partnering with a ministry is about giving just to get—that's why I spent so much time in earlier lessons talking about your heart motives being more important than your gift.

C. But when your heart is right, partnering with a ministry to help it get the Gospel out is going to open doors for you and cause you to prosper.

X. Giving is a powerful part of tapping into God's prosperity.

A. Several different things help determine the harvest you get from your giving—like the attitude you give with, where you give, and trusting God as your source—so there isn't a formula.

B. But you can't really prosper in God's economy until you start sowing into His kingdom.

C. I recommend you do it regularly by tithing and giving from the first fruits of your income.

D. That way, you won't spend your money before you can give, and end up missing out on God's supernatural supply.

E. As you become a deliberate, on-purpose giver—and you do it motivated by love— it will start a flow of God's blessings into your life that will cause you to prosper like never before.

TEACHER'S
—— GUIDE ——

1. Early in his letter to the Philippians, Paul said,

> *I thank my God upon every remembrance of you, Always in every prayer of mine for you all making request with joy, For your fellowship in the gospel from the first day until now.*
>
> PHILIPPIANS 1:3-5

The word translated **"fellowship"** in verse 5 is the Greek word *koinonia*, and it literally means **"partnership"** (*Strong's Concordance*). Paul was thanking the Philippians for their partnership in the Gospel. They were people who gave to Paul in a greater way than any other church had. Paul made specific mention of how eager they were to care for him and provide for his needs. They were helping him take the Gospel to other places around the world. When he said they were careful but lacked opportunity (Phil. 4:10), he was saying they didn't always know where to send their money, but the moment they heard Paul was in Rome, they sent clothes, finances, and things for him to study. But Paul wasn't rejoicing over them just because they took care of him (Phil. 4:11-13); he was rejoicing because he saw their hearts to give, and he knew that by supporting him, they were actually giving to God. He saw that their giving would cause God to pour out a blessing on them and result in a hundredfold return.

 1a. Read Philippians 1:3-5. Why was Paul thanking the Philippians?
   For their partnership in the Gospel
 1b. What is another word for *fellowship*?
   Partnership
 1c. What were the Philippians helping him do?
   Take the Gospel to other places around the world
 1d. Read Philippians 4:11-13. Why wasn't Paul interested in only getting his needs met?
   Because he had learned to be content regardless of his state

2. The amazing thing here is that Paul said no other churches were giving him money to help preach the Gospel (Phil. 4:15). It seems people gave to Paul only while he was in their town preaching: they fed him and gave him a place to stay, but as soon as he left town, he was on his own again. So, every time he went to a new place, he had to start all over financially. I don't think Paul should have had to scrape by like that. People should have been so thankful for what God was doing through him that they took care of him no matter where he was.

 2a. According to Philippians 4:15, the Philippian church was the _____ church that supported him when he departed Macedonia.
   A. First
   B. Best
   C. Largest
   D. Only
   E. Friendliest

3. You can see why Paul was thankful every time he thought about the Philippians and how they helped establish churches in other areas.

> *For even in Thessalonica ye sent once and again unto my necessity. Not because I desire a gift: but I desire fruit that may abound to your account.*
>
> PHILIPPIANS 4:16-17

"Once and again" just means they sent money to Paul more than once. Their giving wasn't just benefiting Paul personally; it was helping to establish God's kingdom abroad, and Paul understood that their giving would result in a supernatural return—because God gives seed to sowers. Paul talked about how their giving caused him to abound, and then he said,

> *But my God shall supply all your need according to his riches in glory by Christ Jesus.*
>
> PHILIPPIANS 4:19

God desires to bless both believers and unbelievers, but this particular verse is talking about people who had partnered with Paul in sharing the Gospel and were helping to establish God's covenant upon the earth. They weren't just giving to Paul because they were receiving from him; they were giving when Paul was blessing people beyond their own city, and they weren't receiving anything in return. In modern terms, you could say they weren't just giving to get books and videos—they were giving toward missionary work.

> 3a. Read Philippians 4:19. Even though God desires to bless both believers and unbelievers, who is the verse specifically talking about?
> **People who partnered with Paul in sharing the Gospel and were helping to establish God's covenant upon the earth**
> 3b. True or false: The Philippians were giving to Paul because they were receiving from him.
> **False**

4. Philippians 4:19 is talking about the special blessing on those who become partners in spreading the Gospel, which means that if you really want to be blessed, then partner with a ministry that has a big vision and is doing a great job of spreading the Gospel. The way God gets money to a ministry is by giving it to the believers who support it. So, one of the best ways to prosper is to find a ministry that is powerfully anointed by God and become a partner with it. I pray that God blesses our partners and causes them to abound, because my ability to accomplish God's will is directly dependent upon other people joining with me and becoming partners. God has made provision for every believer, but there is a special anointing on people who give to help spread the Gospel. When you say "I want to help this church change my city, and I want to help this person go around the world and spread the Gospel," then God is going to prosper you. God gives money to people who will use it to advance the kingdom (Deut. 8:18), and He gives more than enough, so there is always plenty left over for the giver.

> 4a. What's one reason Andrew prays that God blesses his partners and causes them to abound?
> **Because his ability to accomplish God's will is directly dependent upon other people joining with him and becoming partners**
> 4b. True or false: A giver has just enough money to advance God's kingdom.
> **False**

5. Aside from causing a flow of finances to pass through partners' hands, there is an additional benefit to partnering with a ministry:

A man's gift maketh room for him, and bringeth him before great men.
PROVERBS 18:16

I used to think this meant **"gift"** in the sense of God-given ability or anointing. I thought that if I would use my gift of teaching properly, for instance, it would open up doors and bring me before great people. But the Hebrew word used for gift here is *mattan*, and it literally means "a present" (*Strong's Concordance*). It's clear from its other uses in Scripture that it means some kind of monetary gift. This verse is simply saying that even in the natural realm, a gift opens doors. In a negative sense, you could understand this kind of gift to be a bribe, but there is also a positive side to this. You can turn away wrath with a gift or gain favor with people. Gifts also have an effect in the spiritual realm. It can create opportunities and bring you before powerful people. This is different from a bribe, and Scripture gives us an example of a gift being used in this positive sense.

5a. Read Proverbs 18:16. "Gift" in this verse refers to what?
   A. A birthday gift
   B. A monetary gift
   C. A spiritual gift
   D. All of the above
   E. None of the above
5b. What does this kind of gift do?
   It opens doors

6. In the Old Testament, it says that when the Queen of Sheba heard how wise and prosperous King Solomon was, she traveled to Jerusalem to witness it for herself. It says she went up with **"a very great train"** of camels bearing spices, precious stones, and **"very much gold"** (1 Kin. 10:2). The Queen of Sheba was astounded by what she saw in King Solomon's court, and she said,

> *It was a true report that I heard in mine own land of thy acts and of thy wisdom. Howbeit I believed not the words, until I came, and mine eyes had seen it: and, behold, the half was not told me: thy wisdom and prosperity exceedeth the fame which I heard.*
>
> 1 KINGS 10:6-7

Solomon was the wisest and wealthiest man on the face of the earth. The Bible says that people came from all over the world to inquire of him and search out his wisdom. I believe Solomon had more fame and notoriety than the leader of any country today. So, the Queen of Sheba brought a large gift to get Solomon's attention and gain access to him.

> *And she gave the king an hundred and twenty talents of gold, and of spices very great store, and precious stones: there came no more such abundance of spices as these which the queen of Sheba gave to king Solomon.*
>
> 1 KINGS 10:10

A talent is equal to about 75.5 pounds, so that means the queen gave Solomon 9,000 pounds, or 145,000 ounces, of gold. At today's price of $1,730 per ounce, that gold would be worth more than $250,000,000, and there's no telling how much her other gifts were worth. I don't know how long the line was of people waiting to see King Solomon, but the queen's gift moved her right to the front. Not only did she get to spend a little time with him; she ate with him and saw all the different aspects of his kingdom. In a spiritual sense, when you give by partnering with a ministry, it's like you start drawing on the anointing that is on the ministry. You end up partaking of the fruits of that ministry. You receive the benefit of prospering from their blessing.

6a. For what purpose did the Queen of Sheba give a gift to King Solomon?
To get his attention and gain access to him

7. Here's something else to consider: I bet the Queen of Sheba could have used that 250 million dollars for needs within her own kingdom. I bet it raised some eyebrows when people heard that she was planning to give all of that money to a king who was already the richest man on earth. She could have changed entire nations with that money. She could have built buildings and helped farmers in every town she passed through. But the Queen of Sheba decided she was going to use that money to go find out how King Solomon had become so successful in running his kingdom. Then she could apply that knowledge to improving her own land. She did it because she wanted to partake of the success Solomon was experiencing—and it worked.

> *And king Solomon gave unto the queen of Sheba all her desire, whatsoever she asked, beside that which Solomon gave her of his royal bounty. So she turned and went to her own country, she and her servants.*
>
> 1 KINGS 10:13

The queen's gift was only a fraction of King Solomon's yearly earnings, so when it says that Solomon gave to her of his bounty, I think the Queen of Sheba received more from Solomon than she gave. On her return journey, she still had tremendous wealth to use to aid beggars and farmers, but she also had wisdom and anointing she could use to build her entire nation. Benevolent giving would have been a short-term solution, but using wisdom and anointing to lift the kingdom out of need was a long-term solution.

7a. Why did she want access to King Solomon?
Because she wanted to find out how King Solomon had become so successful in running his kingdom, so she could apply that knowledge to improving her own land

8. Sometimes, like the Queen of Sheba did, you should give because you need what a church or minister can give to you. I tell my Bible college students to "sow where you want to go." In other words, if you feel called into missionary work, then find people who are doing good work in that field and support them. By partnering with them, you begin to draw on the anointing and experience they have. It will come to you and help you fulfill your own calling. You find someone who has gone further than you have gone, and you sow into their life to help get yourself to the same place. The Queen of Sheba found a man who had more favor, more wisdom, and greater wealth, and she used a gift to gain access to him in order to glean more wisdom, wealth, and favor for herself. When you do that, it starts a supernatural flow of God's finances toward you so that you are able to both meet your own needs and also abound unto every good work.

8a. Like the Queen of Sheba, what's one reason you should give to a church or minister?
Because you need what that church or minister can give to you
8b. To "sow where you want to go" means what?
Find people who are doing good work in the type of ministry you want to do and support them
8c. What will that do for you?
The anointing and experience of that church or minister will come to you and help you fulfill your own calling

9. God always blesses you back when you show faith in Him by giving of your substance. You will never be more faithful to God than He is to you. I'm not saying that partnering with a ministry is about giving just to get—that's why I spent so much time in earlier lessons talking about your heart motives being more important than your gift. But when your heart is right, partnering with a ministry to help it get the Gospel out is going to open doors for you and cause you to prosper.

   9a. You will _____ be more faithful to God than He is to you.
      Never
   9b. Why did Andrew spent so much time in earlier lessons talking about your heart motives being more important than your gift?
      Because partnering with a ministry is not about giving just to get

10. Giving is a powerful part of tapping into God's prosperity. Several different things help determine the harvest you get from your giving—like the attitude you give with, where you give, and trusting God as your source—so there isn't a formula. But you can't really prosper in God's economy until you start sowing into His kingdom. I recommend you do it regularly by tithing and giving from the first fruits of your income. That way, you won't spend your money before you can give, and end up missing out on God's supernatural supply. As you become a deliberate, on-purpose giver—and you do it motivated by love—it will start a flow of God's blessings into your life that will cause you to prosper like never before.

   10a. What things help determine the harvest you get from your giving?
      The attitude you give with, where you give, and trusting God as your source
   10b. True or false: You can't really prosper in God's economy until you start sowing into His kingdom.
      True
   10c. Why should you regularly tithe and give from your first fruits?
      So that you won't spend your money before you can give, and end up missing out on God's supernatural supply
   10d. To start a flow of God's blessings into your life that will cause you to prosper like never before, what do you need to do?
      Become a deliberate, on-purpose giver—motivated by love

DISCIPLESHIP
—— QUESTIONS ——

1. Read Philippians 1:3-5. Why was Paul thanking the Philippians?

   _____

   _____

   _____

2. What is another word for *fellowship*?

   _____

3. What were the Philippians helping him do?

   _____

   _____

   _____

4. Read Philippians 4:11-13. Why wasn't Paul interested in only getting his needs met?

   _____

   _____

   _____

5. According to Philippians 4:15, the Philippian church was the _____
   church that supported him when he departed Macedonia.
      A. First
      B. Best
      C. Largest
      D. Only
      E. Friendliest

6. Read Philippians 4:19. Even though God desires to bless both believers and unbelievers, who is the verse specifically talking about?

   _____

   _____

   _____

7. True or false: The Philippians were giving to Paul because they were receiving from him.

8. What's one reason Andrew prays that God blesses his partners and causes them to abound?

   _____

   _____

   _____

9. True or false: A giver has just enough money to advance God's kingdom.

10. Read Proverbs 18:16. **"Gift"** in this verse refers to what?
    A. A birthday gift
    B. A monetary gift
    C. A spiritual gift
    D. All of the above
    E. None of the above

11. What does this kind of gift do?
    _____
    _____
    _____

12. For what purpose did the Queen of Sheba give a gift to King Solomon?
    _____
    _____
    _____

13. Why did she want access to King Solomon?
    _____
    _____
    _____

14. Like the Queen of Sheba, what's one reason you should give to a church or minister?
    _____
    _____
    _____

15. To "sow where you want to go" means what?
    _____
    _____
    _____

16. What will that do for you?
    _____
    _____
    _____

17. You will _____ be more faithful to God than He is to you.

18. Why did Andrew spent so much time in earlier lessons talking about your heart motives being more important than your gift?

_____
_____
_____

19. What things help determine the harvest you get from your giving?

_____
_____
_____

20. True or false: You can't really prosper in God's economy until you start sowing into His kingdom.

21. Why should you regularly tithe and give from your first fruits?

_____
_____
_____

22. To start a flow of God's blessings into your life that will cause you to prosper like never before, what do you need to do?

_____
_____
_____

ANSWER
—KEY—

1. For their partnership in the Gospel

2. Partnership

3. Take the Gospel to other places around the world

4. Because he had learned to be content regardless of his state

5. D. Only

6. People who partnered with Paul in sharing the Gospel and were helping to establish God's covenant upon the earth

7. False

8. Because his ability to accomplish God's will is directly dependent upon other people joining with him and becoming partners

9. False

10. B. A monetary gift

11. It opens doors

12. To get his attention and gain access to him

13. Because she wanted to find out how King Solomon had become so successful in running his kingdom, so she could apply that knowledge to improving her own land

14. Because you need what that church or minister can give to you

15. Find people who are doing good work in the type of ministry you want to do and support them

16. The anointing and experience of that church or minister will come to you and help you fulfill your own calling

17. Never

18. Because partnering with a ministry is not about giving just to get

19. The attitude you give with, where you give, and trusting God as your source

20. True

21. So that you won't spend your money before you can give, and end up missing out on God's supernatural supply

22. Become a deliberate, on-purpose giver—motivated by love

——SCRIPTURES——

PHILIPPIANS 4:19

But my God shall supply all your need according to his riches in glory by Christ Jesus.

PHILIPPIANS 1:3-5

I thank my God upon every remembrance of you, [4] Always in every prayer of mine for you all making request with joy, [5] For your fellowship in the gospel from the first day until now.

PHILIPPIANS 4:10-17

But I rejoiced in the Lord greatly, that now at the last your care of me hath flourished again; wherein ye were also careful, but ye lacked opportunity. [11] Not that I speak in respect of want: for I have learned, in whatsoever state I am, therewith to be content. [12] I know both how to be abased, and I know how to abound: every where and in all things I am instructed both to be full and to be hungry, both to abound and to suffer need. [13] I can do all things through Christ which strengtheneth me. [14] Notwithstanding ye have well done, that ye did communicate with my affliction. [15] Now ye Philippians know also, that in the beginning of the gospel, when I departed from Macedonia, no church communicated with me as concerning giving and receiving, but ye only. [16] For even in Thessalonica ye sent once and again unto my necessity. [17] Not because I desire a gift: but I desire fruit that may abound to your account.

PSALM 35:27

Let them shout for joy, and be glad, that favour my righteous cause: yea, let them say continually, Let the LORD be magnified, which hath pleasure in the prosperity of his servant.

MATTHEW 5:45

That ye may be the children of your Father which is in heaven: for he maketh his sun to rise on the evil and on the good, and sendeth rain on the just and on the unjust.

3 JOHN 2

Beloved, I wish above all things that thou mayest prosper and be in health, even as thy soul prospereth.

DEUTERONOMY 8:18

But thou shalt remember the LORD thy God: for it is he that giveth thee power to get wealth, that he may establish his covenant which he sware unto thy fathers, as it is this day.

PROVERBS 18:16

A man's gift maketh room for him, and bringeth him before great men.

PROVERBS 15:27

He that is greedy of gain troubleth his own house; but he that hateth gifts shall live.

——SCRIPTURES——

PROVERBS 19:6

Many will intreat the favour of the prince: and every man is a friend to him that giveth gifts.

1 KINGS 10:6-7

And she said to the king, It was a true report that I heard in mine own land of thy acts and of thy wisdom. [7] Howbeit I believed not the words, until I came, and mine eyes had seen it: and, behold, the half was not told me: thy wisdom and prosperity exceedeth the fame which I heard.

1 KINGS 10:10

And she gave the king an hundred and twenty talents of gold, and of spices very great store, and precious stones: there came no more such abundance of spices as these which the queen of Sheba gave to king Solomon.

1 KINGS 10:13

And king Solomon gave unto the queen of Sheba all her desire, whatsoever she asked, beside that which Solomon gave her of his royal bounty. So she turned and went to her own country, she and her servants.

1 JOHN 3:17

But whoso hath this world's good, and seeth his brother have need, and shutteth up his bowels of compassion from him, how dwelleth the love of God in him?

IN GOD WE TRUST

When it comes to prosperity, the first thing a lot of people teach about is giving. They put the greatest emphasis on "give and it shall be given unto you." Giving is one of the last things I discuss when I teach on finances, because I think the heart attitude you have toward money and the motive you give with are more important. Now I want to tie it all together and show how giving with the right attitude, and in the full knowledge that God is your source, will really prosper you.

A well-known scripture tells us to trust in the Lord with all our hearts and lean not on our own understanding. It's a powerful verse, and we hear it used a lot. In context, the passage is describing how one of the ways you trust in the Lord and lean not on your own understanding is by giving.

> Trust in the LORD with all thine heart; and lean not unto thine own understanding. In all thy ways acknowledge him, and he shall direct thy paths. Be not wise in thine own eyes: fear the LORD, and depart from evil. It shall be health to thy navel, and marrow to thy bones. Honour the LORD with thy substance, and with the firstfruits of all thine increase: So shall thy barns be filled with plenty, and thy presses shall burst out with new wine.
> PROVERBS 3:5-10

People often talk about these verses in the sense of trusting in the Lord, but they overlook the fact that it says to honor the Lord with the first fruits of your income. People will pray all day long for God to direct their paths, but they don't see how giving is connected. Most people who are seeking God's guidance regularly would say they trust in God, but not all of them are giving regularly. Well, if you aren't giving, then you aren't acknowledging and trusting the Lord in all of your ways. And according to this passage, you aren't honoring God.

Finances are an important part of your life and an important part of your relationship with God. Most people work forty or more hours a week, which means they spend more time making a living than anything else they do, and God wants to be involved in all of their ways. If you spend the majority of your time working a job, yet you aren't trusting God with your finances, then you are only trusting God with a small portion of your life. But God wants you to trust Him fully and to let Him into every area of your life.

God doesn't want you plowing through the week, doing your own thing, and then devoting Sunday to church and Bible study. Even if you spend thirty minutes every morning praying and studying the Word but then march into your day without giving God hardly another thought, you aren't letting God into much of your life. God wants to be a part of everything you do.

You don't have to sit around praying or studying the Bible all day to be spending time with God. Even preachers have other things to do besides study the Bible. You have lots of things vying for your attention, but you can still keep your mind focused on God. It doesn't matter what your situation is, you can trust God with all of your heart, even when you're on the job. You might have a boss and quotas to meet, but ultimately God is the one who promotes you.

> *For promotion cometh neither from the east, nor from the west, nor from the south. But God is the judge: he putteth down one, and setteth up another.*
>
> PSALM 75:6-7

In other words, God is the source of everything. You should be looking to God as the source of your prosperity and promotion. Even though you punch a clock and work for someone else, God should be your source. Once you get that mindset, then economic hard times won't bother you. Instead of being fearful about your job security, you'll trust in the Lord—and even if you do lose your job, you'll trust God for something better. Knowing that God is your source gives you a peace and stability in life that a lot of people don't have.

So, how do you make God your source when you are spending most of your time working and fulfilling other responsibilities? It's simple: The Lord says to give the first fruits of all your increase. The way you act on your faith and make God your source is by giving—by tithing and making offerings—because if you don't believe God is going to bless you back, it would be crazy to give away your livelihood.

Unless you factor faith in God into the equation, it makes no sense that giving would lead to prosperity. Taking 10 percent of what you make and giving it away seems foolish to the natural mind—and that is exactly why God asks you to do it. God isn't broke. He doesn't need your 10 percent. Giving is a way of demonstrating that you are in *God's* economy, not the world's.

TAKING 10 PERCENT OF WHAT YOU MAKE AND GIVING IT AWAY SEEMS FOOLISH TO THE NATURAL MIND, AND THAT IS EXACTLY WHY GOD ASKS YOU TO DO IT!

As I've said, God could have set it up differently. He could have made every minister of the Gospel independently wealthy, but He didn't do that, because giving is really about your needs—not keeping the church doors open. Even if I had billions and billions of dollars in a bank somewhere, I would still minister on finances in the exact same way. I would still take up offerings and teach about the need for Christians to give, not because God needs their money, but because they need to trust God! The Lord set up this system of tithes and offerings for your benefit, not His.

Some time ago, I was asked to hold a meeting at the church of a Charis Bible College graduate who was pastor of a church way up in the mountains. I'm not sure, but I think there were around thirty or fifty people in the church. He was concerned that his church wasn't big enough to have me as a guest speaker, so he invited a few other local churches too. Altogether, there were probably around a hundred people who attended the meeting. Still, they were very concerned about finances and thinking they wouldn't be able to give me a good enough offering.

I started the very first meeting by telling them that I wasn't a poor preacher who was there to beg for money. I told them, "I got here on my own, and I'll leave on my own. I don't need you to give." When I said that, you could see the disappointment on the pastor's face. I guess he thought no one was going to give, because I had given them an excuse not to. I went on to teach some of the same things I've written in this study guide. I told them they needed to give to plant a seed for themselves, not because I needed the money. I told them that giving is about recognizing God as your source and trusting in Him.

The week after I left, the pastor called me to say that his church had never given so much as they gave during my meetings. He realized that he had been using the wrong motivation to get his people to give. He had been asking for money apologetically, not understanding what an important part giving plays in trusting God. He told me how he had gotten up in front of his church the following Sunday and repented in front of his congregation for not being strong enough in teaching finances. When he was done talking, his congregation came to the front to hug him, and they just started throwing money on the platform. He said they paid off their entire church indebtedness in that one service—something like ten or fifteen thousand dollars.

It all started from recognizing that tithing and giving have nothing to do with God needing money. God just wants people to trust Him instead of looking to themselves or their employer as their source. It's difficult for the natural mind to handle if you take a portion of what you have and give it away. It seems like you are moving away from your goals by tithing, and you would be if God hadn't promised to give back to you abundantly. Giving is about trusting God in this area that consumes more of your time and energy than any other part of your life. You get there by taking a portion of what God gives you and giving it back to Him.

The scripture we've been looking at about trusting God with our giving says, **"Honour the Lord with thy substance, and with the firstfruits of all thine increase"** (Prov. 3:9). *First fruits* means the very first thing we do—not after we take care of our car payments, food, and entertainment. The Lord is saying that the first thing we should do anytime we get money is set aside some to give. I'm not condemning anyone for not giving. What I'm trying to do is remove the deception that has caused a lot of Christians to compartmentalize their lives and separate serving the Lord from giving.

Some believers are trying to trust God, but they aren't giving, because they don't see how they can squeeze it out of their budget. This is the reason the Lord didn't say to give a specific amount. God put a percentage on giving because everyone can give 10 percent, whether they have a million dollars or a dime.

When you honor God by giving with the first fruits of your increase, then the Lord says, **"So shall thy barns be filled with plenty, and thy presses shall burst out with new wine"** (Prov. 3:10). The way you would say that today is, "I'm going to fill up your checking account, and your savings account is going to burst." Giving is how you wind up with a huge savings—not by hoarding. When you take a portion of what you have and trust God with it, then it becomes a seed that yields greater increase in the future.

You can get strength and sustenance by eating seeds, but you also need enough wisdom to set aside a portion of those seeds for planting. You can't eat those seeds even when you're hungry, because eating all of your seed today means starving tomorrow. Planting seed ensures that you have a crop in the future to feed your family and provide for your needs.

But most people are short-term thinkers. They don't see the wisdom in giving, because the natural mind can't understand the things of the spirit.[1] A lot of people are struggling financially, and their natural minds don't see how they can spare any of their income toward giving. Your mind sees that there isn't enough and concludes that you need to keep everything, but the Word of God says honor the Lord with the first fruits of your substance and your bank account will burst forth with finances.

God says the way to abundance is by giving—or you could say that it's by trusting God, because giving boils down to trust. The Lord asks you to give so that you will learn to rely on Him. Ironically, the people who are most reluctant to give and are most convinced that they need all of their money are the people who need to trust God the most. Faith without works is dead (James 2:26). You have to act on your faith. Don't take this the wrong way, but if you aren't tithing, then you aren't trusting God. Giving is a step of faith that turns your focus to God and moves you into position to receive from Him.

GIVING IS REALLY ABOUT TRUSTING GOD AND ACTING ON YOUR FAITH.

As I've said before, God isn't mad at you if you aren't tithing. He's not going to come and get you. But if you aren't giving, then you aren't really trusting God. It's a scriptural principle that if you want to prosper through God, then you are going to have to learn to give. Look at this verse from Proverbs:

> *There is that scattereth, and yet increaseth; and there is that withholdeth more than is meet, but it tendeth to poverty.*
>
> PROVERBS 11:24

To the natural mind, this doesn't make any sense. How can scattering lead to prosperity, and withholding lead to poverty? Yet that is how God's economy works. You can't understand it with your natural mind. The world prospers by hoarding, but God reveals that the way to supernatural prosperity is through giving. When you don't tithe or give because you think you

---

[1]See 1 Cor. 2:14

need to keep it, you are withholding **"more than is meet,"** and it leads to poverty. If you want to prosper, take a step of faith and start giving.

The longer you have been following the thinking of this world, the less sense any of this is going to make. But according to the promises of Scripture, God gives back to you when you give in faith. It's when you scatter that your barns are filled with plenty and your presses burst forth with new wine. Giving is your way to prosperity! You can't operate in financial prosperity through God's system without trusting God with your finances and being a faithful giver. The next verse in Proverbs says,

> *The liberal soul shall be made fat: and he that watereth shall be watered also himself.*
>
> PROVERBS 11:25

This is stating the same principle discussed earlier about God giving seed to sowers. God gives money to people who are going to sow into His kingdom, not to people who are just going to keep it all. **"The liberal soul shall be made fat"** is another way of saying that when you are a giver, you will have more money than you need. You'll have riches in reserve. God will bless you and multiply you.

This also shows that you reap what you've sown. If you give a little, you get a little—but when you give liberally, you get liberally. When you sow a lot, you reap a lot. Nearly everyone wants to reap a lot, but they try sowing as little as possible. It doesn't work that way. You can't give by the teaspoon and expect to receive by the truckload. If you want to receive by the truckload, then you have to give by the truckload.

Fortunately, God's kingdom is set up on percentages. You don't have to literally give huge amounts of money. God looks at your giving in proportion to how much you have. For instance, Jesus said that the widow who dropped two mites in the offering gave more than all of the rich men who gave to the temple treasury. The rich men gave out of their abundance, but the widow woman gave all that she had.[2] So, it's not just about how much you give, or what percentage of your income it is, it's also about how much money you have left over after giving.

The friend I mentioned earlier who bought a number of cars for me is a pastor and is prosperous—and he lives like it. He lives in an expensive house, has nice clothes, and his "weakness" is nice cars. I was at his house once when a truck drove up and unloaded a brand-new red Corvette. It was hot. It had two ignition keys. If you really wanted to go fast, you started the second ignition. The insurance on that vehicle was a thousand dollars per month.

---

[2]See Luke 21:1-4 and Mark 12:41-44

Many people criticize him for his lifestyle. They only look at what he has and not what he gives. But you should never criticize a person's harvest until you see how much seed they have planted.

I was at his house another time when he gave me twenty thousand dollars for preaching one service at his church. A missionary friend was at church that morning, and he gave him ten thousand dollars. And another minister friend was there, and he gave him a brand-new Cadillac that same morning. Altogether, he gave away over seventy thousand dollars in one day. He probably averaged giving away forty thousand dollars per month. So, his house only cost about sixteen months of his giving. How many of you would want to live in a house that equaled sixteen months of your giving? You might be living in a tent.

And the Corvette was a gift with the insurance included. What should he have done? Turn down a free car with prepaid insurance and go buy something that cost him money just so he could look poor and be humbler? That's not humility; that's stupidity.

God doesn't care what you drive or what kind of house you live in. It's all relative to your giving. This man gave a lot, and he reaped a lot. You can't outgive God. When he took care of others, God took care of him.

The widow gave the equivalent of maybe half a penny, but she gave the most, because she gave her entire livelihood—that's what God calls a liberal giver. If all you have is one dollar and you give it away, then that is a huge gift.

But don't go giving all of your money away! God wants you to take care of your family. He wants you to eat and provide for your needs. He doesn't want you to be broke and living under a bridge. The point here is just that God wants you to trust Him. It's easy for a wealthy person to throw a thousand dollars in the offering plate. Whereas a person who is barely getting by but still tithes with joy is showing trust in God. So, giving liberally isn't about the cash value of your gift.

You can be so wealthy that 10 percent of your income won't even put a dent in your spending. In that case, tithing might not be enough to build trust in God as your source. If you have come to a level of prosperity where giving 10 percent is no skin off your teeth, then you should increase your giving to where you still need to trust God to multiply your finances. Give to where you are relying on God to come through for you financially. It's all about trust. The passage in Proverbs goes on to say,

> *He that trusteth in his riches shall fall: but the righteous shall flourish as a branch.*
> PROVERBS 11:28

This is the same thing Jesus was trying to teach the rich young man whom He told to sell everything he owned and give the proceeds to the poor. The young ruler fell at Jesus' feet and asked what he needed to do to be saved, but Jesus knew that the man wasn't really trusting in Him. The man's trust was in his money. By asking the man to sell everything, Jesus was telling him to start looking to God as his source. It's the same thing the Lord is telling us when He asks us to tithe. He's telling us to stop trusting money and to put our trust in Him. When our trust is in God, we prosper—we flourish as a branch.

I don't see any exception to this. You can try to explain it any way you want, but if you aren't honoring the Lord with your first fruits, the bottom line is that you don't trust God. Fear that God won't come through for you is what is keeping you from giving, and that fear is actually releasing poverty into your life. If that's the case, then all you have to do is start taking steps of faith by giving. Honoring the Lord with your first fruits will release the power and anointing of God in your life, and you will begin to prosper. It's simple.

Many people are praying and asking God to bless them financially, yet they are afraid to follow His instructions about tithing. Giving is an absolutely integral part of godly prosperity, but remember that your motive is more important than the gift. Don't try to give just so you can get— it won't work. Whatever you do, do it heartily as unto the Lord, and God will cause it to prosper.

Giving keeps your heart focused on the Lord. Trusting in God as your source lets Him into your finances. You won't just spend a little devotional time in the morning and then shut God out and go through the rest of the day in your own ability. God doesn't want you to divide your life into a "spiritual" part that prays and a carnal part that works and takes care of day-to-day responsibilities.

One of the ways you can learn to put God first is by taking a portion of what He gives you and giving it back to Him. Your heart will be where your treasure is. Consistently investing money in the kingdom will keep you single-minded on God. Even though you have to work a job, you will know that God is your source. Paul's letter to the Galatians says,

> *Be not deceived; God is not mocked: for whatsoever a man soweth, that shall he also reap.*
>
> GALATIANS 6:7

YOU NOT ONLY REAP WHAT YOU SOW, YOU REAP THE WAY YOU SOW.

The *Amplified Bible* renders this verse as, **"For whatever a man sows, that *and that only* is what he will reap"** (emphasis mine). You don't reap something you haven't sown. You aren't going to reap potatoes if you sow carrots. If you want love, you have to sow love. If you want acceptance, then sow acceptance. And if you want finances, you are going to have to sow finances. To reap a harvest of prosperity, you have to sow resources by giving. Scripture says,

> *Give, and it shall be given unto you; good measure, pressed down, and shaken together, and running over, shall men give into your bosom. For with the same measure that ye mete withal it shall be measured to you again.*
>
> LUKE 6:38

The way you give is how you receive. Are you giving off the top? Is tithing the first thing you do when you get income? If you're slow to give, then you're going to be slow to receive. Some people wait until the last possible moment, and then they give grudgingly or of necessity. They don't really want to give, but they feel like they have to. Then they wonder why their needs aren't supplied right away. It's because of this law: You not only reap *what* you sow; you reap the *way* you've sown.

I know I've already made these points, but I keep coming back to them from different scriptures because I'm hoping that the weight of all this evidence will convince you. I'm hoping you'll get a revelation that if you want to prosper in God's system, then you have to start giving. And you can't just grudgingly give a little bit if you want to get a lot in return. You have to give a lot, you have to do it cheerfully, and you have to give from the first fruits. If you do those things over a prolonged period of time, then you'll start to see a crop come in.

Sadly, the majority of Christians do not tithe and give offerings. Pastors have been saying for a long time that around 20 percent of Christians give 80-100 percent of the churches' finances. From talking to pastors and reading reports on giving, I'd have to say I believe it. So, a lot of believers don't understand this cardinal law that if they want to prosper through God's financial system, then they have to be givers.

I think the main reason people don't give is because of fear—fear that they won't have enough to take care of their families, or fear that God won't come through for them. I hope I have presented enough Scripture to counter that fear and unbelief, and to assure you that once you start giving and trusting God with your finances, He *will* make you prosper!

When the Apostle Paul had something important to say to the believers, he would say, "I beseech ye brethren." It's like saying, "I'm begging you." Well, I'm begging you to start trusting God with your finances—it's for your own good. The whole reason God told you to give is to let Him into your finances.

If you have money, then you can give. It doesn't matter how much you have; trust what God's Word says and begin to give from your first fruits. Don't hold back for fear that you won't have enough. God will provide. He wants to bless you financially, but you have to plant seed. You need to take a step of faith. So, start giving and watch as God's supernatural flow increases your finances and causes you to prosper in every area of your life.

— OUTLINE —

I. Giving is one of the last things I discuss when I teach on finances, because I think the heart attitude you have toward money and the motive you give with are more important.

A. Now I want to tie it all together and show how giving with the right attitude, and in the full knowledge that God is your source, will really prosper you.

B. Proverbs 3:5-10 is describing how one of the ways you trust in the Lord and lean not on your own understanding is by giving:

Trust in the LORD with all thine heart; and lean not unto thine own understanding. In all thy ways acknowledge him, and he shall direct thy paths. Be not wise in thine own eyes: fear the LORD, and depart from evil. It shall be health to thy navel, and marrow to thy bones. Honour the LORD with thy substance, and with the firstfruits of all thine increase: So shall thy barns be filled with plenty, and thy presses shall burst out with new wine.

C. People often talk about these verses in the sense of trusting in the Lord, but they overlook the fact that it says to honor the Lord with the first fruits of your income.

D. They will pray all day long for God to direct their paths, but they don't see how giving is connected.

E. Most people who are seeking God's guidance regularly would say they trust in God, but not all of them are giving regularly.

F. Well, if you aren't giving, then you aren't acknowledging and trusting the Lord in all of your ways.

G. And according to this passage, you aren't honoring God.

II. If you spend the majority of your time working a job, yet you aren't trusting God with your finances, then you are only trusting God with a small portion of your life.

A. God wants you to trust Him fully and to let Him into every area of your life.

B. He wants to be a part of everything you do.

C. You have lots of things vying for your attention, but you can still keep your mind focused on God.

D. It doesn't matter what your situation is, you can trust God with all of your heart, even when you're on the job.

E. You might have a boss and quotas to meet, but ultimately God is the one who promotes you (Ps. 75:6-7).

F. You should be looking to God as the source of your prosperity and promotion.

G. Once you get that mindset, then economic hard times won't bother you.

H. Instead of being fearful about your job security, you'll trust in the Lord—and even if you do lose your job, you'll trust God for something better.

I. Knowing that God is your source gives you a peace and stability in life that a lot of people don't have.

III. So, how do you make God your source when you are spending most of your time working and fulfilling other responsibilities?

A. It's simple: The Lord says to give the first fruits of all your increase.

B. The way you act on your faith and make God your source is by tithing and making offerings.

C. Unless you factor faith in God into the equation, it makes no sense that giving would lead to prosperity—and that is exactly why God asks you to do it.

D. He doesn't need your 10 percent—giving is a way of demonstrating that you are in *God's* economy, not the world's.

E. As I've said, God could have made every minister of the Gospel independently wealthy, but He didn't do that, because giving is really about your needs—not keeping the church doors open.

F. The Lord set up this system of tithes and offerings for your benefit, not His.

IV. Some time ago, I was asked to hold a meeting at the church of a Charis Bible College graduate, and he was very concerned about finances, thinking they wouldn't be able to give me a good enough offering.

A. I started the very first meeting by telling the people, "I got here on my own, and I'll leave on my own. I don't need you to give."

B. When I said that, you could see the disappointment on the pastor's face, because I guess he thought no one was going to give, since I had given them an excuse not to.

C. I went on to teach some of the same things I've written in this study guide and told them they needed to give to plant a seed for themselves.

D. I told them that giving is about recognizing God as your source and trusting in Him.

E. The week after I left, the pastor called me to say that his church had never given so much as they gave during my meetings.

F. He realized that he had been asking for money apologetically, not understanding what an important part giving plays in trusting God.

G. He told me how he had gotten up in front of his church the following Sunday and repented in front of his congregation for not being strong enough in teaching finances.

H. When he was done talking, his congregation came to the front to hug him, and they just started throwing money on the platform.

I. He said they paid off their entire church indebtedness in that one service— something like ten or fifteen thousand dollars.

V. The scripture about trusting God with your giving says, **"Honour the LORD with thy substance, and with the first fruits of all thine increase"** (Prov. 3:9).

   A. The Lord is saying that the first thing you should do anytime you get money is set aside some to give.

   B. I'm not condemning anyone for not giving.

   C. What I'm trying to do is remove the deception that has caused a lot of Christians to compartmentalize their lives and separate serving the Lord from giving.

      i. Some believers are trying to trust God, but they aren't giving, because they don't see how they can squeeze it out of their budget.

      ii. This is the reason the Lord didn't say to give a specific amount but put a percentage on giving, because everyone can give 10 percent, whether they have a million dollars or a dime.

   D. When you honor God by giving with the first fruits of your increase, then the Lord says, **"So shall thy barns be filled with plenty, and thy presses shall burst out with new wine"** (Prov. 3:10).

   E. The way you would say that today is, "I'm going to fill up your checking account, and your savings account is going to burst."

   F. Giving is how you wind up with a huge savings—not by hoarding.

   G. When you take a portion of what you have and trust God with it, then it becomes a seed that yields greater increase in the future.

   H. You can get strength and sustenance by eating seeds, but you also need enough wisdom to set aside a portion of those seeds for planting.

   I. You can't eat those seeds even when you're hungry, because eating all of your seed today means starving tomorrow.

   J. Planting seed ensures that you have a crop in the future to feed your family and provide for your needs.

K. Most people don't see the wisdom in giving, because the natural mind can't understand the things of the spirit.[1]

L. A lot of people are struggling financially, and their natural minds don't see how they can spare any of their income toward giving.

M. But the Word of God says honor the Lord with the first fruits of your substance and your bank account will burst forth with finances.

VI. God says the way to abundance is by giving—or you could say that it's by trusting God, because giving boils down to trust.

A. The Lord asks you to give so that you will learn to rely on Him.

B. Ironically, the people who are most reluctant to give and are most convinced that they need all of their money are the people who need to trust God the most.

C. Faith without works is dead (James 2:26).

D. Don't take this the wrong way, but if you aren't tithing, then you aren't trusting God.

E. Giving is a step of faith that turns your focus to God and moves you into position to receive from Him.

VII. As I've said before, God isn't mad at you if you aren't tithing.

A. Look at this verse from Proverbs:

There is that scattereth, and yet increaseth; and there is that withholdeth more than is meet, but it tendeth to poverty.

PROVERBS 11:24

B. To the natural mind, this doesn't make any sense, yet that is how God's economy works.

C. When you don't tithe or give because you think you need to keep it, you are withholding **"more than is meet,"** and it leads to poverty.

D. If you want to prosper, take a step of faith and start giving.

E. The longer you have been following the thinking of this world, the less sense any of this is going to make.

F. But according to the promises of Scripture, God gives back to you when you give in faith.

G. The next verse in Proverbs says,

---

[1] See 1 Cor. 2:14

The liberal soul shall be made fat: and he that watereth shall be watered also himself.

PROVERBS 11:25

H. This is stating the same principle discussed earlier about God giving seed to sowers.

I. **"The liberal soul shall be made fat"** is another way of saying that when you are a giver, you will have more money than you need, you'll have riches in reserve, and God will bless you and multiply you.

J. This also shows that you reap what you've sown: If you give a little, you get a little—but when you give liberally, you get liberally.

K. Nearly everyone wants to reap a lot, but they try sowing as little as possible.

L. You can't give by the teaspoon and expect to receive by the truckload.

VIII. Fortunately, God's kingdom is set up on percentages.

A. Jesus said that the widow who dropped two mites in the offering gave more than all of the rich men who gave to the temple treasury.

B. The rich men gave out of their abundance, but the widow woman gave all that she had.[2]

C. So, it's not just about how much you give, or what percentage of your income it is, it's also about how much money you have left over after giving.

D. The friend I mentioned earlier who bought a number of cars for me is a pastor and is prosperous—and he lives like it.

E. I was at his house once when a truck drove up and unloaded a brand-new red Corvette.

F. Many people criticize him for his lifestyle.

G. They only look at what he has and not what he gives.

H. But you should never criticize a person's harvest until you see how much seed they have planted.

I. He probably averaged giving away forty thousand dollars per month.

J. And the Corvette was a gift with the insurance included.

K. What should he have done? Turn down a free car with prepaid insurance and go buy something that cost him money just so he could look poor and be humbler?

L. That's not humility; that's stupidity.

---

[2]See Luke 21:1-4 and Mark 12:41-44

M. God doesn't care what you drive or what kind of house you live in.

N. It's all relative to your giving.

O. This man gave a lot, and he reaped a lot.

P. When he took care of others, God took care of him.

Q. The widow gave the equivalent of maybe half a penny, but she gave the most, because she gave her entire livelihood—that's what God calls a liberal giver.

R. If all you have is one dollar and you give it away, then that is a huge gift.

S. Giving liberally isn't about the cash value of your gift.

T. You can be so wealthy that 10 percent of your income won't even put a dent in your spending.

U. In that case, you should increase your giving to where you still need to trust God to multiply your finances.

V. Give to where you are relying on God to come through for you financially.

IX. The passage in Proverbs goes on to say,

> *He that trusteth in his riches shall fall: but the righteous shall flourish as a branch.*
> PROVERBS 11:28

A. This is the same thing Jesus was trying to teach the rich young man who fell at Jesus' feet and asked what he needed to do to be saved.

B. Jesus knew that the man wasn't really trusting in Him.

C. By asking the man to sell everything, Jesus was telling him to start looking to God as his source.

D. It's the same thing the Lord is telling us when He asks us to tithe.

E. He's telling us to stop trusting money and to put our trust in Him.

F. When our trust is in God, we prosper—we flourish as a branch.

G. I don't see any exception to this.

X. You can try to explain it any way you want, but if you aren't honoring the Lord with your first fruits, the bottom line is that you don't trust God.

A. Fear that God won't come through for you is what is keeping you from giving, and that fear is actually releasing poverty into your life.

B. If that's the case, then all you have to do is start taking steps of faith by giving.

C. Honoring the Lord with your first fruits will release the power and anointing of God in your life, and you will begin to prosper.

D. Many people are praying and asking God to bless them financially, yet they are afraid to follow His instructions about tithing.

E. Giving is an absolutely integral part of godly prosperity, but remember that your motive is more important than the gift.

F. Whatever you do, do it heartily as unto the Lord, and God will cause it to prosper.

XI. Giving keeps your heart focused on the Lord.

A. Trusting in God as your source lets Him into your finances.

B. God doesn't want you to divide your life into a "spiritual" part that prays and a carnal part that works and takes care of day-to-day responsibilities.

C. One of the ways you can learn to put God first is by taking a portion of what He gives you and giving it back to Him.

D. Your heart will be where your treasure is.

E. Consistently investing money in the kingdom will keep you single-minded on God.

F. Even though you have to work a job, you will know that God is your source.

XII. Paul's letter to the Galatians says,

> *Be not deceived; God is not mocked: for whatsoever a man soweth, that*
> *shall he also reap.*
> GALATIANS 6:7

A. The *Amplified Bible* renders this verse, **"For whatever a man sows, that *and that only* is what he will reap"** (emphasis mine).

B. Scripture says,

> *Give, and it shall be given unto you; good measure, pressed down, and shaken*
> *together, and running over, shall men give into your bosom. For with the*
> *same measure that ye mete withal it shall be measured to you again.*
> LUKE 6:38

C. The way you give is how you receive.

D. Are you giving off the top? Is tithing the first thing you do when you get income?

E. If you're slow to give, then you're going to be slow to receive.

F. Some people wait until the last possible moment, and then they give grudgingly or of necessity.

G. They don't really want to give, but they feel like they have to.

H. Then they wonder why their needs aren't supplied right away.

I. It's because of this law: You not only reap *what* you sow; you reap the *way* you've sown.

XIII. I know I've already made these points, but I keep coming back to them from different scriptures because I'm hoping that the weight of all this evidence will convince you.

A. I'm hoping you'll get a revelation that if you want to prosper in God's system, then you have to start giving—and you can't just grudgingly give a little bit if you want to get a lot in return.

B. You have to give a lot, you have to do it cheerfully, and you have to give from the first fruits.

C. If you do those things over a prolonged period of time, then you'll start to see a crop come in.

XIV. Pastors have been saying for a long time that around 20 percent of Christians give 80-100 percent of the churches' finances.

A. From talking to pastors and reading reports on giving, I'd have to say I believe it.

B. I hope I have presented enough Scripture to counter fear and unbelief, and to assure you that once you start giving and trusting God with your finances, He *will* make you prosper!

C. When the Apostle Paul had something important to say to the believers, he would say, "I beseech ye brethren"—it's like saying, "I'm begging you."

D. Well, I'm begging you to start trusting God with your finances—it's for your own good.

XV. If you have money, then you can give.

A. It doesn't matter how much you have; trust what God's Word says and begin to give from your first fruits.

B. Don't hold back for fear that you won't have enough—God will provide.

C. He wants to bless you financially, but you have to plant seed—you need to take a step of faith.

D. So, start giving and watch as God's supernatural flow increases your finances and causes you to prosper in every area of your life.

TEACHER'S
──── GUIDE ────

1. Giving is one of the last things I discuss when I teach on finances, because I think the heart attitude you have toward money and the motive you give with are more important. Now I want to tie it all together and show how giving with the right attitude, and in the full knowledge that God is your source, will really prosper you. Proverbs 3:5-10 is describing how one of the ways you trust in the Lord and lean not on your own understanding is by giving:

Trust in the LORD with all thine heart; and lean not unto thine own understanding. In all thy ways acknowledge him, and he shall direct thy paths. Be not wise in thine own eyes: fear the LORD, and depart from evil. It shall be health to thy navel, and marrow to thy bones. Honour the LORD with thy substance, and with the firstfruits of all thine increase: So shall thy barns be filled with plenty, and thy presses shall burst out with new wine.

People often talk about these verses in the sense of trusting in the Lord, but they overlook the fact that it says to honor the Lord with the first fruits of your income. They will pray all day long for God to direct their paths, but they don't see how giving is connected. Most people who are seeking God's guidance regularly would say they trust in God, but not all of them are giving regularly. Well, if you aren't giving, then you aren't acknowledging and trusting the Lord in all of your ways. And according to this passage, you aren't honoring God.

    1a. Read Proverbs 3:5-10. What does this passage describe?
        It describes how one of the ways you trust in the Lord and lean not on your own
        understanding is by giving
    1b. How do you honor the Lord?
        A. By coming to church on time
        B. With singing when the music's playing
        C. With the first fruits of your income
        D. All of the above
        E. None of the above
    1c. True or false: Giving is connected to God directing your path.
        True
    1d. If you aren't giving, you aren't what?
        Acknowledging, trusting, and honoring the Lord

2. If you spend the majority of your time working a job, yet you aren't trusting God with your finances, then you are only trusting God with a small portion of your life. God wants you to trust Him fully and to let Him into every area of your life. He wants to be a part of everything you do. You have lots of things vying for your attention, but you can still keep your mind focused on God. It doesn't matter what your situation is, you can trust God with all of your heart, even when you're on the job. You might have a boss and quotas to meet, but ultimately God is the one who promotes you (Ps. 75:6-7). You should be looking to God as the source of your prosperity and promotion. Once you get that mindset, then economic hard times won't bother you. Instead of being fearful about your job security, you'll trust in the Lord—and even if you do lose your job, you'll trust God for something better. Knowing that God is your source gives you a peace and stability in life that a lot of people don't have.

3. So, how do you make God your source when you are spending most of your time working and fulfilling other responsibilities? It's simple: The Lord says to give the first fruits of all your increase. The way you act on your faith and make God your source is by tithing and making offerings. Unless you factor faith in God into the equation, it makes no sense that giving would lead to prosperity—and that is exactly why God asks you to do it. He doesn't need your 10 percent—giving is a way of demonstrating that you are in *God's* economy, not the world's. As I've said, God could have made every minister of the Gospel independently wealthy, but He didn't do that, because giving is really about your needs—not keeping the church doors open. The Lord set up this system of tithes and offerings for your benefit, not His.

   3a. How do you make God your source when you are spending most of your time working and fulfilling other responsibilities?
      Give the first fruits of all your increase

   3b. It makes no sense that giving would lead to prosperity if you didn't factor in what?
      A. Time
      B. Non-profit tax deductions
      C. Reasoning
      D. Faith
      E. Basic mathematics

   3c. Why did God set up the system of tithes and offerings?
      For your benefit

4. Some time ago, I was asked to hold a meeting at the church of a Charis Bible College graduate, and he was very concerned about finances, thinking they wouldn't be able to give me a good enough offering. I started the very first meeting by telling the people, "I got here on my own, and I'll leave on my own. I don't need you to give." When I said that, you could see the disappointment on the pastor's face, because I guess he thought no one was going to give, since I had given them an excuse not to. I went on to teach some of the same things I've written in this study guide and told them they needed to give to plant a seed for themselves. I told them that giving is about recognizing God as your source and trusting in Him. The week after I left, the pastor called me to say that his church had never given so much as they gave during my meetings. He realized that he had been asking for money apologetically, not understanding what an important part giving plays in trusting God. He told me how he had gotten up in front of his church the following Sunday and repented in front of his congregation for not being strong enough in teaching finances. When he was done talking, his congregation came to the front to hug him, and they just started throwing money on the platform. He said they paid off their entire church indebtedness in that one service—something like ten or fifteen thousand dollars.

   4a. What plays an integral part in trusting God?
      Giving

   4b. True or false: The Lord said everyone is to give a specific amount when they give.
      False

5. The scripture about trusting God with your giving says, **"Honour the LORD with thy substance, and with the first fruits of all thine increase"** (Prov. 3:9). The Lord is saying that the first thing you should do anytime you get money is set aside some to give. I'm not condemning anyone for not giving. What I'm trying to do is remove the deception that has caused a lot of Christians to compartmentalize their lives and separate serving the Lord from giving. Some believers are trying to trust God, but they aren't giving, because they don't see how they can squeeze it out of their budget. This is the reason the Lord didn't say to give a specific amount but put a percentage on giving, because everyone can give 10 percent, whether they have a million dollars or a dime. When you honor God by giving with the first fruits of your increase, then the Lord says, **"So shall thy barns be filled with plenty, and thy presses shall burst out with new wine"** (Prov. 3:10). The way you would say that today is, "I'm going to fill up your checking account, and your savings account is going to burst." Giving is how you wind up with a huge savings—not by hoarding. When you take a portion of what you have and trust God with it, then it becomes a seed that yields greater increase in the future. You can get strength and sustenance by eating seeds, but you also need enough wisdom to set aside a portion of those seeds for planting. You can't eat those seeds even when you're hungry, because eating all of your seed today means starving tomorrow. Planting seed ensures that you have a crop in the future to feed your family and provide for your needs. Most people don't see the wisdom in giving, because the natural mind can't understand the things of the spirit.[1] A lot of people are struggling financially, and their natural minds don't see how they can spare any of their income toward giving. But the Word of God says honor the Lord with the first fruits of your substance and your bank account will burst forth with finances.

    5a. In regards to giving, what can everyone do?
       Give 10 percent, whether they have a million dollars or a dime
    5b. Read Proverbs 3:10. What happens when you give with the first fruits of your increase?
       "So shall thy barns be filled with plenty, and thy presses shall burst out with new wine." [In other words, God is going to fill up your checking account, and your savings account is going to burst]
    5c. If you hoard, you won't end up with what?
       A. A huge savings
       B. A clean house
       C. A lot of friends
       D. All of the above
       E. None of the above
    5d. What does eating all of your seed today mean?
       Starving tomorrow
    5e. What does planting seed ensure?
       That you have a crop in the future to feed your family and provide for your needs
    5f. Why don't people see the wisdom in giving?
       Because the natural mind can't understand the things of the spirit [1 Cor. 2:14]

6. God says the way to abundance is by giving—or you could say that it's by trusting God, because giving boils down to trust. The Lord asks you to give so that you will learn to rely on Him. Ironically, the people who are most reluctant to give and are most convinced that they need all of their money are the people who need to trust God the most. Faith without works is dead (James 2:26). Don't take this the wrong way, but if you aren't tithing, then you aren't trusting God. Giving is a step of faith that turns your focus to God and moves you into position to receive from Him.

    6a. Giving boils down to _____.
        <u>Trust</u>

7. As I've said before, God isn't mad at you if you aren't tithing. Look at this verse from Proverbs:

> *There is that scattereth, and yet increaseth; and there is that withholdeth*
> *more than is meet, but it tendeth to poverty.*
> PROVERBS 11:24

To the natural mind, this doesn't make any sense, yet that is how God's economy works. When you don't tithe or give because you think you need to keep it, you are withholding **"more than is meet,"** and it leads to poverty. If you want to prosper, take a step of faith and start giving. The longer you have been following the thinking of this world, the less sense any of this is going to make. But according to the promises of Scripture, God gives back to you when you give in faith. The next verse in Proverbs says,

> *The liberal soul shall be made fat: and he that watereth shall be watered*
> *also himself.*
> PROVERBS 11:25

This is stating the same principle discussed earlier about God giving seed to sowers. **"The liberal soul shall be made fat"** is another way of saying that when you are a giver, you will have more money than you need, you'll have riches in reserve, and God will bless you and multiply you. This also shows that you reap what you've sown: If you give a little, you get a little—but when you give liberally, you get liberally. Nearly everyone wants to reap a lot, but they try sowing as little as possible. You can't give by the teaspoon and expect to receive by the truckload.

7a. True or false: God is mad at you if you don't tithe.
False
7b. The way God's economy works cannot be understood by _____ .
A. Recent statistics
B. Businessmen
C. Politicians
D. A new Christian
E. The natural mind
7c. According to Proverbs 11:24, what leads to poverty?
Not tithing or giving because you think you need to keep it
7d. How do you know God gives back to you when you give in faith?
Because of the promises of Scripture
7e. Read Proverbs 11:25. What does **"the liberal soul shall be made fat"** mean?
It means that when you are a giver, you will have more money than you need, you'll have riches in reserve, and God will bless you and multiply you
7f. You can't give by the _____ and expect to receive by the
_____ .
Teaspoon, truckload

8. Fortunately, God's kingdom is set up on percentages. Jesus said that the widow who dropped two mites in the offering gave more than all of the rich men who gave to the temple treasury. The rich men gave out of their abundance, but the widow woman gave all that she had. So, it's not just about how much you give, or what percentage of your income it is, it's also about how much money you have left over after giving. The friend I mentioned earlier who bought a number of cars for me is a pastor and is prosperous—and he lives like it. I was at his house once when a truck drove up and unloaded a brand-new red Corvette. Many people criticize him for his lifestyle. They only look at what he has and not what he gives. But you should never criticize a person's harvest until you see how much seed they have planted. He probably averaged giving away forty thousand dollars per month. And the Corvette was a gift with the insurance included. What should he have done? Turn down a free car with prepaid insurance and go buy something that cost him money just so he could look poor and be humbler? That's not humility; that's stupidity. God doesn't care what you drive or what kind of house you live in. It's all relative to your giving. This man gave a lot, and he reaped a lot. When he took care of others, God took care of him. The widow gave the equivalent of maybe half a penny, but she gave the most, because she gave her entire livelihood—that's what God calls a liberal giver. If all you have is one dollar and you give it away, then that is a huge gift. Giving liberally isn't about the cash value of your gift. You can be so wealthy that 10 percent of your income won't even put a dent in your spending. In that case, you should increase your giving to where you still need to trust God to multiply your finances. Give to where you are relying on God to come through for you financially.

8a. How is it that the widow woman gave more than the rich men?
    Because the widow woman gave all that she had
8b. Until you see how much seed someone has planted, what shouldn't you do?
    Criticize their harvest
8c. True or false: The cash value of your gift doesn't determine how liberally you gave.
    True
8d. If giving 10 percent of your income is not enough for you to trust God, what should you do?
    Increase your giving

9. The passage in Proverbs goes on to say,

He that trusteth in his riches shall fall: but the righteous shall flourish as a branch.
PROVERBS 11:28

This is the same thing Jesus was trying to teach the rich young man who fell at Jesus' feet and asked what he needed to do to be saved. Jesus knew that the man wasn't really trusting in Him. By asking the man to sell everything, Jesus was telling him to start looking to God as his source. It's the same thing the Lord is telling us when He asks us to tithe. He's telling us to stop trusting money and to put our trust in Him. When our trust is in God, we prosper—we flourish as a branch. I don't see any exception to this.

9a. What is the Lord telling you when He asks you to tithe?
    To stop trusting money and to put your trust in Him
9b. According to Proverbs 11:28, what happens when you trust in God?
    You prosper—you flourish as a branch
9c. Andrew doesn't see any _____ to this.
    Exception

10. You can try to explain it any way you want, but if you aren't honoring the Lord with your first fruits, the bottom line is that you don't trust God. Fear that God won't come through for you is what is keeping you from giving, and that fear is actually releasing poverty into your life. If that's the case, then all you have to do is start taking steps of faith by giving. Honoring the Lord with your first fruits will release the power and anointing of God in your life, and you will begin to prosper. Many people are praying and asking God to bless them financially, yet they are afraid to follow His instructions about tithing. Giving is an absolutely integral part of godly prosperity, but remember that your motive is more important than the gift. Whatever you do, do it heartily as unto the Lord, and God will cause it to prosper.

10a. _____ that God won't come through for you is what is keeping you from giving, and that _____ is actually releasing poverty into your life.
Fear, fear

10b. If you want God to bless you financially, then you shouldn't be _____ to follow God's instructions about tithing.
A. First
B. Unfaithful
C. Afraid
D. All of the above
E. None of the above

11. Giving keeps your heart focused on the Lord. Trusting in God as your source lets Him into your finances. God doesn't want you to divide your life into a "spiritual" part that prays and a carnal part that works and takes care of day-to-day responsibilities. One of the ways you can learn to put God first is by taking a portion of what He gives you and giving it back to Him. Your heart will be where your treasure is. Consistently investing money in the kingdom will keep you single-minded on God. Even though you have to work a job, you will know that God is your source.

11a. In order to let God into your finances, what do you have to do?
Trust in Him as your source

11b. You will know that God is your source when you what?
Consistently invest money in the kingdom

12. Paul's letter to the Galatians says,

> *Be not deceived; God is not mocked: for whatsoever a man soweth, that shall he also reap.*

GALATIANS 6:7

The *Amplified Bible* renders this verse, **"For whatever a man sows, that *and that only* is what he will reap"** (emphasis mine). Scripture says,

> *Give, and it shall be given unto you; good measure, pressed down, and shaken together, and running over, shall men give into your bosom. For with the same measure that ye mete withal it shall be measured to you again.*

LUKE 6:38

The way you give is how you receive Are you giving off the top? Is tithing the first thing you do when you get income? If you're slow to give, then you're going to be slow to receive. Some people wait until the last possible moment, and then they give grudgingly or of necessity. They don't really want to give, but they feel like they have to. Then they wonder why their needs aren't supplied right away. It's because of this law: You not only reap *what* you sow; you reap the *way* you've sown.

12a. Read Galatians 6:7 and Luke 6:28. If you're slow to _____ , then you're going to be slow to _____ .
Give, receive

12b. Why is this the case?
Because of this law: You not only reap what you sow; you reap the way you've sown

13. I know I've already made these points, but I keep coming back to them from different scriptures because I'm hoping that the weight of all this evidence will convince you. I'm hoping you'll get a revelation that if you want to prosper in God's system, then you have to start giving—and you can't just grudgingly give a little bit if you want to get a lot in return. You have to give a lot, you have to do it cheerfully, and you have to give from the first fruits. If you do those things over a prolonged period of time, then you'll start to see a crop come in.

13a. What do you have to do over a prolonged period of time to see a crop come in?
You have to give a lot, you have to do it cheerfully, and you have to give from the first fruits

14. Pastors have been saying for a long time that around 20 percent of Christians give 80-100 percent of the churches' finances. From talking to pastors and reading reports on giving, I'd have to say I believe it. I hope I have presented enough Scripture to counter fear and unbelief, and to assure you that once you start giving and trusting God with your finances, He *will* make you prosper! When the Apostle Paul had something important to say to the believers, he would say, "I beseech ye brethren"—it's like saying, "I'm begging you." Well, I'm begging you to start trusting God with your finances—it's for your own good.

    14a.   Twenty percent of Christians give what?
          80 to 100 percent of the churches' finances
    14b.   Why is Andrew begging you to start trusting God with your finances?
          Because it's for your own good

15. If you have money, then you can give. It doesn't matter how much you have; trust what God's Word says and begin to give from your first fruits. Don't hold back for fear that you won't have enough—God will provide. He wants to bless you financially, but you have to plant seed—you need to take a step of faith. So, start giving and watch as God's supernatural flow increases your finances and causes you to prosper in every area of your life.

    15a.   Does it matter how much you have to start giving?
          No
    15b.   Why shouldn't you hold back for fear that you won't have enough?
          Because God will provide

DISCIPLESHIP
—— QUESTIONS ——

1. Read Proverbs 3:5-10. What does this passage describe?

    _____
    _____
    _____

2. How do you honor the Lord?
    A. By coming to church on time
    B. With singing when the music's playing
    C. With the first fruits of your income
    D. All of the above
    E. None of the above

3. True or false: Giving is connected to God directing your path.

4. If you aren't giving, you aren't what?

    _____
    _____
    _____

5. How do you make God your source when you are spending most of your time working and fulfilling other responsibilities?

    _____
    _____
    _____

6. It makes no sense that giving would lead to prosperity if you didn't factor in what?
    A. Time
    B. Non-profit tax deductions
    C. Reasoning
    D. Faith
    E. Basic mathematics

7. Why did God set up the system of tithes and offerings?

    _____
    _____
    _____

8. What plays an integral part in trusting God?

    _____
    _____
    _____

9. True or false: The Lord said everyone is to give a specific amount when they give.

10. In regards to giving, what can everyone do?

    _____
    _____
    _____

11. Read Proverbs 3:10. What happens when you give with the first fruits of your increase?

    _____
    _____
    _____

12. If you hoard, you won't end up with what?
    A. A huge savings
    B. A clean house
    C. A lot of friends
    D. All of the above
    E. None of the above

13. What does eating all of your seed today mean?

    _____
    _____
    _____

14. What does planting seed ensure?

    _____
    _____
    _____

15. Why don't people see the wisdom in giving?

    _____
    _____
    _____

16. Giving boils down to _____.

17. True or false: God is mad at you if you don't tithe.

18. The way God's economy works cannot be understood by _____ .
    A. Recent statistics
    B. Businessmen
    C. Politicians
    D. A new Christian
    E. The natural mind

19. According to Proverbs 11:24, what leads to poverty?

    _____
    _____
    _____

20. How do you know God gives back to you when you give in faith?

    _____
    _____
    _____

21. Read Proverbs 11:25. What does **"the liberal soul shall be made fat"** mean?

    _____
    _____
    _____

22. You can't give by the _____ and expect to receive by the

    _____ .

23. How is it that the widow woman gave more than the rich men?

    _____
    _____
    _____

24. Until you see how much seed someone has planted, what shouldn't you do?

    _____
    _____
    _____

25. True or false: The cash value of your gift doesn't determine how liberally you gave.

26. If giving 10 percent of your income is not enough for you to trust God, what should you do?

    _____
    _____
    _____

27. What is the Lord telling you when He asks you to tithe?

_____

_____

_____

28. According to Proverbs 11:28, what happens when you trust in God?

_____

_____

_____

29. Andrew doesn't see any _____ to this.

30. _____ that God won't come through for you is what is keeping you from giving, and that _____ is actually releasing poverty into your life.

31. If you want God to bless you financially, then you shouldn't be _____ to follow God's instructions about tithing.
    A. First
    B. Unfaithful
    C. Afraid
    D. All of the above
    E. None of the above

32. In order to let God into your finances, what do you have to do?

_____

_____

_____

33. You will know that God is your source when you what?

_____

_____

_____

34. Read Galatians 6:7 and Luke 6:28. If you're slow to _____ , then you're going to be slow to _____ .

35. Why is this the case?

_____

_____

_____

36. What do you have to do over a prolonged period of time to see a crop come in?

_____
_____
_____

37. Twenty percent of Christians give what?

_____
_____
_____

38. Why is Andrew begging you to start trusting God with your finances?

_____
_____
_____

39. Does it matter how much you have to start giving?

_____
_____
_____

40. Why shouldn't you hold back for fear that you won't have enough?

_____
_____
_____

ANSWER
—KEY—

1. It describes how one of the ways you trust in the Lord and lean not on your own understanding is by giving

2. C. With the first fruits of your income

3. True

4. Acknowledging, trusting, and honoring the Lord

5. Give the first fruits of all your increase

6. D. Faith

7. For your benefit

8. Giving

9. False

10. Give 10 percent, whether they have a million dollars or a dime

11. **"So shall thy barns be filled with plenty, and thy presses shall burst out with new wine."** (In other words, God is going to fill up your checking account, and your savings account is going to burst)

12. A. A huge savings

13. Starving tomorrow

14. That you have a crop in the future to feed your family and provide for your needs

15. Because the natural mind can't understand the things of the spirit (1 Cor. 2:14)

16. Trust

17. False

18. E. The natural mind

19. Not tithing or giving because you think you need to keep it

20. Because of the promises of Scripture

21. It means that when you are a giver, you will have more money than you need, you'll have riches in reserve, and God will bless you and multiply you

22. Teaspoon, truckload

23. Because the widow woman gave all that she had

24. Criticize their harvest

25. True

26. Increase your giving

27. To stop trusting money and to put your trust in Him

28. You prosper—you flourish as a branch

29. Exception

30. Fear, fear

31. C. Afraid

32. Trust in Him as your source

33. Consistently invest money in the kingdom

34. Give, receive

35. Because of this law: You not only reap what you sow; you reap the way you've sown

36. You have to give a lot, you have to do it cheerfully, and you have to give from the first fruits

37. 80 to 100 percent of the churches' finances

38. Because it's for your own good

39. No

40. Because God will provide

—SCRIPTURES—

PROVERBS 3:5-10

Trust in the LORD with all thine heart; and lean not unto thine own understanding. [6] In all thy ways acknowledge him, and he shall direct thy paths. [7] Be not wise in thine own eyes: fear the LORD, and depart from evil. [8] It shall be health to thy navel, and marrow to thy bones. [9] Honour the LORD with thy substance, and with the firstfruits of all thine increase: [10] So shall thy barns be filled with plenty, and thy presses shall burst out with new wine.

PSALM 75:6-7

For promotion cometh neither from the east, nor from the west, nor from the south. [7] But God is the judge: he putteth down one, and setteth up another.

1 CORINTHIANS 2:14

But the natural man receiveth not the things of the Spirit of God: for they are foolishness unto him: neither can he know them, because they are spiritually discerned.

JAMES 2:26

For as the body without the spirit is dead, so faith without works is dead also.

PROVERBS 11:24-25

There is that scattereth, and yet increaseth; and there is that withholdeth more than is meet, but it tendeth to poverty. [25] The liberal soul shall be made fat: and he that watereth shall be watered also himself.

LUKE 21:1-4

And he looked up, and saw the rich men casting their gifts into the treasury. [2] And he saw also a certain poor widow casting in thither two mites. [3] And he said, Of a truth I say unto you, that this poor widow hath cast in more than they all: [4] For all these have of their abundance cast in unto the offerings of God: but she of her penury hath cast in all the living that she had.

MARK 12:41-44

And Jesus sat over against the treasury, and beheld how the people cast money into the treasury: and many that were rich cast in much. [42] And there came a certain poor widow, and she threw in two mites, which make a farthing. [43] And he called unto him his disciples, and saith unto them, Verily I say unto you, That this poor widow hath cast more in, than all they which have cast into the treasury: [44] For all they did cast in of their abundance; but she of her want did cast in all that she had, even all her living.

PROVERBS 11:28

He that trusteth in his riches shall fall: but the righteous shall flourish as a branch.

GALATIANS 6:7

Be not deceived; God is not mocked: for whatsoever a man soweth, that shall he also reap.

—SCRIPTURES—

LUKE 6:38

Give, and it shall be given unto you; good measure, pressed down, and shaken together, and running over, shall men give into your bosom. For with the same measure that ye mete withal it shall be measured to you again.

RECEIVE JESUS AS YOUR SAVIOR

Choosing to receive Jesus Christ as your Lord and Savior is the most important decision you'll ever make!

God's Word promises, **"That if thou shalt confess with thy mouth the Lord Jesus, and shalt believe in thine heart that God hath raised him from the dead, thou shalt be saved. For with the heart man believeth unto righteousness; and with the mouth confession is made unto salvation"** (Rom. 10:9-10). **"For whosoever shall call upon the name of the Lord shall be saved"** (Rom. 10:13).

By His grace, God has already done everything to provide salvation. Your part is simply to believe and receive.

Pray out loud, *"Jesus, I confess that You are my Lord and Savior. I believe in my heart that God raised You from the dead. By faith in Your Word, I receive salvation now. Thank You for saving me!"*

The very moment you commit your life to Jesus Christ, the truth of His Word instantly comes to pass in your spirit. Now that you're born again, there's a brand-new you!

It doesn't really matter whether you felt anything or not when you prayed to receive the Lord. If you believed in your heart that you received, then God's Word promises that you did. **"Therefore I say unto you, What things soever ye desire, when ye pray, believe that ye receive them, and ye shall have them"** (Mark 11:24). God always honors His Word. Believe it!

Please contact me and let me know that you've prayed to receive Jesus as your Savior . I would like to rejoice with you and help you understand more fully what has taken place in your life. *Welcome to your new life!*

RECEIVE THE HOLY SPIRIT

As His child, your loving heavenly Father wants to give you the supernatural power you need to live this new life.

"For every one that asketh receiveth; and he that seeketh findeth; and to him that knocketh it shall be opened...how much more shall your heavenly Father give the Holy Spirit to them that ask him?" (Luke 11:10 and 13).

All you have to do is ask, believe, and receive!

Pray, *"Father, I recognize my need for Your power to live this new life. Please fill me with Your Holy Spirit. By faith, I receive it right now! Thank You for baptizing me. Holy Spirit, You are welcome in my life!"*

Congratulations—now you're filled with God's supernatural power!

Some syllables from a language you don't recognize will rise up from your heart to your mouth (1 Cor. 14:14). As you speak them out loud by faith, you're releasing God's power from within and building yourself up in your spirit (1 Cor. 14:4). You can do this whenever and wherever you like.

It doesn't really matter whether you felt anything or not when you prayed to receive the Lord and His Spirit. If you believed in your heart that you received, then God's Word promises that you did. **"Therefore I say unto you, What things soever ye desire, when ye pray, believe that ye receive them, and ye shall have them"** (Mark 11:24). God always honors His Word—believe it!

Please contact me and let me know that you've prayed to be filled with the Holy Spirit. I would like to rejoice with you and help you understand more fully what has taken place in your life. *Welcome to your new life!*

ABOUT THE AUTHOR

For over four decades, Andrew Wommack has traveled America and the world teaching the truth of the Gospel. His profound revelation of the Word of God is taught with clarity and simplicity, emphasizing God's unconditional love and the balance between grace and faith. He reaches millions of people through the daily *Gospel Truth* radio and television programs, broadcast both domestically and internationally. He founded Charis Bible College in 1994 and has since established Charis Bible College extension schools in other major cities of America and around the world. Andrew has produced a library of teaching materials, available in print, audio, and visual formats. And, as it has been from the beginning, his ministry continues to distribute free audio materials to those who cannot afford them.